Contents

The Troubled Century

British and World History
1914–1993

Mark Hichens

The Pentland Press
Edinburgh – Cambridge – Durham

First published in 1994 by
The Pentland Press Ltd
1 Hutton Close
South Church
Bishop Auckland
Durham

British Library
Cataloguing in Publication Data

A catalogue record for this book
is available from the British Library.

ISBN 1-85821-193-X

Typeset by Carnegie Publishing, 18 Maynard St., Preston
Printed and bound by Antony Rowe Ltd., Chippenham

Table of Maps

Acknowledgements

The author expresses his thanks to the following who have supplied copyright illustrations for this book:

The Imperial War Museum on pages 22, 26, 30, 40, 41, 43, 53, 115, 135, 136, 141, 142, 150, 154, 164, 165, 166, 167, 168, 171, 190, 192, 198, 199, 200, 215, 220, 225, 232, 237, 241, 243, 248, 259, 297.

Topham Picture Source on pages 3, 51, 80, 85, 93, 134, 276, 287, 289, 292, 300, 302, 316, 327, 349, 352, 354, 357, 359, 360.

Popperfoto on pages 75, 138.

Hulton Deutsch on pages 65, 68, 96, 121, 123.

Evening Standard on page 126.

The Illustrated London News on pages 138, 183.

Magnum Photos on pages 212, 237, 312, 313, 345.

Imperial Science Museum on page 82.

Foreword

The author believes strongly that history is to be enjoyed and that it is the task of the historian to entertain as well as to edify.

Many histories of the twentieth century already exist, but it is so vast a subject and contains so much that is fascinating that new books will always be appearing. *The Troubled Century* is a narrative history, British based but including much world history, essential as Britain's involvement with other countries becomes closer. There are also a large number of maps and carefully chosen illustrations which add vitally to the text.

Although *The Troubled Century* is intended mainly for younger readers, it will also be of interest to adults, especially to those (and there seem to be many of them) who learned little or no modern history at school; it will provide for them a useful background for many present day events.

In schools *The Troubled Century* should be a valuable addition to the library and will be a useful supplementary reader for GCSE exams. With this in mind an appendix has been added with comprehension tests and suggested projects for each chapter.

In a book of this size it is not possible to do more than give a general account of the main events and personalities of the century or, more particularly, of the years 1914 to 1993. Much has had to be left out and much covered only lightly. Special prominence has been given to the two world wars as these are of great interest to younger readers, and it is surely right that the great sacrifices and sufferings of those years should be fully realised. But the book contains much else as well including, among other subjects, the rise of the European dictators, the dissolution of the British Empire and the rise and fall of Communism.

The author's main purpose in writing the book has been to arouse curiosity as well as to satisfy it and to help readers discover those areas of history which interest them most.

Chapter 1

'THE LAMPS GO OUT'

The Assassination of an Archduke

On 28th June 1914 the Archduke Franz Ferdinand, heir to the Emperor of Austria and commander-in-chief of the Austrian army, paid a formal visit to Sarajevo, capital of Bosnia, which had recently become a province of the Austro–Hungarian Empire.[1] At the time there was much discontent in the province as most of the inhabitants were Slavs and strongly opposed to Austrian rule. The wish of many of them was to unite with the neighbouring independent state of Serbia from whom they received a certain amount of secret help and encouragement. In spite of the discontent no special precautions had been taken about the safety of the Archduke, and the details of his visit, including his movements, had been made public. To six young students this seemed an ideal opportunity to strike a blow for the freedom of Bosnia, and they hatched a plot to assassinate the Archduke; and in this they were assisted by a secret Serbian society known as the Black Hand. At first the students' plans miscarried; four of them lost their nerve and another threw a bomb which went off under the wrong car. The Archduke was shaken but otherwise unhurt, and if he had cancelled the remainder of his visit he might have survived. He insisted on continuing, however, with only a small change to his scheduled route, and by chance this brought him close alongside the sixth assassin, Gavrilo Princip, who did not fail to take the opportunity thus presented to him, and both the Archduke and his wife were killed.

At the time few people foresaw that this incident would lead to a European war. Assassinations of royalty, particularly in the Balkans, were not uncommon and, after an initial uproar, they had not had

---

[1] The Austrian Empire, one of the oldest in Europe, had been known as Austria–Hungary since 1867.

Central Europe in 1914

far-reaching consequences, but in 1914 it was to be different. At the time Austria's relations with Serbia were very unfriendly. For some time Serbians had been stirring up trouble in the eastern provinces of the Austro–Hungarian Empire, and the Austrian government was seeking an occasion for war with Serbia so that she could be humiliated and 'taught a lesson'. For a month after the death of Franz Ferdinand there was a lull while the Austrians tried to find evidence involving the Serbian government in the assassination; but this they were unable to do. However, they were not prepared to let the matter drop and presented the Serbian government with an ultimatum which contained ten demands. Most of these concerned the arrest of the assassins and the suppression of secret societies, and the Serbians agreed to all of them

*The arrest of Gavrilo Pricip, the man who set in motion the events
leading to the ourbreak of war.*

except one – that Austrian officials should be allowed into Serbia to
'collaborate' in the carrying out of the demands. This the Serbians
regarded as an affront to their national sovereignty and refused to agree
to it. To most people in Europe the Serbian reply seemed satisfactory,
and there was a general feeling that the crisis was over; but the Austrians, still looking for a showdown with Serbia, decided to push the
matter further, and on 28th July declared war. A week later nearly the
whole of Europe was at war.

Europe Divided into Two Camps

There was, of course, more to this catastrophe than the murder of an
Archduke. Europe had been on the brink of war for some years. At the
time the Continent was divided into two camps with a system of alliances
which meant that two countries going to war would almost certainly
involve others as well. On the one hand there were the 'Central Powers'

consisting of Germany and the Austro–Hungarian Empire, and on the other the 'Allied Powers' of France and Russia with Great Britain moving in their direction. And so when Austria declared war she looked to Germany for support, while Serbia looked to Russia who, it was believed, would not stand by while fellow Slavs in a neighbouring state were overwhelmed. And Russia, in turn, would look for help to France. At first the great powers acted with caution. The Russians were anxious to avoid war, but felt they owed it to the Serbs to make some gesture of support, and so they started to mobilise part of their army. At this the rulers of Germany took fright; they were convinced that in modern warfare victory would go to the side which first mobilised its full army and brought it into action. By this reasoning, therefore, they believed they could not remain inactive while the Russians mobilised and delivered the first blow. And so, after some hesitation, the German government sent an ultimatum to Russia demanding that mobilisation should cease at once. To this the Russians could not agree without great loss of face, and on 1st August Germany declared war on Russia.

The question then arose as to whether France would fulfil her treaty obligations and come in on the side of Russia. But in the event Germany gave her no choice. Some years before, German army chiefs had drawn up a plan to be put into operation in the event of war, and this involved attacking and defeating France first and then turning on Russia afterwards. So complicated was this plan (involving the transport of 3,000,000 men in 4,278 trains) that it could not be altered. The Germans were tied to it. And so on 3rd August Germany declared war on France. The question then arose as to whether Britain would come into the war. This was not certain, for although Britain and France had been drawing closer together lately and their service chiefs had been drawing up plans for joint action, Britain was bound by no treaty to come to France's help, and the Liberal government was divided on the issue. However, its hand was forced; for the German master plan[1] provided that their armies should invade France through Belgium, and to Belgium Britain did have firm treaty obligations. In 1839 when Belgium had been separated from Holland, Britain had been one of the countries which had guaranteed her independence; and

---

[1] Known as the Schlieffen Plan after the soldier who devised it.

although a German leader was said to have referred to this scornfully as 'a scrap of paper', it removed British doubts, and on 4th August Britain declared war on Germany.

And so suddenly out of a clear sky all the major powers of Europe were at war. There was no clear cut reason for it; except for Serbia no country's safety was threatened, yet all were passionately convinced that they were fighting in defence of their homelands. Differences between the great powers certainly existed but these had become less acute lately, and none of Europe's leaders wanted a major war. However, in 1914 they found themselves powerless to prevent it, and Europe was carried over the brink.

At the time few people in Europe realised the scale of the disaster. In most countries they went to war gladly even joyously. To the Germans it was the coming of 'The Day', the end of a long stagnating peace and the beginning of an era when their hopes for a new and greater Germany would be fulfilled. To most Frenchmen too it was a moment of exhilaration – their long-awaited opportunity for revenge for their defeat by Prussia in 1870 and for making France once again the foremost power in Europe. War fever was rampant in England too. Young men rushed to enlist, terrified that the fighting would be over before they had struck their blow. To them the war was an exciting challenge, a crusade, an opportunity for heroism and adventure. The poet, Rupert Brooke, only just out of university (and soon to lose his life in the war), described this exultation:

> Honour has come back, as a king, to earth
> And paid his subjects with a royal age;
> And nobleness walks in our ways again;
> And we are come into our heritage.

There were some, of course, too, who were deeply depressed by the coming of war. To them it was a day of doom. 'The lamps are going out all over Europe,' Sir Edward Grey, the British foreign secretary, said sadly. 'We shall not see them lit again in our lifetime.'

The Two Sides Compared

At the beginning of the war there were six principal countries involved. On the one side there were the empires of Germany, Austria–Hungary and Turkey, known as the Central Powers. On the other were the empires of Great Britain, France and Russia, known as the Entente Powers or the Allies. At first sight they seemed very unequal. The population of the Allies was nearly twice that of the Central Powers and their economic resources much greater. Also they had command of the seas so that they could blockade their enemies, while they themselves could trade with the rest of the world and get help from abroad, notably from the British dominions of Canada, Australia, New Zealand and South Africa, all of which had joined in the war at once of their own accord. The advantages of the Central Powers were few by comparison. In some industries, notably steel and chemicals, German production was higher than that of the Allies; also at the beginning of the war the Germans had a larger and better trained army.

The Central Powers

Austria–Hungary

The Austro–Hungarian Empire consisted of many different races – Slavs, Croats, Germans, Magyars and Italians – which had been drawn together originally to combat the menace from the Turks. But by 1914 this menace had long since disappeared and many of the subject races were clamouring for their independence. This had already been achieved by the provinces in Italy and to some extent by the Hungarians, but the Austrian government was determined that this disintegration should go no further. It was for this reason that it felt such a deadly hostility towards the Serbians who had been encouraging the Slavs of Eastern Europe to rise in revolt and break away from Austrian rule.

The nominal ruler of Austria in 1914 was the Emperor Francis Joseph, then in his 84th year and the 67th of his reign. A gaunt, wooden, lonely figure, his life had been dogged by tragedy; his only son had committed suicide, his wife had been assassinated in Switzerland, as also had his brother in Mexico and his nephew in Bosnia. Left to himself it is likely that he would not have allowed the Serbian crisis to get out of hand, but he was an old man, aware that times were changing and unwilling to overrule his ministers who were determined to exaggerate the crisis and, if necessary, to fight a local war with Serbia, although they had no wish for a war with Russia and certainly not with Britain and France.

During the war Austria was not to play an important or heroic part. Her armies, though large, had little stomach for the fight and were often in trouble and had to be rescued and bolstered up by the Germans. At the end of the war, with the defeat of the Central Powers, the Empire of Austria–Hungary was broken up.

Turkey

Following their capture of Constantinople in 1453 the Ottoman Turks had established a large empire in Eastern Europe and for many years had posed a serious threat to the rest of the Continent. By 1914, however, they had been expelled from Europe and the rest of their empire was crumbling away.

There was no adequate reason for Turkey coming into the war on the side of Germany and Austria. She was, it is true, the historic enemy of Russia whose aims in the direction of the Dardanelles and the Mediterranean she still feared. It is true too that in the years before the war the Turkish government had been having dealings with German leaders who were planning to build a Berlin to Baghdad railway. Nevertheless there was every reason for Turkey to remain neutral: her vital interests were not affected, she stood to gain little in the event of a German victory and to lose heavily if the Allies won.

In the war Turkey was to play only a subsidiary role. She successfully warded off an Allied attack on Gallipoli (see p. 24) and tied down large Allied forces in Greece and the Middle East where she posed a threat to the Suez Canal and the Persian (Iranian) oilfields. At the end of the war she had to pay the penalty for being on the losing side and was deprived of the remaining parts of her empire in the Middle East.

Germany

The German Empire was the newest in Europe, having come into existence in 1870 following Prussia's swift and overwhelming victory over France. After that all German states became united, with the king of Prussia as their Emperor or Kaiser, and became the strongest country in Europe. Her population was growing the fastest, her industrial output was the greatest and her army was the most powerful. Also since 1897 she had started to build a battlefleet which had momentous consequences as it brought her into conflict with Britain. The young Kaiser William II, a grandson of Queen Victoria, seems to have thought that a battlefleet was necessary for his prestige and that of the new German Empire. He also thought that it would keep Britain neutral if a war were to break out on the Continent, but in the event it had the opposite effect. It caused great alarm and strong anti-German feelings in Britain and a determination to maintain the country's naval superiority at all costs. And so there ensued an arms race with each country trying to build larger and more powerful ships than the other, and with relations between the two countries becoming ever worse. Increasingly Germans came to resent Britain and to be jealous of her power and prestige; Britain, they felt, was hemming them in and preventing them from expanding their overseas empire. The British, for their part, became more and more suspicious of the Germans. Why did they need to build a fleet? It was not necessary to defend their country. They did not need it to defend their trade routes. They were not, like Britain, dependent on overseas trade. Could it not only be a deliberate threat to Britain?

At the same time Germany made other enemies in Europe and caused much alarm by the arrogant and blustering talk of some of her leaders. There was much glorification of war and loud assertions of the 'duty' to wage it, and of Germany's right to expand and dominate Europe. Much of this talk was, of course, 'hot air' and not to be taken too seriously. In more sober moods Germans spoke in a different tone. To many foreigners, however, as indeed to some Germans, this bombastic militarism was frightening and repulsive.

Perhaps typical of Germany at that time was the dual personality of the Kaiser. On the one hand the family man – father of seven and a dutiful and devoted grandson of Queen Victoria – and the statesman who had given Germany twenty-five years of peace. On the other hand the fanatic – excitable and irresponsible, throwing tantrums and ranting about Germany's destiny. The First World War is sometimes known as the Kaiser's War, but this is inappropriate. Left to himself, he would probably have found a way to peace, but the pressures on him, particularly from the army, were too great. Basically he was a weak man carried along by the flood.

The Allies

Russia

In 1914 the Communist revolution had not yet come to Russia and its system of government was still the most old-fashioned and despotic in Europe. It was only 50 years since the serfs had been freed and eight since the first parliament had been convened. The Tsar Nicholas II, a gentle, shy, bewildered man, had a great wish to improve the lot of his people and to give the country a more democratic form of government; but he was weak-minded and incapable and dominated by a formidable and unbalanced wife who, in turn, was under the influence of a fanatical monk called Rasputin. Tragedies and problems beset the unfortunate Nicholas on every side. Most of his ministers and, indeed, most people in government service were corrupt and inefficient; most Russian people were desperately poor; the country abounded in secret revolutionary societies; and riots and assassinations were frequent.

Abroad Russian prestige was very low. She had few friends and had just fought a disastrous war with Japan in which her armies had been defeated and her fleet sunk.

However, when war came in 1914 there was a surge of loyalty to the Tsar, and the Russian people rallied not only to the defence of their own country but also to the aid of their only ally, France, which was bearing the brunt of the German attack. In the course of the war Russian armies were to fare miserably on the battlefield; defeat followed defeat until the situation became so desperate that not even the Russian people could bear it any longer. Revolution broke out in the course of which the Communists, at the time a tiny minority, were able to seize power (see p. 37) and make a humiliating peace with Germany.

France

France's defeat by Prussia in 1870 and the subsequent loss of the provinces of Alsace and Lorraine had been a bitter blow to French pride, and many Frenchmen were thirsting for revenge. For a long time, however, this was impossible; Germany was too strong for France to tackle alone and the wily German chancellor, Otto von Bismarck, had seen to it that France should have no allies to help her.

In some ways France had recovered marvellously from her defeat. Reparations and war debts were soon paid off, and Paris had resumed her position as the cultural and artistic capital of Europe with a golden age of writers, painters and composers.[1] At the same time the French built up an extensive overseas empire in Central and Northern Africa and Indo-China. However, there was a murky side to the picture, particularly on the political scene; presidents and prime ministers had come and gone rapidly, some committing suicide, some being assassinated and some disgraced. There had been a number of political scandals, one of which had rocked the nation as never before. This concerned a Jewish army officer, Captain Dreyfus, who had been wrongly convicted on a charge of treason and who for a long time was denied justice. The 'Dreyfus Affair' caused a tremendous division in the country: on one side were the government and the army who felt their honour was at stake and strongly opposed any retrial; on the other were liberal elements, mainly from intellectual and artistic circles, who thought that an injustice had been done and was being covered up and must be remedied at all costs.[2]

By the beginning of the twentieth century, however, France's fortunes were beginning to revive. By then Bismarck had been removed from power and, as has been seen, the rash and foolish behaviour of Kaiser William II was bringing enemies for Germany and friends for France. The first of these friends was Russia. Many thought it strange that the French Republic, the most democratic state in Europe, should ally itself to the Continent's most despotic monarchy, but the alliance worked without difficulty, and when war came Germany had to fight on two fronts; and if this was not the disaster for Germany it was once thought it would be, it saved France from defeat in the opening months of the war. The other country with which France became on more friendly terms was Britain. For a long time the two countries had been kept apart by rivalry in the scramble for new colonies, and at the end of the nineteenth century had nearly gone to war about a remote outpost

---

[1] This was the age of the Impressionist painters and such great composers as Debussy and Fauré.

[2] Eventually, after three years on Devil's Island, a prison off the coast of French Guiana, Dreyfus was pardoned and restored to his rank.

in southern Sudan called Fashoda. However, with the building of the German fleet and the growing aggressiveness of the Kaiser the two countries had been drawn together. No alliance was signed, but there was an understanding, or *Entente Cordiale*, by which it was tacitly agreed that the two countries' defence chiefs would collaborate to draw up plans in the event of war with Germany.

When war came it was France which had to bear the main onslaught of the German army. Parts of her country were occupied throughout the war, and most of the fighting took place on French soil; her losses on the battlefield were vast, and at times it was a desperate struggle to keep going. The cost of final victory was far greater than anyone had thought possible.

Great Britain

In 1914 the British Empire still covered one quarter of the earth's surface, and Britain was still the world's wealthiest nation. However, this situation was changing. Britain's industry was no longer the world's greatest, her supremacy at sea was being challenged, and her prestige in the world had recently suffered a heavy blow by a war in South Africa against the Boers, a settlement of farmers mainly of Dutch origin, who for a time defied the might of the great British Empire and could only be defeated in the end by the use of ruthless and, as many saw it, inhuman methods.

For much of the nineteenth century Britain had remained aloof from Europe in so-called 'splendid isolation'. But in view of her declining position this was something she could no longer afford. It was necessary for her to find friends in Europe and, as has been seen, since the building of the German battlefleet she had been drawing closer to the enemies of Germany. When war came it was greeted in Britain, as in other countries, with enthusiasm. Few had little idea of the fearsome bloodbath in which they would become involved.

Timescale

1914

June 28   Assassination of Archduke Franz Ferdinand.
July 26   Austria declares war on Serbia.

	30	Russian mobilisation.
August	1	Germany declares war on Russia.
	3	Germany declares war on France and invades Belgium.
	4	Great Britain declares war on Germany.

Chapter 2

FIRST WORLD WAR 1914–15
Heavy Losses and Deadlock

Invasion of Belgium

When war broke out in August 1914 the mobilisation plans of the great powers worked efficiently and within a few weeks more than six million men were under arms. By then both Germany and France had already launched attacks which, they hoped, would taken them into the opposing side's capital by Christmas.

At that time there was a general belief that in modern warfare advantage lay with the side which attacked first; it was thought that the country which first mobilised its armies and brought them into the battle area would then carry all before it by sheer weight of numbers. In the event this belief proved mistaken and resulted in immense loss of life. For in the last forty-five years, while Europe had been at peace, the science of war had been transformed by new inventions which gave advantage to the defenders rather than the attackers. In 1914 it was soon demonstrated how deadly was the newly developed machine gun when mounted in a dug-out trench surrounded with barbed wire. Later it was estimated that two machine guns could hold up the advance of a thousand men. In other ways too, conditions of modern warfare favoured the defence, notably in the matter of transport. Vast armies needed vast supplies, and for these they depended on the railways. But railways could only supply attacking armies as far as the country's frontier; once they were into enemy territory, where retreating armies would have made the railways behind them unusable, they would have to rely on horse-drawn transport, and horses required large and bulky supplies of fodder. The defenders, on the other hand, were at no such disadvantage; they would be able to use their railways to bring reinforcements to any threatened area.

It was because of these great advantages of the side on the defensive

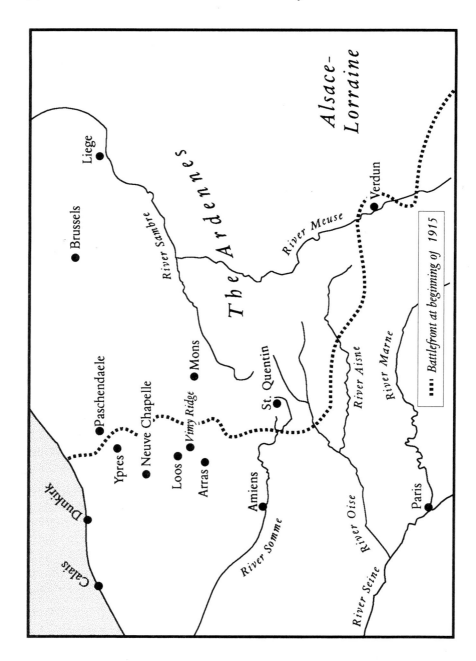

The Western Front

that nearly all land fighting in the war became deadlocked; and in France and Belgium two vast armies confronted each other in long lines of trenches, hardly ever winning or losing more than a few hundred yards of territory. This stalemate did not, however, occur at once. During the opening months of the war there was considerable movement by the opposing armies. Both France and Germany lost no time in launching long-planned offensives; but the Germans attacked first and had greater success.

As has been seen, the Germans had planned that their invasion of France was to be carried out through Belgium. This was the easiest route and the Germans were confident that, provided they gave certain guarantees and promised to evacuate the country at the end of the war, the Belgians would offer no resistance. How could they with their small ill-equipped forces[1] stand up to the most powerful army in Europe? It came as an unpleasant shock to the Germans, therefore, when the Belgians resisted stubbornly. Not only did the Belgian army stand in their way, but civilians too played their part, blowing up bridges and tunnels, tearing down telegraph wires and occasionally making good use of their sporting rifles. German reaction to this was swift and terrible. For some years German war chiefs had been declaring that terror should be used to shorten war. In the German Conduct of War Manual it was stated: 'War cannot be conducted merely against the combatants of an enemy state but must seek to destroy the total and material and intellectual resources of the enemy.' In Belgium in 1914 the Germans proceeded to put this fearful doctrine into practice. Whole villages were destroyed and their inhabitants massacred; hostages were taken and shot; and, a grim sign of things to come, Zeppelins[2] bombed defenceless civilians. However, the Germans were to discover then, as others were to discover later, that terrorism does not always have the intended effect. Instead of cowing people into submission it makes them obstinate and angry and so tends to lengthen wars rather than shorten them. Certainly Germany's use of terror in 1914 appalled world opinion and strengthened the resolve of her enemies to fight the war to the end.

---

[1] Some Belgian guns were reported to be drawn by dogs.

[2] Large cylindrical airships named after their inventor. At that time they had a much longer range than aeroplanes and a much larger bomb-carrying capacity.

Belgian resistance could not, of course, last long. The German army was much too powerful. Heroic as it was, it held up the German advance into France for no more than two days.

Arrival of the British Army

In 1914 Britain's army was highly trained and efficient, having recently learned some hard lessons in the war in South Africa; but it numbered no more than 100,000 men as compared with the millions of the French and the Germans. At first there was some disagreement as to how and where the British army should be brought into action. Should it be tacked on to the French army? Or should it operate independently in other theatres of war?

There were many, including the mighty Lord Kitchener,[1] who favoured the latter course of action, but it was found to be impracticable if the British army was to come into action at once. Moving an army required long and detailed planning, and the only plan in existence at the time was one which placed the British army side by side with the French. And so this was agreed and within three weeks of the outbreak of war British forces were in position on the left flank of the French army on the Belgian frontier, and so directly in the way of the oncoming German invasion. Almost at once they found themselves in action in the bleak Belgian mining town of Mons. Here their fighting spirit and accurate rapid rifle fire soon dispelled some lighthearted German notions about the amateurishness of the British army.[2] But they were hopelessly outnumbered, and as the French forces on their right had just met with disaster and were in headlong retreat, it was necessary for them too to make a long and rapid withdrawal.

---

[1] Field-Marshal Lord Kitchener of Khartoum had gained a great reputation as a soldier in India, Egypt and South Africa. Because of this, he was brought into the government in 1914 as Secretary of State for War. However, like most soldiers, he was not a skilful politician and was soon at odds with his colleagues in the cabinet whom he tended to treat as subordinates. Later in the war, he was drowned when making a sea voyage to Russia.

[2] At that time there was a tendency in Germany to look on the British army as something of a joke – a small force of no consequence dressed in red tunics and bearskins. They remembered Bismarck's quip about sending in the police force to round up the British army if it ever landed in Germany.

Failure of French Offensive

When it became clear that the main German offensive was being launched through Belgium, the French commander-in-chief, General Joffre, felt no dismay. This must mean, he thought, that troops had been taken away from other parts of the German front, notably in the Ardennes and Lorraine where he was about to launch his own offensive. Resistance there in that case would be all the weaker. Like other French generals at that time Joffre was convinced that French armies only won victories when they were on the attack. Defence did not come naturally to them; but when they took the offensive they carried all before them. What mattered in war, they believed, was not so much planning and weapons as the fighting spirit and the will to win. Thus in 1914 the French army had plenty of cavalry but little artillery; and the infantry, still dressed in blue tunics and red trousers, relied on bayonets rather than machine guns.

The result was tragic. The French made their attack as planned and fought with great gallantry, but no amount of fighting spirit could prevail against modern weapons. What could cavalry and bayonets achieve against machine guns and artillery? Everywhere the French were driven back. Their losses were appalling, not only in numbers but in quality; the finest troops of their army were lost. It was a devastating blow from which they never recovered.

The Battle of the Marne

For two weeks after their defeat in the Battle of the Frontiers the French armies, along with the British, had to make a long and dispiriting retreat. At any time during this period, if the Germans had broken through and the French line had collapsed, the war could have been lost. That this did not happen was in part due to the calmness and confidence of the French commander-in-chief. After the war Joffre was to come in for harsh criticism; he was accused, among other things, of being slow-thinking, unimaginative and complacent.[1] However, at this supreme

---

[1] Much has been made of how much time he spent every day, even at times of greatest crisis, at his meals.

The Eastern Front

crisis his nerve held. Had he shown the least sign of panic or defeatism, this would have spread like wildfire and French resistance could have broken down. As it was he did not waver; in spite of his fearsome responsibility and the endless reports of defeats and heavy losses he remained composed and optimistic.

Keeping the French armies intact at this time meant, as events proved, that they were assured of final victory. For time was running out for the Germans. For fourteen days they had advanced rapidly; they had crossed the river Marne and were within striking distance of Paris. But by then the problems of an attacking army were beginning to tell: the troops were exhausted, their supply lines were growing ever-longer, and railways could no longer be used. Moreover there was doubt and indecision in the German High Command. The commander-in-chief, Von Moltke, was of a different calibre to his uncle who had led the Prussians to victory in 1870. Weak and hesitant, he had allowed the German master plan to go wrong. The essence of this was that the German attacking forces were to be concentrated on the right wing of the army for the drive through Belgium; other forces on the remainder of the front were to do no more than carry out a holding operation, that is to engage the enemy forces opposite them so that they could not be moved elsewhere, but no more than this. This was not, however, to the taste of the commanders of these forces and they put great pressure on Von Moltke to allow them to join in the main attack, and he agreed. Also at a crucial time he allowed vital divisions to be taken away from France to go to the Russian front. The consequence of this was that the main German attack ran out of steam and was driven back, and in front of Paris the French managed to catch them at a disadvantage. All available troops poured out of the city[1] to join in the Battle of the Marne, the result of which was that the Germans pulled back in full retreat. For a time there were hopes that the war had been won as the Allies set out in pursuit. However, five days later when they reached the river Aisne, they found that the Germans had dug in and set up machine gun posts, and their advance came to a halt. There then took place something of a scramble while the Allies gained possession of the Channel Ports, and a fearful battle was fought at the Belgian town

---

[1] Some in requisitioned taxicabs.

of Ypres. From then on stalemate set in, and the position of the two sides did not alter significantly for the next four years.

The Eastern Front

On the Eastern Front neither the Germans nor the Russians had made plans for attack. Here the German intention was to fight a defensive war until their armies had been victorious in the west and then to transfer enough forces to defeat the Russians. For their part the Russians were unready: their armies were ill-equipped, and the general staff had not yet come round to planning a campaign. However, in response to an urgent appeal for help from the French, two armies were sent from Poland into East Prussia. At first they had some success but later (29th August) they were routed at the battle of Tannenburg and sent reeling back.

The Russians had more success against the Austrians. They occupied the Austrian province of Galicia (now part of the Ukraine) and reached the Carpathians. But the position was restored when German troops arrived on the scene. Soon afterwards both sides began digging trenches, and for the time being the battle came to a halt and fighting was stalled.

Before the war German military leaders had been apprehensive at the thought of fighting a war on two fronts, but thanks to the nearly impregnable defence provided by machine guns and barbed wire, this was to prove possible. It did mean, however, that, until the Russians made peace in 1917 following the Bolshevik revolution, large German forces were tied down in the east when they were badly needed in the west.

War at Sea

On the outbreak of war many people expected a tremendous showdown between the British and German battlefleets. But in the event this did not occur. In the pre-war 'race' to build most battleships Britain had maintained her superiority and entered the war with twenty of the new Dreadnought battleships as against Germany's fifteen. For the time being, therefore, the main German fleet stayed in port while the British navy drove nearly all German shipping from the seas and took possession of Germany's overseas colonies. However, this did not occur without some opposition and, before they were finally sunk, German cruisers, roaming the oceans alone or in small groups, did much damage. The *Emden* sank fourteen merchant ships in the Indian Ocean before being sunk by the Australian cruiser *Sydney*. In the Pacific and later in the South Atlantic a squadron of five ships under Von Spee was at large for four months in the course of which it sank an inferior British force off the coast of Chile at Coronel. A month later, however, it was itself caught off the Falkland Islands by more powerful British ships and destroyed.

Although Britain's superiority in battleships had been maintained, the effectiveness of this superiority was beginning to be impaired by the appearance of new weapons. Already the movements of big ships were being restricted by the danger from mines and submarines; and these caused the loss of several battleships. For most of the war the main British and German battlefleets remained in harbour, but this was in itself an important British victory. It meant that Britain's communications with the rest of the world were kept open,[1] while the blockade of Germany gradually tightened. It was estimated that during the war British ships transported across the oceans some 33 million people, two and a half million horses and mules, half a million vehicles and 49 million tons of stores and equipment.

1915

The Western Front – Stalemate and Further Losses

In 1915 the German commander-in-chief, Von Falkenhayn, made a major decision: he would remain on the defensive in the west and transfer troops to the east for a decisive blow against Russia.

The Germans did attack once on the Western Front at Ypres in April, but this aimed only to strengthen their position in the area and to experiment with a new weapon – poison gas. Despite the deadliness of this weapon the attack was withstood, but British casualties were nearly twice those of the Germans. Otherwise all attacks in 1915 were made by the Allies, and all were costly failures. It seemed that the Germans

---

[1] As will be seen later Britain's sea routes were to be gravely threatened by an all-out U-boat campaign.

Australian troops waiting to go 'over the top'. What is the man nearest the camera doing?

Blinded by poison gas.

were adapting more quickly than the Allies to the technique of trench warfare. British and French commanders still failed to realise the deadly effectiveness of machine guns, and some of them clung to the belief that cavalry still had a part to play in war. But their most dangerous delusion was that the way through the opposing trenches was by means of heavier and heavier artillery barrages; they failed to see that these could not destroy opposition completely and served as a warning to the enemy where an attack was coming.

Perhaps the most successful attack of 1915 was the first, that of the British at Neuve Chapelle. Here there was only a short artillery barrage so that the enemy was taken by surprise and the infantry broke through their front line. However, reinforcements were not at hand to exploit this success. Later in the year the British commanders, under great pressure from the French, mounted another offensive over the coalfields of Loos. Their army was not properly prepared and the commanders regarded the area as unsuitable, but the French were desperate and the attack went ahead. In the ensuing battle the infantry again broke through the front line, but could not get through the second, and once again the Germans were able to rush reinforcements to the area more quickly than the attackers. On this occasion it was the British who used poison gas, but the wind was not always in the right direction and it blew back on them, proving almost as dangerous to them as to the Germans. When the attack was finally called off British casualties amounted to some 50,000 men as opposed to about 20,000 Germans.

Great as were British losses in 1915 they were small compared to those of the French. As a result of their offensives, none of which gained more than a few hundred yards of territory, nearly 200,000 men were lost. But Joffre was not unduly disheartened. He was beginning to think in terms of a 'war of attrition', that is gradually wearing down the strength of the enemy and relying on the greater number of the Allies to prevail in the end. But in 1915 Allied casualties were twice those of the Germans.

The Eastern Front

It has been seen that it was in the east that Germany was to make her main effort in 1915. Von Falkenhayn had two main objectives: to force

Russia to make a separate peace and to overrun Serbia, thereby opening up communications with Germany's new ally, Turkey.

The campaign against Russia achieved great success. The Germans broke through the Russian lines and overran Poland and Galicia. The Russians suffered immense losses and were forced to make a long retreat. But their armies, starving and ill-equipped though they were, remained intact, and the longer the retreat went on and the nearer they were to home, the easier their position became. At the same time the German lines of communication grew longer. Finally the Russians dug in some 300 miles further east and the German advance was halted. For two years yet Russia was to remain in the war.

It did not take the Germans long to conquer Serbia. At the beginning of the war Austrian attempts to invade the country had been repulsed, but in the autumn of 1915 when they received help both from Germany and from their new ally, Bulgaria, the country was soon overrun. For the time being Serbia disappeared from the map, not to return till the end of the war, somewhat enlarged, as Yugoslavia.

Gallipoli – A Gamble That Nearly Came Off

The apparent deadlock and heavy losses on the Western Front soon led some people to believe that Britain should not be tied down to fighting the war in France and Belgium alone. Even before the setbacks of 1915 ideas were circulating about campaigns in other parts of the world. Of these the one which aroused most support and which was eventually carried out was the one to force a passage through the Dardanelles – the straits separating the Aegean Sea and the Sea of Marmora.

Turkey had come into the war on Germany's side in October of 1914. She was not able to do much to help but imposed an additional strain on Russia and constituted a threat to Britain's position in the Middle East, particularly to the Suez Canal and the Persian oilfields. It was believed by some that if British battleships were to force their way through the Dardanelles and appear off the Golden Horn,[1] Turkey would be intimidated into suing for peace. At a stroke the threat to the Middle East would be removed and a badly needed supply route to

---

[1] A fiord dividing the city of Constantinople into two parts.

Russia opened up. It was in the nature of a gamble, and it nearly came off, but not quite.

At the beginning of 1915 the British War Cabinet decided that no troops could be spared for the operation, whereupon Winston Churchill, the First Lord of the Admiralty, decided that the Navy would undertake it alone; and a force of old and nearly obsolete battleships was despatched to the Dardanelles. The Turks were caught by surprise and the operation nearly succeeded, but the British suffered some losses from mines and U-boats, and the attempt was abandoned.

At the same time the British government decided that it could after all spare some troops and another attack should be made. It was planned that infantry would be landed on the Gallipoli peninsula; these forces would overcome the Turkish shore batteries and so clear the way for the battleships. However, the Turks had by now been warned of what was coming and had rushed reinforcements to the area; and when the first landings were made on 25th April the British troops were pinned down by heavy fire from the steep cliffs above. Almost at once it was necessary for them to dig in, and so once again, as on the Western Front, it became a matter of trench warfare and deadlock. But so close had the operation come to success that the British government decided that for reasons of morale it should be continued and brought to a victorious conclusion. More troops were sent out for another landing further up the coast. This took place in August and, like the first, came near to success, but the British generals in charge of it were elderly and out of touch with modern methods of warfare, and did not press home the attack with enough speed, and here too there was deadlock.

For four months the British army in Gallipoli, which included Australian and New Zealand contingents, the famous ANZAC, held out in very unfavourable conditions; but at the end of the year it was decided to make a complete withdrawal. This at least was a success; it could have cost many lives, but in the event not a man was lost.

Italy Joins the Allies

If 1915 was a year of failures for the Allies, they did have one success, a diplomatic one, when Italy was persuaded to come into the war on their side. Back in 1882 Italy had formed a Triple Alliance with Germany and Austria, but by 1914 she was drifting away from them. Italian

British soldiers with wounded German prisoners.

leaders made it clear that their policy was one of 'sacred egoism', that is, Italy would join whichever side promised her greater rewards in the event of victory. At the time the lands most coveted by Italy belonged to Austria which firmly refused to give up any of them. The Allies, on the other hand, had little hesitation in promising them away, and the secret Treaty of London was concluded. Italy declared war on Austria in May but not on Germany until a year later.

Although she suffered heavy casualties, Italy did not play a decisive role in the war. Her troops were unable to break through the mountains which surrounded her on her northern border and remained hemmed in. However, she did tie down a large number of Austrian troops which could have been used elsewhere.

The Home Front

On the outbreak of war the people of Britain had been quick to put aside their differences and unite behind the government. In the early part of 1914 there had been great unrest and violence in the country: there had been strikes and bitter disputes in industry; the campaign of the

'Suffragettes' for the right of women to vote was growing in intensity; and in Ireland a civil war between Roman Catholics and Protestants seemed imminent. But on the outbreak of war these dissensions were stilled. The Irish party in Parliament gave full support to the war and thousands of Irishmen (Protestant and Catholic) came forward to enlist in the armed forces. The Suffragettes dropped their campaign for the right to vote and demanded instead 'the right to work'. And in industry, for the time being, strikes died down and there was greater cooperation between management and workers to produce what was needed for the war effort.

All over the country men rushed to join the army, and at first it was unnecessary for the government to introduce compulsory military service. Urged on by the stern figure of Lord Kitchener beckoning them from thousands of posters and by patriotic songs sung in hundreds of music halls, three million volunteers came forward. This was more than the authorities could deal with, and many men were kept hanging around through the winter in tents without uniforms and drilling with walking sticks.

At first there was little disruption of ordinary life. Everything went on much as before with the war as something of a sideline. But then the casualty lists became longer, some foods were in short supply, and from December there were Zeppelin raids on London which caused some destruction and necessitated a black-out. For a time there was no all-out war effort, but the defeats and setbacks of 1915, notably the failure at Gallipoli, were to change this. A great clamour arose for a more intensive war, and the cry was raised that soldiers were dying because of a shortage of arms, particularly shells. This outcry greatly weakened the position of the Liberal government headed by Mr Asquith, and it became necessary for him to form a coalition with the Conservatives. In this government the Minister of Munitions was David Lloyd George whose responsibility it was to reorganise the whole of British industry to provide for the needs of the war. This was a task needing all Lloyd George's dynamic energy, involving, among other things, the recruitment of millions of new workers, particularly women, and persuading trade unions to waive their rules about non-members. From this time a new spirit was abroad; Britain was going to war in earnest.

Timescale

1914	
August 23	British troops in action at Mons.
29	Russians defeated at Tannenberg.
September 5	Battle of the Marne begins.
14	Germans dig in on the river Aisne.
1915	
March 10	British attack at Neuve Chapelle.
April 22	Germans attack at Ypres using poison gas.
25	British troops land at Gallipoli.
May 23	Italy declares war on Austro–Hungary.
September 25	British attack at Loos.
October	Serbia overrun.
December 18	British troops evacuated from Gallipoli.

Chapter 3

FIRST WORLD WAR 1916–18
War of Attrition and Final Victory
1916

The Western Front – Verdun and the Somme

In 1916 the German High Command decided that the main effort for that year was to be made in the west, and the principal objective would be to knock France out of the war. Although Von Falkenhayn considered Britain to be Germany's prime enemy, he thought that she would not be overcome only by the defeat of her armies in France. But if crippling losses were inflicted on the French army, which had already suffered grievously, the French government might be compelled to sue for peace.

Von Falkenkayn was aware that in trench warfare the defenders usually suffered lighter losses than the attackers, but that this was only the case when the defence was prepared to give a little ground and abandon weak positions when necessary. He, therefore, chose as his point of attack a place which he knew the French would defend to the last – this historic fortress of Verdun. The military importance of Verdun was slight, but its emotional importance to the people of France was tremendous and, sure enough, the French government ordered it to be defended at all costs.

The struggle for Verdun was to be one of the greatest bloodbaths of history. The French commander, General Pétain,[1] declared: 'They shall not pass', and pass they did not, but the cost of preventing them was horrendous – some 315,000 men killed. The Germans too suffered immense losses. If for reasons of morale it was necessary for the French

---

[1] In the Second World War, when he was over eighty, he was to be head of the French government which made peace with the Germans.

On their way to the trenches.

Troops resting near the front.

to defend Verdun, so also for reasons of morale was it necessary for the Germans to capture it. Troops were poured in recklessly, and losses in the end amounted to over 281,000.

While the battle for Verdun was raging desperate appeals were sent to France's allies to create a diversion, and the British responded by launching an attack on the river Somme. A plan for a joint Franco–British attack in this area had already been drawn up, and this now became a mainly British undertaking.

The Battle of the Somme was to prove even more of a bloodbath than Verdun. The British high command had still not grasped the elements of trench warfare. It still believed that the way through the enemy lines was by a tremendous artillery bombardment followed by a massed infantry attack followed by cavalry to pursue the fleeing enemy. It still failed to realise that the most important element of all was surprise, that massed infantry attacks would collapse in face of a small number of machine guns, and that there was no role for cavalry in modern warfare. In consequence the Battle of the Somme proved an appalling catastrophe. The preliminary bombardment lasted five days and so gave the Germans plenty of warning as to where the attack was coming. At the same time it failed to penetrate the enemy dug-outs, and so, when it was over, the German machine-gunners emerged from these, shaken, but still able to fire their guns. On the first day of the battle (1st July) British losses amounted to 60,000 men. As the new men of 'Kitchener's Army', carrying over half a hundredweight of equipment, came stumbling over the shell-torn 'no man's land' between the trenches, they presented all too easy a target for the machine-gunners. Again and again the attacks were repeated. When the battle was finally called off four months later British losses had risen to 420,000 men. The French lost 200,000 and the Germans 450,000.

The Battle of the Somme had a profound effect on the morale of British troops. Up till then the war had been a crusade which most men had joined eagerly and happily. Even in the worst situations troops had laughed and joked and sung humorous songs about Blighty,[1] Tipperary and Sister Susie Sewing Shirts for Soldiers. After the Somme the mood changed and the humour turned sour. Jokes then were about staff officers in safe, comfortable jobs behind the lines and men back at home

---

[1] The troops' name for England.

who had not joined the army. The war became a fearsome endurance test and men came to loathe it, and yet, such was their comradeship and loyalty to each other that they did not wish to be away from it.

The Eastern Front

In answer to French appeals for help the Russians also took the offensive in 1916. Their main attack, complete with artillery bombardment and massive troop concentrations, was an expensive failure, their losses being in the proportion of 5–1 to those of the Germans. However, a later attack in Galicia, known after its commander as the Brusilov Offensive, had considerable success. Here, from necessity rather than design, there was no artillery barrage; Russian troops simply made a number of surprise attacks, and the Austrian line was overrun. However, as usual there were no reserves to follow this up and German troops were able to restore the position. But these German troops had been intended for Verdun.

War at Sea – The Battle of Jutland

It has been seen that in the first years of the war there was no great showdown between the British and German battlefleets. British superiority was acknowledged and both fleets remained in harbour, watching and waiting. The Germans knew that if the whole of their fleet met the whole of the British fleet, they would be outgunned, but the hope of the new German commander-in-chief, Admiral Scheer, was that the British fleet could be forced to divide up and then parts of it could be brought to battle separately. The British commander-in-chief, Admiral Jellicoe, was aware of this danger and aimed to keep his fleet together, but there were difficulties in this. For the only harbour on the east coast of the British Isles which could hold the whole of the Grand Fleet in safety was in the far north in the Orkney Islands at Scapa Flow. This meant that it was possible for the German fleet to make raids into the North Sea, sink merchant shipping, even bombard the east coast of England and then escape back to Germany before the arrival of the British Grand Fleet. With the appointment of Scheer these raids increased in number, and it became necessary for Jellicoe to detach his battle cruisers[1] under Admiral Beatty and station them further south.

Scheer's plan was to bring these battle cruisers into action and destroy them. He would come to sea with the whole of his fleet and send his battle cruisers on ahead to bombard the coast of England. This would bring Beatty steaming south, whereupon the German battle cruisers were to retreat and draw Beatty on to the main German fleet following up behind. In the event the plan miscarried, as the British admiralty got wind that something big was happening and ordered the whole Grand Fleet to put to sea. But at first everything went according to the German plan. Beatty was brought to battle, heavy losses were inflicted on him and he was then lured southwards. In time he made contact with the main German fleet, but he then turned round and retreated, and now it was the turn of the Germans to be lured into a trap. For Scheer was quite unaware of the movements of the Grand Fleet.

Jellicoe, steaming south, was desperate for news about the position and course of the German fleet so that he could bring his twenty-four Dreadnought battleships into battle to the best possible advantage; but for a time Beatty failed to give him this vital information. When eventually he did, Jellicoe made his dispositions immediately so that his fleet was deployed to trap the Germans. All seemed set for the most tremendous naval battle of all time. But then it did not come off. Jellicoe was certainly cautious, and rightly so. He well knew that, as Winston Churchill later wrote, he could 'lose the war in an afternoon'. For Germany the loss of her fleet would be a disaster but not necessarily a death blow. But for Britain such a loss must mean total defeat.

Accordingly Jellicoe took no risks. He knew that in a straight fight his fleet could out-gun the Germans, but he had to guard against the dangers from mines, submarines and torpedoes. Inevitably this slowed down the movements of his ships so that Scheer was able to escape from his trap. At the end of the battle Scheer sent in destroyers under a smoke screen to launch torpedoes at the British battleships, and Jellicoe turned away to avoid them and then made no attempt to pursue the retreating German fleet. He contented himself with placing the Grand Fleet between the German fleet and its way back to Germany.

---

[1] Large ships with heavy guns and great speed, but little protective armour.

Once again Scheer seemed trapped. But by then darkness was falling and Jellicoe would not risk a night engagement. But for Scheer, if he were to avoid total destruction, this was essential, and he ordered his battle cruisers to break through the rear of the British line at all costs. This, in the confusion of darkness, they succeeded in doing, the British ships at that point failing to realise what was happening and to inform the commander-in-chief.

And so the German fleet was able to get back to port, and the Battle of Jutland petered out. At first sight it might seem to have been a British defeat. Their losses were heavier: three battle cruisers, three cruisers and eight destroyers, as against one German battleship, one battle cruiser, four cruisers and five destroyers. But battles are not decided by losses alone. The essential point was that the oceans of the world remained open to Allied shipping and closed to the Germans, also when confrontation came, the German fleet had withdrawn and did not put to sea again before the end of the war when it came out to surrender and then to scuttle itself.

The Home Front

At the end of 1916 the war seemed as firmly deadlocked as ever. On the Western Front both sides had suffered immense losses with little to show for them; and at sea, when at last the two battlefleets came face to face, the result had been indecisive. In view of this it is not surprising that there should have been a feeling in all countries at that time, that the war should be brought to an end by a negotiated peace settlement. Only a few people, however, dared to voice these views in public. In Britain most people were totally opposed to such an idea and wanted to win the war at all costs, and at the end of the year a new government took office dedicated to this purpose. In this, another coalition of Liberals and Conservatives, Asquith was replaced as prime minister by Lloyd George.

In everyday life there were further signs of change as the war effort intensified. Compulsory military service (conscription) had been introduced and as a result there was a great increase in the number of women doing men's jobs, not only in shops and offices but also as police officers, bus conductors and ambulance drivers.

Although the war brought most people in Britain together in a common cause, peace did not last long in Ireland. Open revolt broke out in 1916 in Dublin with the so-called Easter Rising. This was soon put down, but the severity with which the ringleaders were treated created more Irish martyrs and built up more trouble for the future.

1917

All-out U-boat Campaign

In 1915 Germany had directed her main effort against Russia and in 1916 had delivered what she hoped would be a knock-out blow against France. In 1917 it was to be the turn of Britain to receive the main onslaught. For this Ludendorff [1] planned a full-scale offensive against British shipping. He considered that this would be more effective than defeating the British armies in France, for Britain was completely dependent on overseas supplies of food and raw materials, particularly oil, and if these were cut off, she would be starved into surrender. There was, however, a serious drawback to this plan: to be effective it would be necessary to sink all ships sailing to Britain, both Allied and neutral including those of America. Ludendorff realised that this was likely to bring America into the war, but he hoped that Britain would be forced to make peace before America could intervene.

The Germans had used U-boats earlier in the war but, partly owing to American protests and partly because they did not have enough of them for a really effective blockade, the campaign had been abandoned. In 1917, however, some 300 U-boats were available, and American protests were to be ignored.

At first the onslaught was highly successful. In April over a million tons of shipping were sunk, and it was reckoned that one ship in four leaving the British Isles never returned. Neutral ships refused to sail to Britain and supplies in the country ran dangerously low. The position was extremely critical and it seemed that Ludendorff's gamble might be going to pay off; but then, quite suddenly, the situation began to

---

[1] Von Falkenhayn had been replaced as Chief of the General Staff by Hindenburg, but he was elderly and little more than a figurehead, and most decisions were taken by his right-hand man, Ludendorff.

improve as British counter-measures took effect. Of these the most important was the introduction of convoys with merchant ships sailing together protected by anti-submarine vessels. There were great difficulties here and some naval experts had said it was impossible to implement; but Lloyd George insisted and in the event he was justified. Quite soon shipping losses were cut from 25 per cent to 1 per cent. At the same time urgent steps were taken to increase the building of new ships both in Britain and America, so that in time it became possible for all shipping losses to be replaced. At home to counter the shortage of food, rationing was introduced and efforts were made to increase home production.

America Enters the War

When war broke out in 1914, and many times since, President Wilson of the United States had declared categorically that his country would always remain neutral. Even after the sinking of the liner *Lusitania* with a hundred United States citizens on board he had reaffirmed American neutrality and proclaimed that there was 'such a thing as being too proud to fight'. However, more and more, America became involved in the war. American businessmen could not ignore the large profits that were to be made by selling war materials to both sides. Inevitably each side tried to prevent all trading with its enemies. For Germany this was difficult but for Britain it was comparatively easy; her navy intercepted all ships, searched them and prevented war equipment from reaching Germany. This caused some resentment in America but nothing like the furious indignation that erupted when American lives were lost as a result of German U-boats sinking American ships at sight. During the years when the U-boats had been called off American trade with Britain had increased considerably and had become of great importance to both countries. It was when Germany threatened to sink all ships and cut off this trade that America came into the war (6th April).

The entry of the United States into the war was an event of major importance in world history. Not only did it make certain the ultimate victory of the Allies but it marked the beginning of the American connection with Europe. Until then the United States had held aloof from European affairs, and its policy had been one of 'isolation'. From

1917, however, this began to change, and American influence in Europe and the world began to grow.

It would be some time before American entry into the war had full effect, but there were some immediate benefits to the Allies. The US navy cooperated fully with Britain in hunting down the U-boats and tightening the blockade of Germany. But above all it gave a much needed boost to Allied morale which in 1917 had sunk low after a series of defeats and heavy losses. American intervention brought new hope. In time American forces would play a decisive part on the Western Front but, as the Germans had calculated, there would be a time lag. For although the United States had a large navy, it had only a small army. Manpower it had in plenty but this would first have to be trained and equipped, and before it started arriving in Europe in large numbers the Germans hoped that they would have won the war.

The Russian Revolution

If in 1917 Britain and France were to gain an ally in the West they were to lose one in the East. After immense loss of life and human suffering the people of Russia had had enough of the war. At first they had shown great patriotism and enthusiasm; but then when defeat followed defeat, and conditions at home, owing to an inefficient and corrupt government, became ever more chaotic, there were many who looked for new leaders who would be ready to make peace.

Since before the outbreak of war Russia had been ripe for revolution. For years the tsars and their ministers had shown themselves incapable of governing their vast territories – although always interested in adding to them. They had seemed to show complete indifference to the sufferings of the people, and had always striven to obstruct any movements for change: liberty had been repressed and any form of democracy denied. Also the worst features of the Industrial Revolution had been left unchecked so that at the beginning of the twentieth century men, women and children were still working as many as eighteen hours a day. Inevitably there had been considerable revolutionary activity, but until the war this had achieved little; outbreaks of rebellion had been severely put down and the leaders imprisoned or driven into exile abroad.

The supreme ruler of Russia since 1894 had been the Tsar Nicholas II.

No-one could have been less fitted to lead Russia into the twentieth century, nor to have been her leader in a European war. With the situation growing ever more desperate insurrections broke out. In March 1917 the people of Petrograd,[1] then the capital of Russia, rioted for food and the soldiers, instead of suppressing them, joined them. At the time the tsar was at the front with his army and was prevented from returning by railwaymen who stopped his train. A week later he was to abdicate, and in the following year he and his family were put to death.

The Russian Revolution came in two stages. The first, the March Revolution, had little connection with Communism. After the deposition of the tsar power passed to a council of workers and soldiers known as a Soviet, most of whose leaders were moderate men pledged to continuing the war. In the following months, however, the war went from bad to worse; war weariness grew and mutiny broke out in the army. At the same time the more extreme revolutionary leaders returned to Russia from abroad. Lenin, the Bolshevik leader, was provided by the Germans with a special sealed train to convey him from Switzerland, while Trotsky made his way from New York.

The second revolution, masterminded by Lenin, occurred in October. The Bolsheviks gained control of Petrograd and of the Soviet; Lenin became its chairman with Trotsky as Commissar for Foreign Affairs. The new government immediately set about 'the building up of socialism'; decrees were issued handing over factories to the workers and urging the peasants to seize the lands of the landowners. At the same time negotiations began for the making of a separate peace with Germany, and on 15th December an armistice was agreed. In the following year at Brest-Litovsk the new Russian leaders were compelled to agree to harsh and humiliating terms with the cession of vast territories including Poland and the Ukraine.

The Western Front

On the Western Front in 1917 the war of attrition went on remorselessly, with both sides continuing to suffer heavy losses; otherwise the position remained unchanged. The pattern was depressingly similar to

---

[1] Known for seventy years subsequently as Leningrad.

previous years: massive attacks on strongly fortified positions, ample warning having first been given by prolonged and ineffective artillery bombardments. Sometimes the enemy lines were penetrated but, as before, resources were not at hand to exploit the situation.

At the beginning of the year Joffre was replaced as French commander-in-chief by Nivelle, a younger man, who had ideas for a new large-scale offensive, but unfortunately these were foiled at the outset by the action of the Germans – not, as in 1916, by attacking first but by withdrawing. For Ludendorff had decided to go on the defensive in the west in 1917, and had ordered a withdrawal to a shorter and stronger line which became known to the Allies as the Hindenburg Line.[1] This had meant giving up a large area of territory, but Ludendorff had ordered this to be devastated – houses to be destroyed, roads mined and wells poisoned. This operation completely upset the plans for Nivelle's offensive, but it went ahead all the same.

The British attacked first at Arras and initially had some success, notably a brilliant action by Canadian troops at Vimy Ridge. Later the main attack was launched by the French on the river Aisne, but this failed. Losses again were fearsome, and it seemed for a time that the spirit of the French army had been broken: mutiny broke out, trenches were left unmanned, and troops went into action bleating like sheep being led to the slaughter. Nivelle was replaced by Pétain who by firmness, thoroughness and, above all, by promising no more offensives managed to restore discipline and, to some extent, morale.

With the French army in a state of collapse it was necessary for the British to take urgent action to distract the Germans' attention. And so the British commander-in-chief, Sir Douglas Haig, put into operation a plan he had long cherished for a big attack in Belgium. This was strongly opposed by some people, notably the British prime minister, Lloyd George; but in the end Haig got his way. Since becoming commander-in-chief Haig had been in command of far larger forces than any other British general in history. During that time he had had little success and enormous losses but, unlike Joffre, Nivelle and Von Falkenhayn, he was still at his post, still full of

---

[1] The Germans called it the Siegfried Line.

Stretcher party wading through the mud of Passchendaele.

confidence and totally convinced that his method of fighting the war was the only one possible.

Haig's attack in Belgium, sometimes known as The Third Battle of Ypres and sometimes as Passchendaele, was to be another tragedy. The place for the attack was badly chosen, as Haig himself might have discovered if he had ever visited it. For much of the land had been reclaimed from the sea, and the water was held back by an elaborate system of drainage which was destroyed during the battle by the artillery bombardment. This, combined with heavy rains, turned the battlefield into a quagmire. The attack began on 31st July and was soon bogged down; guns sank in the mud while men waded about in it waist-deep. But Haig persisted and the operation was not finally called off until November by which time losses amounted to a further 300,000 men.

Soon afterwards on another part of the front it was shown what could be achieved if new ideas were permitted and, above all if the element

British tank as it might have appeared to Germans in trench.

of surprise in making an attack was fully appreciated. On 20th November without any preliminary bombardment 381 tanks[1] attacked the German lines at Cambrai and completely overran them, thereby achieving greater success than the massive attacks at Ypres and on the Somme at a fraction of the cost. As before, however, there were not the reserves to follow up the success and in time the Germans were able to recapture most of the ground they had lost. But it was clear that a means of penetrating enemy trenches had been found.

The Italian Front

Although it was Ludendorff's policy to remain on the defensive in the west in 1917 it became necessary for him to strike what he hoped would

---

[1] The British had been developing these for some time. Most top military commanders thought they would be of little practical use, but others, including Winston Churchill, then Minister of Munitions, insisted that production of them should go ahead.

be a decisive blow against Italy, for his Austrian allies were becoming increasingly war-weary and recalcitrant and needed a victory to boost their morale. An attack was launched at the end of October and at the Battle of Caporetto the Italians were defeated. They were forced to retreat for 70 miles, but then were able to set up a new line which proved strong enough to halt the German and Austrian advance. The effect of a heavy defeat had been to rouse Italy's fighting spirit.

The Middle East

1917 had been another disastrous year for the Allies, but at the end of it came a welcome success when British forces under General Allenby achieved the feat – long attempted by Crusaders – of capturing Jerusalem from the Turks. In this Allenby had great assistance from Colonel Lawrence (later known as 'Lawrence of Arabia') who stirred up the Arabs in revolt against the Turks and led them on a number of raids and ambushes.

Throughout the war Britain had maintained large forces in the Middle East: an army of half a million men had been stationed in Palestine to protect the Suez Canal; and another army of the same size was eventually built up in Mesopotamia (now Iraq) to protect the Persian oilfields. In time both these armies were to undertake operations which were ultimately successful. There were, however, those who thought these efforts misplaced. This 'mopping up' of the outlying provinces of the Turkish Empire was, they maintained, a heavy drain on resources and had little effect on the main outcome of the war.

1918

Repulse of Final German Offensive

In 1917 the Germans had had great success: they had knocked Russia out of the war; they had dealt a heavy blow to Italy; their U-boats had inflicted calamitous damage to Allied shipping; and their losses on the Western Front had again been less than those of the Allies. However, the German high command realised that time was running out for them. The ever-tightening blockade was causing serious shortages of food and

Canadians passing through the battered remains of Ypres.

raw materials, and American troops were arriving in Europe in increasing numbers. At the beginning of 1918, for the first time in the war, it would be possible for Germany to have superiority of numbers on the Western Front as, with Russia at peace, large forces could be transferred from the east. But this situation would not last.

Accordingly Ludendorff resolved to make an all-out bid for victory early in 1918. For this he planned first a series of attacks in the southern part of the front, and then a main attack in the north at Ypres which aimed to capture the Channel Ports and threaten the Allies' communications. In this offensive no new tactics were to be used – no tanks or aeroplanes – but great reliance was to be placed on the element of surprise. Artillery bombardments were to be short and sharp, and troop movements were to take place at night in the greatest secrecy.

The first attack was launched on 21st March. It was greatly helped by a thick mist and was very successful: the Allied line was overrun and Allied forces pushed right back. Other attacks too broke through so that by June the Germans had reached the river Marne and were only 56 miles from Paris. In the north 300,000 casualties had been inflicted on the British, and there was a danger that they would be cut off from the French to the south of them. However, great as was the German success, it was not great enough. For the Allied line, though it had sagged and bulged, had not broken; and the deeper the German troops advanced into French territory, the more difficult it became to keep them supplied. Also the great 'bulge' created by the German advance proved extremely vulnerable when the Allies mounted their counter-attack. That the Allies were able to do this was due to the formation of a large reserve, and the appointment at last of a supreme commander of all Allied forces. It seems strange that this had not been done before, but until April 1918 the three commanders-in-chief – Pétain, Haig and Pershing (c-in-c of the American armies) – had been independent and there had been little cooperation between them. But in the crisis caused by the German breakthrough jealousies and national pride receded, and the French Marshal Foch became Supreme Allied Commander.

Foch then took command of all forces in reserve and these he proceeded to use to great effect. When the last German attack was halted in July a counter-attack was launched against the flank of one of the German 'bulges'. The Germans were driven back and their position became so dangerous that Ludendorff had to call off his main attack at Ypres. The Allies were quick to follow up their success and further attacks were made of which one of the most successful was that of the British at Amiens. On 8th August they attacked and advanced six miles in one day. But it was then the turn of the Allies to discover that, although they had found the means of breaking through enemy trenches, they had not yet solved the problem of maintaining the momentum of an attack after the first success. Infantry could not keep up with tanks nor could supplies of petrol and ammunition, and in the meanwhile the Germans had had time to re-establish their lines.

The Germans were, however, in full retreat. By early September they were back in the positions they had occupied at the beginning of the year. Then at the end of the month the British broke through the Hindenburg Line. But still the German front remained intact, and the war could have dragged on into 1919. But then the end came suddenly, not because of the total defeat of the German armies, but because of a general collapse of German morale.

The Collapse of Germany

Ludendorff was one of the first to lose his nerve. He had been greatly disheartened by the failure of his offensive and the success of the Allied counter-attacks. Moreover American troops were now arriving in Europe at the rate of 300,000 a month. At the end of September too came serious news from Eastern Europe where the Allied army in Greece,[1] after three years of inactivity, had attacked the Bulgarians (allies of Germany) who had promptly capitulated. At the same time Ludendorff became convinced that the German soldier had lost his will to win, and he told the Kaiser that he must make peace at once.

The first overture for peace came on 4th October and was addressed to President Wilson from whom it was hoped generous terms might be obtained. Negotiations went on for over a month while Germany's remaining allies – Austria and Turkey – dropped out of the war. On the Western Front, however, the position was still under control, and Ludendorff now proposed to go on fighting if the right terms could not be agreed. But he was to find that he had stirred up forces he could no longer control. The desire for peace among the German people had become overwhelming; the loss of their allies, the defeat of their armies in France and the desperate shortages caused by the naval blockade brought home to them the hopelessness of their position. They demanded peace on almost any terms, and on 11th November an armistice was signed pending a final peace treaty.

The terms of the armistice were severe: Allied forces were to occupy part of Germany; as a token of good faith the Germans were to hand over at once large quantities of armaments including their fleet; they were to withdraw at once from all lands they had invaded as well as from Alsace–Lorraine, an area that had long been in dispute. These terms were agreed in Foch's railway carriage in the Forest of Campiègne on 11th November, and at 11 a.m. on that day all fighting ceased.

Conclusion

And so the war at last came to an end. There has, perhaps, never been such a human tragedy. Altogether some eight and a half million men were killed and over twenty million wounded. And even this was not

---

[1] An Allied army of 500,000 men had been stationed in Salonika since 1915. It had originally been sent to give help to Serbia. When Serbia was overrun it was decided for reasons of prestige to leave the army in the area. Until 1918 it took no part in the war, and the Germans referred to it as 'their largest internment camp'.

the full count for several millions more died because of famine and disease brought about by the war. Also the war had aroused great hatred, fear and bitterness, and the effect of these would be felt for many years to come.

Timescale

1916

February 21	German offensive at Verdun begins.
April 25	Easter Rising in Dublin.
May 31	Battle of Jutland.
June 4	Brusilov offensive opened.
July 1	Battle of Somme begins.
November 13	Battle of Somme called off.
December 7	Lloyd George becomes prime minister.

1917

March	First Russian Revolution. Abdication of Tsar.
April 1	U-boat offensive begins.
6	United States declares war on Germany.
9	British attack at Arras. Canadians capture Vimy Ridge.
July 31	Battle of Passchendaele (Third Ypres) begins.
October	Second Russian Revolution. Bolsheviks take over.
24	Italians defeated at Caporetto.
November 20	Battle of Cambrai.
December 9	British capture Jerusalem.
15	Russia makes peace with Germany at Brest-Litovsk.

1918

March 21	German offensive on Western Front begins.
July 18	French counter-attack begins.
August 8	British attack at Amiens.
October 4	First peace overtures.
November 11	Armistice agreed.

Chapter 4

THE MAKING OF PEACE

Confusion and Misery in Europe

The war had taken a terrible toll in Europe: as well as the millions of dead and wounded, there were millions more who were hungry and homeless.[1] In the last months of the war there had been violent upsets and the map of the Continent had been transformed: old empires had disappeared and in their place had come new democratic republics, uncertain of their ability to survive and with their frontiers still unsettled. And fighting was not yet entirely over; in Russia the civil war between Red Russian and White (Communist and anti-Communist) still dragged on, protracted by foreign intervention.[2]

A wise and just peace settlement was needed, but the people of Europe were not in the right mood for this. The French and Belgians were deeply embittered by the devastation of their countries by the German army. In Britain during the war there had been sensational propaganda campaigns with lurid accounts of German atrocities, and the hatred stirred up by these would not disappear at once. In the press and on political platforms there were such cries as 'Hang the Kaiser' and 'Make Germany Pay'; and in democratic countries statesmen could not ignore these outcries. It was in this atmosphere that Europe's leaders assembled in Paris to make peace.

---

[1] On top of everything else there occurred in 1918 and 1919 the worst ever influenza epidemic. Some 150,000 people in England and Wales died of it and perhaps as many as 30,000,000 worldwide including 14,000,000 in India – more than were killed on both sides in the whole of the war.

[2] Britain supplied the White Russians with armaments, and in 1918 there were British forces in the north of Russia in Archangel and Murmansk.

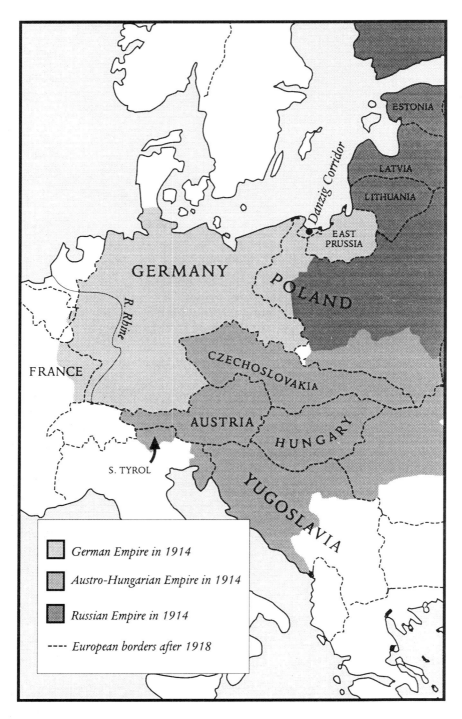

Central Europe 1918

Hopes for a Better World

The overwhelming wish of all people at that time was for a lasting peace and a better world. At the worst times of the war people had dared to hope that it was going to be 'a war to end wars', and Britain's prime minister, Lloyd George had promised British servicemen 'a land fit for heroes'. The greatest idealist had been the American president, Woodrow Wilson. It was he who had enunciated eloquently the war aims of the Allies in his Fourteen Points, and had talked of 'making the world safe for democracy' and of 'establishing a universal dominion of right by such a concert of free peoples as shall bring peace and safety to all nations and make the world itself at last free.' Hopes, alas, which were not to be fulfilled.

In the task he set himself Wilson resolved to make a break with old-fashioned methods of peacemaking. At the last great peace conference in Europe, at Vienna in 1815, the statesmen had met together in secret and had concluded a settlement whereby nearly all lands were returned to their hereditary rulers. Wilson was determined that this time negotiations would be open and there would be no indiscriminate handing over of peoples and provinces to countries against their wills. Everything would be settled by 'self-determination', that is the wishes of the people concerned.

In 1919 Wilson had much in his favour. He was the leader of the world's most powerful country, and had not only a great fund of idealism but also of armed force. He himself sought to gain nothing out of the war for the United States – neither territory nor indemnities (financial compensation). At the outset of the talks he had every hope that a peace treaty based on justice and human rights would be concluded. Disillusionment and frustration were not long in coming.

Difficulties of Peacemakers

Although the delegates had great opportunities in Paris in 1919, they also had formidable, perhaps insuperable, difficulties. In the first place Paris was surely not the right place to hold the peace talks. The atmosphere was too highly charged and emotional; France had suffered devastating losses during the war and anti-German feelings were running high, and in Paris particularly there was not the necessary calm in which peace talks should be held. There were feelings of fear and, at times, hysteria, which were bound to have their effect on the delegates. Also the delegates had too little time for their work; all too often they had to make snap decisions on inadequate information and with too little consideration. The Armistice had come with great suddenness and European leaders had not had time to work out their aims and policies; they had not even discussed among themselves President Wilson's Fourteen Points on the basis of which Germany had surrendered. And they could not afford to delay as it was necessary to confront Germany with a peace treaty at once. The Allied armies were being demobilised and the only way in which pressure on Germany could be maintained was by a naval blockade which was inhuman as it caused starvation among German civilians. As well as being overstrained and unprepared, the Paris delegates were also hampered by the pressure always being brought to bear on them by public opinion at home. Because negotiations were held in public they were not free agents and on occasions had to take decisions against their better judgement.

Decline of Idealism

On arrival at the Peace Conference President Wilson soon found many obstacles in the way of a treaty based on idealism. It was one thing to declare that all questions would be settled according to the wishes of the majority of the people concerned, but there were great complications about putting it into practice. In some places different races were so intermingled that the wishes of the majority could not be clearly determined. There was also the serious problem of the secret treaties made between the Allies during the war. These could not be scrapped, but to honour them would be a breach of self-determination. The most important of these was that made between the Allies and Italy in which Italy had been promised, as the price of her entry into the war, several ports in the Adriatic, some Greek islands and the South Tyrol which would extend her northern frontier to the crest of the Alps. At the conference Italy claimed her due, but to grant it would be to defy the wishes of the inhabitants of these places, for the South Tyrol included a quarter of a million Austrians and the territory in the Adriatic over a

*Georges Clemencau, Woodrow Wilson and David Lloyd George
at the Paris peace talks.*

million Yugoslavs. In the end Italy's demands were reduced, but still large numbers of Austrians and Yugoslavs were put under her rule against their wishes.

French Point of View

If the principle of self-determination had to be sacrificed in order to satisfy Italy, it looked at one time as if a much greater sacrifice would be necessary to satisfy France.

At the end of the war the French were determined to obtain for their country the maximum security against another German attack; and with this in mind they were not so much interested in a treaty based on idealism as one based on force. Twice in the last fifty years German armies had invaded France, and in the last war damage done had been massive; the northern part of the country had been occupied for four years and at the end of that time had been ravaged – farms laid waste, mines ruined and factories and machinery destroyed. It was not surprising then that Frenchmen attached more importance to an easily defended frontier than to the principle of self-determination. They, therefore, demanded that the French frontier be extended to the Rhine. This would mean not only the return to France of the provinces of Alsace–Lorraine, which was generally agreed, but also the annexation of the Rhineland which contained several million Germans.

The French delegate at the peace conference was the prime minister, Georges Clemenceau, a fiery and formidable seventy-nine-year-old, who had been nicknamed 'the tiger'. In the last desperate years of the war it was he more than anyone who had maintained France's fighting spirit and will to win. With the coming of peace he was determined the reap the fruits of victory. He realised that he had an opportunity which would not last for long. In a few years Germany would have recovered and, with her larger population and faster birth rate, would again constitute a threat to France. And by then British and American forces would have returned to their own countries and France would be on her own. At first Clemenceau insisted on the Rhine frontier, but eventually he was dissuaded, it being pointed out to him that the loss of the Rhineland would be as great a grievance to Germany as the loss of Alsace–Lorraine had been to France, and would inevitably lead to a war of revenge. Instead it was enacted that the Rhineland would be occupied for fifteen years, that Germany should disarm and that France should be secured by an Anglo–American Treaty of Guarantee.[1]

British Point of View

Of all the European delegates at the peace conference the one who gave most support to President Wilson was the British prime minister, David Lloyd George. This he could afford to do as at an early stage he had obtained all that was necessary for British interests. The German navy had been surrendered and soon after had scuttled itself, so that once again, apart from the United States, British supremacy at sea was unchallenged. Britain had also obtained new colonial territory; but this had come in the form of 'mandates' which meant that certain conditions were attached. It was necessary for Britain to submit an annual report

---

[1] It will be seen later that this never came into force as the American Senate refused to ratify the Treaty of Versailles.

German battleship scuttled in Scapa Flow.

on these colonies to the League of Nations, and to show that the rights of the native populations were being safeguarded, and that they were being prepared for self-government. On these terms Britain obtained mandates for the German colony of Tanganyika in East Africa (later Tanzania) and the Turkish colonies of Iraq, Transjordan and Palestine in the Middle East.

On most of the issues at the peace conference Lloyd George was on the side of moderation, and he tried hard to prevent a harsh and punitive peace, fully realising that this would only lead to another war. But like other delegates from democratic countries he did not have a free hand; it was necessary for him to listen to loud, intemperate voices at home. Soon after the Armistice he decided to hold a general election and in order to be sure of winning this he had to take a tough line about Germany. As has been seen, people at that time were in an ugly mood. Urged on by a clamorous and irresponsible press campaign, they were calling for revenge, and much as Lloyd George might deplore this, he had, to some extent, to go along with it.

The Treaty of Versailles

Altogether five treaties were signed in Paris in 1919: Versailles with Germany, St Germain with Austria, Trianon with Hungary, Neuilly with Bulgaria and Sèvres (not ratified) with Turkey.

It was realised by President Wilson that a just and lasting peace was unlikely to be concluded until the passions stirred up by the war had died down. He, therefore, insisted that all five treaties should include the setting up of the League of Nations. This had been one of his Fourteen Points and was the one to which he attached most importance, for it meant that mistakes or injustices committed at the Conference could be rectified later. And so he saw to it that the first task of the delegates was to draw up the Covenant of the League.

The remaining provisions of the treaties fall under three main headings.

Disarmament. It has been seen that France would only withdraw her claim to the Rhineland if Germany was disarmed, and this was generally agreed. Accordingly the German army was limited to 100,000 men, there was to be no compulsory military service, no aircraft were to be built for military purposes, and the German navy was restricted with a ban on submarines. Also the Rhineland was declared a neutral zone and was to be occupied by Allied troops for fifteen years. At the same time, in order not to seem too vindictive, it was declared that German disarmament was to be a prelude to general disarmament; but this did not occur.

Reparations. This proved to be one of the thorniest problems of the Conference and was to drag on for many years. It was generally agreed that Germany, who had suffered little material damage, should pay for the devastation inflicted by her armies in the occupied countries. However, this would leave Britain out, so it was agreed that war pensions should be included. It was suggested by some that Germany should be made to pay for the whole cost of the war, but this would have been an astronomic figure, far beyond Germany's capacity. In the end the exact amount of reparations was left open, to be decided at a later date when, it was hoped, statesmen would tackle the problem more realistically.

Germany was also required to pay reparations in the form of coal and ships. In order to make amends for the destruction of French and Belgian coalmines it was agreed that a French army should occupy the

Saar Valley coalfield for fifteen years. Also, as compensation for British shipping losses, all vessels over 1600 tons should be handed over. These, however, were to prove a doubtful blessing as they were to cause unemployment in British shipyards.

Territorial Changes. President Wilson's hope, then, to redraw the map of Europe according to the wishes of the people encountered many setbacks, and by the time he arrived in Paris the people of Europe had, to some extent, settled matters themselves. Thus the Austrian provinces of Bohemia and Moravia along with some Hungarian territory had been formed into the country of Czechoslovakia. Serbia with some Austrian and Hungarian provinces had proclaimed itself the kingdom of Yugoslavia; and the old kingdom of Poland had been re-established as a republic with territory from Russia, Austria and Germany. The creation of these new countries was presented to the peacemakers as a *fait accompli*, and all that was left to them was to fix the frontiers and arrange for plebiscites (direct vote of the whole electorate) in disputed areas.

In the end Germany did not lose much territory. Alsace–Lorraine was restored to France, and a few villages were ceded to Belgium. It was, of course, necessary for Germany to give up the land gained from Russia at the Treaty of Brest-Litovsk (see p. 38). All of this was generally agreed. More contentious was the ceding to Poland of part of Upper Silesia which had been part of the conquests of Frederick the Great. In 1919 it contained much German industry, and its loss caused great resentment, as also did the arrangements concerning the port of Danzig; this was predominantly German, but was essential to Poland as her main outlet to the Baltic. In the end it was declared a Free City and Poland was granted means of access by way of a corridor which went through German territory and cut off part of East Prussia. This awkward arrangement was to cause much friction and was one of the causes of the Second World War.

The most notable feature of the new map of Europe was the disappearance of the Empire of Austria–Hungary. These two countries were now separated, stripped of their provinces and cut down to size. All that remained of Austria was a small land-locked republic which was forbidden to unite with Germany without the consent of the League of Nations.

Another empire to vanish from Europe was that of Turkey – apart from Constantinople. A final peace treaty with Turkey was delayed until 1923 when at the Lausanne Conference she regained some European territory, but by then her previous provinces in Europe had been distributed and those in the Middle East had been mandated to Britain and France.

Merits and Defects of Peace Treaty

When the Allies eventually came to an agreement about the terms of the Peace Treaty these were presented to Germany for her to accept. Objections to them could be made in writing, but there were to be no negotiations. The German government must either take them or leave them in which case the blockade of the country would remain in force, and the German people would be faced with starvation. Much as they disliked some of the terms and much as they resented the manner in which they were imposed on them, the German leaders knew they had no choice but to accept. Their delegates were marched, prisoner fashion, into the Palace of Mirrors at Versailles and commanded to sign.

In later years the Treaty of Versailles was to come in for strong criticism, inevitably so perhaps, as it failed in its main objective – to preserve the peace and prevent a war of revenge. There were several reasons for this failure, but perhaps the fundamental one was that in the peacemaking in Paris there were two crucial absences – Germany and Russia. Was it realistic to make a treaty about the future of Europe and expect it to last when it was not signed by the two largest countries in the continent? It was true that at the time Germany was in the throes of defeat and Russia engaged in civil war, but they would emerge from these in time, and recover and seek a leading role in European affairs; and they would have little regard for a treaty in which they had had no part.

Later the Versailles treaty was dealt a mortal blow by the withdrawal of America. As has been seen it had been constructed on the assumption that it would be guaranteed by the United States which would continue to be involved in European affairs. By the end of 1919, however, it had become clear that President Wilson was no longer representative of the feelings of the majority of American people who were wanting to be quit of Europe and to return once again to a policy of 'isolation'. Soon afterwards the US Senate refused to ratify the Treaty which meant that in future its only guarantors would be Britain, France and Italy, and they lacked the power to implement it. All too soon the question would arise as to how the Treaty should be enforced. By the time Britain and France had demobilised and Germany had recovered how would it be possible to insist that Germany should carry out the treaty provisions on such matters as reparations and disarmament?

Although much can be said against Versailles and the other Paris peace treaties, they did, nevertheless, achieve much that was good. In the first place they established the League of Nations which, although not a permanent success, was of great importance and brought about a new phase in international cooperation. Also the treaties provided that millions of Europeans were liberated from foreign domination. The subject races of Austria, Hungary, Russia and Turkey became independent, and for the first time in history nearly all the peoples of Europe (perhaps over 95 per cent) belonged to the country of their choice free from foreign rule.

Chapter 5

BRITAIN BETWEEN THE WARS

Post-War Turmoil

In Britain, as in other countries, the years after the war were an ill-fated period with much industrial strife, unemployment and disappointed hopes. Unemployment, the great curse of the inter-war years, did not come at once. At first trade was lively as people bought all the things they had been unable to obtain during the war, ex-servicemen spent their gratuities, and European countries, which had suffered greater war damage and had not yet recovered from it, were obliged to buy more goods than usual from Britain. For the first two years, therefore, there was little unemployment in spite of the demobilisation of some four million servicemen. But in spite of these 'boom' conditions there was great unrest in industry, and numerous strikes occurred. Prices rose faster than wages, and ex-servicemen found few signs of the 'land fit for heroes' which they had been promised. But worse was to come. By 1921 the post-war spending spree had come to an end and was followed by a slump in which the number of unemployed rose to two million. Especially badly hit were the coalmines; demand for coal fluctuated considerably and miners were always being laid off; and mine owners were trying to reduce wages which was strongly resisted. To strengthen their position the miners had made an agreement with the railwaymen and dockers (known as the Triple Alliance) whereby if one went on strike, they all came out. However, when this was put to the test the railwaymen and dockers backed out at the last moment, and the miners, left alone, were compelled to give in.

Downfall of Lloyd George

For four years after the war Britain continued to be governed by a coalition of Conservatives and Liberals headed by Lloyd George. But in 1922 the Conservatives decided to go it alone and in the general election of that year they gained a majority and took office under their leader, Andrew Bonar Law. But Bonar Law was a sick man and after a few months was obliged to resign and was succeeded by Stanley Baldwin.

On becoming prime minister Baldwin adopted a policy of 'Protection', that is charging duties on foreign goods coming into the country, including some foods, which made them more expensive. At that time this was a matter which stirred men's passions. During the nineteenth century Britain's wealth had been based on Free Trade which to some people, especially Liberals, had become sacred. In the twentieth century, however, some people had come to think that in the new conditions of trade, in which Britain was no longer the predominant industrial nation but only one of several, Free Trade was no longer an advantage, and that British and some Empire products should have a measure of 'protection' in the form of tariffs (import duties). In the first years of the century the Conservative leader, Joseph Chamberlain, had tried to introduce protection, whereupon his opponents accused him of wanting to raise the price of food and the Conservatives were heavily defeated at the next general election. But in 1922 Baldwin came to the conclusion that unemployment and Britain's other economic problems could only be solved by a policy of Protection and giving preference to goods coming from the Empire (known as Imperial Preference). He fully realised that in doing this he would be stirring up a hornets' nest; he also knew that his predecessor, Bonar Law, had given a pledge not to bring in Protection. He considered, therefore, that a general election should be held, and in this the Conservatives lost a lot of ground; they were still the largest party in Parliament, but their majority over all other parties had been lost. The second largest party was now the Labour Party with the Liberals holding the balance and the power to decide which party should take office. The leader of the Liberals was once again Herbert Asquith, who had been displaced by Lloyd George during the war (see p. 34), and partly because of the Conservative threat to Free Trade, he decided to back Labour. And so in January 1924 King George V sent for the Labour leader, James Ramsay Macdonald, and the first Labour government took office.

The First Labour Government

Since the war the fortunes of the Labour Party had risen dramatically. In 1919 its representation in Parliament was 39, and in the general election of that year it increased to only 59; but in 1922, with the Liberals still divided,[1] it shot up to 142, and then in 1923 to 191. And then suddenly the Labour Party was in office.

The leader of the Labour Party in 1924 and certainly its dominant personality was James Ramsay Macdonald. Born in a small Scottish fishing village, the son of a domestic servant, he had been in the course of his career a teacher, clerk and journalist; but, unlike other Labour leaders, never a manual worker. In 1900 he had been one of the founder members of the Labour Party and was its first secretary. In the building up of the Party during its formative years his influence had been outstanding, but in 1914 he became separated from it when he declared himself opposed to the war. During the war years he had been a lonely and unpopular figure and, like all pacifists, had been charged with lack of patriotism. But with the coming of peace he was reunited with his Labour colleagues, and in 1922 they elected him their leader. In the following year he was prime minister.

Ramsay Macdonald had many gifts: these included a fine presence, a quick understanding and impassioned, if long-winded, oratory. In addition he had what so many politicians of that time lacked – a burning idealism. With him politics became less humdrum and sordid; he gave them a glow and made them exciting. His predominant interest was foreign affairs, and he insisted on taking the post of foreign secretary as well as that of prime minister. Here he had considerable success; during the eight months he held the office the question of German reparations was settled, Britain's relations with France were mended, and steps were taken to bring back Germany and Russia into the family of nations.

Macdonald's achievements at home, however, were less notable: unemployment remained woefully high and trade depressed. At first there had been some who had looked with dread on the coming of a

---

[1] As between the supporters of Lloyd George and Asquith.

Labour government, expecting confiscation of private property, crippling taxation and other revolutionary changes. But they need not have worried; even if he had had the inclination for such measures, which he did not, Macdonald's hands were tied. His government depended entirely on the support of the Liberal Party which could turn it out at any time. It was 'in office but not in power'. Sweeping socialist changes were impossible.

It was unlikely that the Liberals would support the Labour government for long. Macdonald's modest, sensible rule was doing much to establish Labour as the new party of the Left. And so, after only nine months, the first Labour government came to an end. Those nine months, however, had been of great importance. Fears that some people had of the Labour Party had been removed and it had been demonstrated that Labour was able to govern.

Stanley Baldwin

In the general election which followed the resignation of the Labour government, the third in two years, the Conservatives won a sweeping victory with a large majority over all other parties. This was a great triumph for their leader, Stanley Baldwin who for the next twelve years was to be the dominant influence in British politics.

Baldwin had not come into politics until he was over forty. Until then he had been a successful and prosperous owner-manager of an ironworks in Worcestershire. At first sight he might seem unremarkable – stolid, straightforward and phlegmatic – apparently an ordinary, unexceptional Englishman. It might suit him to present this image to the public, but underneath he was sensitive and nervous and a shrewd politician. Lloyd George considered him 'the most formidable antagonist whom I ever encountered'.

In later years the reputation of Baldwin was to be blackened, as he was to be held responsible for Britain's unpreparedness for the Second World War, and his name was associated with the policy of 'appeasement', that is of giving way to European dictators and agreeing to their demands. These charges have some validity. It is true that during the 'Baldwin era' Britain's defences were allowed to run down; it is also true that Baldwin neglected foreign affairs; he was not interested in them and was content to leave them to his foreign secretaries who were

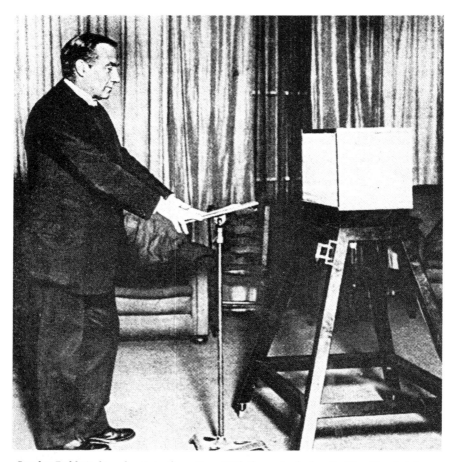

Stanley Baldwin braodcasts to the nation. With the arrival of radio 'fireside chats' over the air were to take the place of fiery speeches at political meetings.

not always up to the job. Because of these failures abroad Baldwin's achievements at home have often been under-estimated, and these were considerable. He overcame three major crises – The General Strike (see p. 63), the Great Depression (see p. 66) and the Abdication (see p. 72). He also did much to calm down the industrial unrest and class warfare of that time. It was his great ambition to draw the people of Britain together and make of them one nation, and in this he had some success; his fair-mindedness, calmness and avoidance of provocative measures were much appreciated by his political opponents, particularly in the Labour Party. If it is true that he was mainly responsible for Britain's unreadiness when war came, he was also mainly responsible for Britain entering the war a united nation with all parties agreeing to fight it out to the end.

It has been said of Baldwin that he was 'a miser with power', that is that he was highly successful in gaining it, but then hoarded it and was unwilling to use it. This was clearly evident after the 1924 election. Following this, with his large majority in Parliament, Baldwin had the power to do great deeds, but instead he did nothing. After his failure in the previous election he had renounced Protection, and now he seemed to be content to pause and wait on events. These were not long in coming.

The General Strike

With the continued rise in unemployment the belief took hold among some politicians and economists that it could only be cured by more exports which could only be achieved by lower prices which in turn could only be achieved by lower wages. Baldwin stated bluntly: 'All the workers of this country have got to take reductions in wages to help put industry on its feet.' Inevitably this policy caused great resentment among the workers and especially so among the coalminers.

Coalmining at that time was Britain's largest industry, employing over a million men. In recent years it had had many ups and downs. During the war and immediately afterwards demand for coal had been strong, and there had been full employment and higher wages. In 1921, however, when the German and Polish mines came into full production the industry had to face stiff competition. Then in 1923, when the French occupied the Ruhr and German miners went on strike (see p. 108) prosperity returned for a time, but disappeared when German mines came back into full production in 1925. Many mines were then being run at a loss, and the mine owners gave notice of an overall reduction in wages which was flatly rejected by the mineworkers' union.

It was this deadlock which was to lead eventually to the General Strike. For the miners then appealed for help to the Trades Union Congress which offered to bring out on strike workers in other key industries in sympathy. At the same time the TUC sought to negotiate a settlement not with the mine owners but with the government in the hope that a subsidy would be forthcoming to maintain wages at their present level. But this aroused strong opposition from some government members, as it seemed to them that a general strike was being threatened in order to exact a subsidy for the coalmines. Baldwin, however, partly because he hoped that a settlement would be agreed and partly because he was not yet ready for a showdown, agreed to the TUC demand and a subsidy of £24,000,000 was paid to maintain wages at their present level while a royal commission investigated the overall problems of the mining industry. At the same time the TUC arranged for further workers to join the strike, and the government made emergency plans to deal with the situation. The commission made its report early in 1926. It recommended many changes in the industry which were welcome to the miners, but it also stated that for the time being there would have to be either a reduction in wages or an increase in working hours. The government tentatively agreed to these proposals, but they were rejected by both the miners and the mine owners. The latter objected to the recommended changes in the industry, and the reaction of the former was summed up in the words of one of their leaders: 'Not a cent off the pay, not a minute on the day.'

Once again a deadlock had been reached and this time there was to be no reprieve. The miners came out on strike on 1st May 1926. Negotiations then took place between the government and the TUC, and it is said that they were near to agreement when the government abruptly brought the talks to an end. The reason given for this was that undue pressure was being brought to bear on it. It was reported that some printers on the *Daily Mail* had refused to set up an article critical of the strikers which led the government to suppose that a general strike had actually begun, which it had not. But for the government it was the last straw; it had never liked negotiating under duress and it maintained that for a body outside Parliament, like the TUC, to attempt to force the democratically elected government of the country into a certain course of action was a threat to the constitution. Accordingly it refused to negotiate any further. The TUC then felt obliged to call a national strike including road transport and railway workers, printers and workers in heavy industry, building and gas and electricity undertakings.

The strike was to last for only nine days and during that time there was little serious interruption to everyday life. Troops unloaded food and

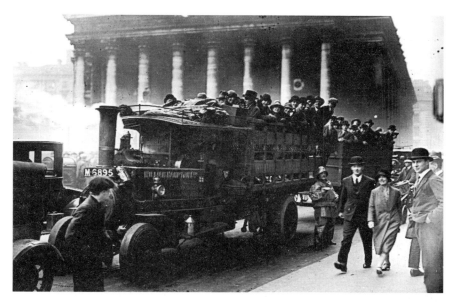

City workers in unconventional transport during the General Strike.

Bus with new driver and protection.

other essential goods at the docks and these were moved to distributing centres. Thousands of people came forward to volunteer to drive lorries, buses and even trains; thousands more enrolled as special constables; and well-to-do ladies did their bit by undertaking such jobs as packing newspapers or cleaning out railway carriages. In some quarters it was believed that revolution had come to Britain, but this was far from the case. The TUC had never had any intention of taking over the government of the country, and the men on strike had no idea that they were posing a threat to the constitution; all they wanted was to prevent a cut in miners' wages. Throughout the strike Baldwin was careful to avoid panic measure which might have provoked the strikers or have won sympathy for their cause. By appearing at all times to be calm and reasonable and by resting his case simply on the fact that the government could not negotiate under duress he won great support in the country. Altogether there was surprisingly little violence; some did occur in the docks and some was prompted by the running of buses by 'blackleg' labour. But generally tempers were restrained and in places police and strikers played football together.

It soon became clear to the TUC that the strike was not going to achieve its object, and on 12th May it was called off unconditionally. The miners, however, still refused to budge an inch and they went it alone for another six months before being forced back to work on the employers' terms. But this 'victory' was to cost the employers dear, for it so embittered the miners that they became more determined than ever that mines should be taken into public ownership. Otherwise the General Strike had no momentous consequences. The showdown which both sides of industry had been expecting proved to be a mild affair. When it was over there was a feeling that the air had been cleared.

The Great Depression

Mr Baldwin's government ran its course until 1929 but in the general election of that year the Conservatives lost their large majority and in the new parliament the Labour Party had more seats. However, to form a government it once again had to depend on support from the Liberals and so was again much restricted in what it could do. It was to have little luck; after less than a year it found itself embroiled in one of the worst economic crises the country has ever known.

Today there are many opinions about the basic causes of the Great Depression. Only a few general points will be mentioned here. At the root of the problem was the situation that greater mechanisation in industry had led to greater production of goods; but these could not be sold, not because they were not needed but because there were not enough people who could afford to buy them. Thus came about the tragic and absurd spectacle of poverty in the midst of plenty. On the one hand were people hungry, poorly clothed and ill-equipped; and on the other were farmers burning their crops, fishermen throwing their catches back into the sea and manufacturers cutting production of badly needed goods and making yet more workers redundant. What was needed at the time was more purchasing power but, unfortunately, the measures taken to remedy the situation tended to reduce this rather than increase it. Perhaps the greatest mistake had been the return to the Gold Standard in 1925. When this was done the pound had been overvalued in relation to foreign currencies with the result that Britain's exports became more expensive and, therefore, fewer, while imports became cheaper and so flooded the country, bringing ruin to British manufacturers and farmers.

The Great Depression originated in the United States where in the late 1920s there had been a wave of frantic speculation similar to that in England at the time of the South Sea Bubble. Dazzled by prospects of getting rich quickly, people had rushed to buy shares – often with borrowed money. This had great dangers: as long as the shares continued to rise in price, which at first they did, all was well, but inevitably there came the day of reckoning when the grossly inflated values of the shares began to fall and then, as more and more people tried to sell, the fall became an avalanche and many shares became totally valueless with thousands of people being ruined.

The Great Depression in America inevitably had repercussions in Europe where there was great reliance on American loans which suddenly came to an end. The economies of many European countries came under strain, particularly so in Britain which was in no condition for such an ordeal. In 1930 there was a further fall in exports and a further rise in unemployment. And then in the late summer came a run on the pound; foreigners rushed to get rid of their English money, and there was the prospect that the pound might become valueless as the German mark had done a few years before (see p. 108). This had been an appalling catastrophe for Germany, and it was this nightmare that was to haunt men's minds in the ensuing crisis.

The Labour government was not well equipped to deal with the situation. Ramsay Macdonald knew nothing of finance and depended entirely on the views of experts who were unanimous that in order to stop the run on the pound and preserve its value large loans would be needed from abroad, and in order to obtain these the budget would have to be balanced. This would mean drastic economies: severe cuts would have to be made in the salaries of government employees – judges, ministers, teachers, civil servants and the armed services. In addition there would have to be cuts in social services, particularly the large sums being spent on unemployment relief. To most members of the Labour government such measures were unthinkable; it was a denial of everything Labour stood for, and many took the line that, if it had to be done, it would be better to resign and let the Conservatives do it. But this was not the view of Ramsay Macdonald. He had little inclination to run away from the crisis. He was convinced that cuts in unemployment relief, though drastic and cruel, were the lesser of two evils. Without them the value of the pound might be halved and so too would

'Hunger Marchers'. Unemployed from Jarrow on their way to London.

the living standards of the whole country. And so Macdonald tried to persuade his ministers to accept the necessary cuts, but in this he was unsuccessful, and everyone expected that he would then resign and make way for a Conservative government. However, without consulting his cabinet colleagues he agreed to form a coalition with the Conservatives and Liberals to overcome the crisis. In this he was supported by only a few of his ministers; the rest resigned; and Macdonald came to be regarded by the main body of his party as a traitor.

Soon after the formation of the National Government, as the coalition was called, measures were taken to balance the budget and for the time being the run on the pound died down. But soon afterwards it began again partly as a result of the mutiny of a small number of naval ratings in Invergordon in protest against the cuts in their pay. This time, having no more resources with which to prop up the value of the pound, the government made a U-turn and did what it had been formed to prevent and suspended the Gold Standard. Experts had predicted fearful consequences of this, but these did not occur. The pound did drop in value, but generally life went on much as before.

Although the National Government was supposed to last for a limited period only, until the crisis of the pound had been overcome, its leaders soon decided that it should be prolonged. In 1931 a general election was held in which it won an overwhelming victory, the Labour Party being all but obliterated.[1] In some form or other the National Government, predominantly Conservatives, was to last until the Second World War.

A New Outlook – Maynard Keynes

With the onset of one economic crisis after another there were more and more people who were beginning to think that the capitalist system, which in the previous century had made Britain the world's wealthiest country, was now out of date and incapable of dealing with modern problems. At the heart of the capitalist system was the doctrine of *laissez-faire* (leave alone) the essence of which was that everyone should have freedom to build up his own property (capital) without interference from government. Trade and industry should sort out their

---

[1] The figures were: National Government 521, Labour 52.

own problems and all business should be strictly governed by the laws of supply and demand ('market forces'), and government interference would do more harm than good. But already, in the last century and since, there had been many departures from *laissez-faire*: cautiously and belatedly the government had felt bound to intervene to protect workers (particularly women and children) from being exploited. There had also been widespread growth of the doctrine diametrically opposite to Capitalism – Socialism – which deplored private property and laid down that everyone should work for the common good. In the years following the Great Depression Socialism and its more extreme form, Communism, gained further ground, and some became convinced that in time they must, inevitably, replace Capitalism altogether. That this did not happen in England was due in part to the evolution of a new type of Capitalism associated mainly with a British economist, John Maynard Keynes.

Keynes found great faults with the way the capitalist system was operating in the twentieth century. He was convinced that great changes had to be made. 'We have,' he wrote, 'to invent new wisdom for a new age. And in the meantime we must, if we are to do any good, appear unorthodox, troublesome, dangerous, disobedient to them that begat us.' Although Keynes found old-fashioned Capitalism out of date, he did not regard Socialism as the answer. His solution was a blend of the two.

It seemed to Keynes that there were two main problems which had to be addressed. The main one was that the law of supply and demand was not working out. Supply was far outstripping demand; with modern methods of production huge quantities of goods could be produced but could not be sold as not enough people had enough money to buy them. The problem, therefore, was to increase demand by getting more money into more pockets; and the way to do this, according to Keynes, was by large-scale expenditure on public works such as roads, railways and houses. This led on to the other great failing of *laissez-faire* which was that it did not provide enough money for projects of this sort. The old idea had been that it should come from private savings, but Keynes saw that these were completely inadequate and that credit (borrowings) should be used, and this credit should be controlled by a central institution.

If, then, the main problem was lack of demand, it followed that the usual methods of dealing with financial depressions – rigorous economies, cuts in wages and laying workers off – would do more harm than good. Such measures might bring about lower costs of goods, but at the same time they would create less spending power and less demand for those goods. The cure, therefore, lay not so much in the reduction of wages as in their expansion; put one man in work and you help to put another in work. Therein, according to Keynes, in what came to be known as the Economics of Expansion, lay the answer to unemployment.

The Monarchy

Few British monarchs have had a more tumultuous and difficult reign than George V who came to the throne in 1910 at the height of a major political crisis concerning the passing of the Parliament Act which aimed to reduce the powers of the House of Lords. This resulted in a deadlock between Lords and Commons which only the king, inexperienced and unsure of himself, could resolve. A few years later there loomed the threat of civil war in Ireland and then came the outbreak of the First World War. During the war the king shared to the full the anxieties of the country's leaders, and in addition he had to endure malignant talk about his German ancestry, so that he felt it necessary to change the name of his dynasty from Hanover to Windsor. And after the war came further troubles – another Irish crisis, the General Strike and the Great Depression. Throughout these the king was a model of what a constitutional monarch ought to be – impartial, fair-minded and unwaveringly loyal to his ministers of whatever party. To the first Labour Government in particular he showed great consideration and did all he could to ease its difficulties. In private life the king tended to be autocratic and intolerant, but in affairs of state he was always reasonable and on the side of moderation. With no intellectual gifts and few interests[1] he had, nevertheless, great common sense and a capacity for hard work. He also had a deep and genuine love for the British people, and in spite of his shyness and occasional bad temper, the British people sensed this love and returned it. During the Silver Jubilee celebrations of 1935 many, including the king himself, were surprised by the warmth and spontaneity of popular feeling. 'I'd no idea they felt like that about

---

[1] Apart from sailing, shooting and stamp collecting.

me,' he said after returning from a drive through some of the poorer parts of London.

George V died in 1936 and was succeeded by his eldest son who became Edward VIII. The new king was acclaimed with delight. As Prince of Wales he had won many hearts with his charm and lack of pomposity. He was a very different man from his father – unconventional, imaginative and with a great distaste for the ceremonial side of monarchy. It was expected that he would make some changes to the style of monarchy, but he was not to reign for long. Almost at once he was confronted by a major crisis caused by his proposed marriage to Wallis Simpson, an American lady, who was in the process of obtaining a divorce from her second husband. At that time views on divorce were much stricter than they are today, and the Church of England, of whom the king was titular head, did not allow it. At first the prime minister, Stanley Baldwin, tried hard to dissuade the king from such a marriage, but when this was unavailing, he had to tell him that Mrs Simpson could never be accepted as queen. In this he was backed not only by the main British political parties but also by those of the British Dominions. In these circumstances the king, still as determined as ever to marry Mrs Simpson, decided that he must abdicate which he did on 10th December 1936, leaving the throne to his younger brother, Albert, who became George VI. He was given the title of the Duke of Windsor.

Social Change

It has been seen that post-war Britain was far from being 'a land fit for heroes'. All too many of the heroes were queuing for the dole and struggling to make two ends meet. But the picture was not all black. For the majority of people in Britain life was better than it had been before the war – more secure and more comfortable. More people had more money than ever before. And although poverty in some areas was desperate and a disgrace to the country, it was, nevertheless, not so extreme and so agonising as it had been at the beginning of the century; some of the edge had been taken off it by measures of social security.

After the war it was the wish of many people to return to the way of life as it had been before. But this was impossible. In order to survive during the war great social changes had been necessary, and many of these had come to stay. Most fundamental, perhaps, was the change in moral standards. Even before the death of Queen Victoria these were beginning to be relaxed and people were questioning those things the Victorians had held sacred – family life, the British Empire, Christianity and respectability. During the inter-war years this move away from Victorian values gathered pace, and, increasingly, people were leading lives much less restricted by convention and morality.

One of the most striking changes in post-war Britain was the new status and behaviour of women. During the war the lives of millions of women had been revolutionised when they had undertaken jobs previously done only by men – in factories, offices, hospitals and public transport. After the war many of these women had returned home to the life of a wife and mother; but there were some who were determined to hold on to the opportunities and freedoms they had won. Increasing numbers of them were going to the universities, qualifying as doctors and lawyers, and even becoming members of parliament. Before the war women did not have the right to vote, and there were many, including the Liberal government, who were strongly opposed to granting it. But after the part women had played in the war their right to vote was generally accepted, although they did not get it on full equality with men until 1928. Some women, particularly among the well-to-do, displayed their new-found freedom in their life-styles, doing things their mothers would never have dreamed of doing – smoking cigarettes, drinking cocktails, making up their faces and wearing new and daring clothes.

Men's clothes too at this time became much simpler; top hats, frock coats and tails began to disappear to be replaced by lounge suits, soft collars and pullovers. And in life generally there was more informality, notably in manners and language. To some extend this was due to the American influence which was especially strong at that time owing to the large number of American films pouring into the country (see p. 85). Many Americanisms (such as 'Oh Boy!' and 'OK') came into general use, and American dance music, known as jazz,[1] became widely popular. To America too people were indebted for labour-saving appliances in the home, such as the vacuum cleaner and the refrigerator

---

[1] Strictly speaking 'jazz' should only refer to the negro music of the Southern States of America with a particular type of rhythm; but the word was usually used to describe all dance music.

which did much to relieve the housewife of her drudgery and to take the place of domestic servants.

Another notable change in lifestyles was that the population was becoming more mobile. More people were driving cars and riding bicycles so that holidays by the sea, touring the countryside and visits abroad were becoming more widespread. And most exciting of all were the developments which came at this time in air travel.

Early Advances in Aviation

Great advances in flying had been made during the First World War, and when it was over there were many attempts to establish new records. Great Britain had taken little part in the first experiments in flight, but after 1919 British aviators were well to the fore. The English Channel had been crossed by the Frenchman, Louis Blériot, in 1909, but the Atlantic crossing remained, and the *Daily Mail* offered a prize of £10,000 for the first direct non-stop flight. The challenge was soon taken up. There remained over from the war a large number of bombers which had been built to bomb Berlin, and in one of these, with extra fuel tanks added, two RAF officers, John Alcock and Arthur Whitten-Brown, set out from Newfoundland in June 1919 and sixteen hours later crash-landed in a bog in Ireland. Their journey was later described by Winston Churchill, then Secretary of State for Air, as being of

The Vickers-Vimy, in which Alcock and Brown flew across the Atlantic, crash-landed in Ireland.

comparable importance to that of Columbus. It was not until 1927 that the Atlantic was crossed again by aeroplane when Charles Lindbergh of America made his sensational flight, alone and without radio, in his little monoplane, *The Spirit of St Louis*. But only a month after Alcock and Brown a crossing was made, more comfortably and more easily, by the British airship, *R34*.

In the construction of airships, or Zeppelins as they called them, the Germans had a long lead, and during the war they launched a number of them in air raids on England. Some of these had been shot down and much was learned from the wreckage, and by the end of the war two British airships, the *R33* and *R34*, had nearly been completed. These beautiful craft had many advantages over aeroplanes at that time: they had a longer range, were generally safer and quieter and more comfortable. However, although the Atlantic crossing of *R34* was achieved safely, it was not a total success, as it was found that it could not carry a heavy enough load of passengers and freight to be commercially

The Hindenburg *in flames in New Jersey.*

viable. The future of airships, therefore, became uncertain, especially after the crash with heavy loss of life of the *R38*. For a time they were not much seen in England, but they continued to be used with success in Germany and America, and they made a comeback in England in 1930 when two splendid craft were built – the *R100* and *R101*. The former made a successful maiden flight to Canada, but the latter crashed while on a prestige flight to India with the Minister for Air on board. The result was a complete and final stop to all work on airships in Britain. In other countries they lingered on for a time, even after the terrible crash of the greatest ever airship, *The Hindenburg*, in 1937. They did not finally disappear from the scene until the coming of the Second World War.

Opening Up of the World's Airways

At the same time as the airship had been declining, there had been great advances in aircraft design so that it had been possible to make a start in the opening up of the world's airways.

The establishment of regular international air services in Britain had not come as soon as might have been expected. For the British public had been slow to take to air travel. For a long time flying was regarded by many as a sport or hobby, but not as a means of transport. People were not to be lured away easily from their ships, railways and motor cars. And so at first regular flights abroad were few and only over short distances. They were undertaken by small, private firms, and how different they were from air travel today is shown by the following description:

> The pilot sat in the open in a little cockpit and ran the aeroplane single-handed. Before the days of uniform the pilots came to work indulging their own sartorial fancies, in plus-fours and tweed caps, or in a dark suit, bowler hat and spats. The passengers sat on flimsy chairs in a little canvas-sided cabin, and they could open or shut the windows if they liked, but they had no service at all during the flight.

These small firms had great difficulty in keeping going and would have disappeared altogether but for help from the government which in 1924 joined many of them together to form Imperial Airways, a monopoly company with financial backing from public funds. During the following years this company made some progress but by 1926 its range was no more than 500 miles. The task of establishing landing fields, wireless stations and meteorological services did not proceed quickly. However, British aviation received a great boost at this time from the pioneering work of one of the great aviators, Sir Alan Cobham who made flights to all parts of the world including one to Australia and back in a seaplane which on its return landed on the Thames outside the Houses of Parliament. Many other efforts were made at this time to make the British people more 'air-minded', and some exciting flights and air races took place, notably a sensational nineteen-day flight in 1930 by a young English secretary, Amy Johnson, from England to Australia with some hair-raising adventures including a sandstorm in Persia, a monsoon in Burma and a crash landing in Timor.

By the mid-thirties the aeroplane had overtaken the airship as the main means of aerial transport. This had been made doubly certain by the invention of a young RAF officer, Frank Whittle. As far back as 1928, when he was only twenty-one, Whittle had been thinking of an aeroplane flying in the stratosphere at speeds of over 500 miles an hour. Such an aeroplane, Whittle knew, would have to have an entirely new sort of engine without propellers. By 1930 he had designed the first jet engine and taken out a patent. On 15th May at Cranwell the first jet plane made its first flight.

Timescale

1922 End of coalition under Lloyd George. Bonar Law becomes prime minister, succeeded by Stanley Baldwin.
1924 First Labour Government.
1926 General Strike.
1929 Second Labour Government.
1931 Formation of National Government.
1936 Abdication of Edward VIII.

Chapter 6

ENTERTAINMENT AND THE MEDIA

Newspapers

New Opportunities

With the expansion of education so that nearly the whole population could read, and with the development of new transport facilities and the invention of the electric telegraph and the telephone, tremendous opportunities were opening up for British newspapers. Demand for them was rising all the time, and particularly for newspapers of a new sort – less serious in tone, more chatty and full of such things as society gossip, atrocities and, above all, sporting news. In Britain between the wars more newspapers were read per head of population than in any other country.

Newspapers had played a vital role in British history since they first started to appear in the seventeenth century; they had been one of the main instruments in the struggle for freedom. For this reason governments had disliked them and tried to suppress them and create difficulties for them.[1]

But by the time of the 'newspaper explosion' at the end of the nineteenth century the battle had been won and freedom of the press from government interference had been established. However, in time other threats to a fully independent press were to emerge. For newspapers were to become big business, concentrated in the hands of fewer and fewer proprietors. With the coming of cheap, national daily papers many of the old local papers had been forced out of business. The trend soon became clear: the large were getting larger and the small were disappearing.

There were obvious dangers in this concentration of press power; it

---

[1] As for example by imposing a heavy duty on newsprint.

made it possible for the great newspaper owners, the so-called 'press lords', to bombard the country with their own views and to ignore or distort those of their opponents. But the owners too were not free agents. From the 1920s onwards a new force appeared in the newspaper world – the large advertisers. Up to then advertising had been on a small scale and mainly local; but first the big department stores and then other businesses discovered the effectiveness of mass advertising on a national scale. This was a development of major importance, for proprietors came to rely completely on advertisements for the viability of their papers, and circulation became all-important, and newspapers with small circulations were unable to compete.[1] Another consequence of this dependence on advertising was that large advertisers found themselves in a position to influence the policies of the newspapers in which they advertised. They had the power to bring influence to bear on the editor.

The 'Press Lords'

The first person to show how great were the possibilities for newspapers in the modern world was Alfred Harmsworth, later Lord Northcliffe. He was to introduce a new form of journalism with prodigious success. Following the appearance of the *Daily Mail* in 1896, the first halfpenny daily newspaper, he became the dominating force in British journalism, but by the time he died in 1922 other proprietors had entered the field, and in the 1920s and 1930s there was fierce competition between them.

Of the new press lords one of the most successful and certainly the most ambitious was Max Aitken, better known as Lord Beaverbrook. Born in New Brunswick, the son of a Presbyterian minister, Aitken displayed at an early age a genius for making money and became a millionaire before he was thirty. He then left Canada and came to England, bent on a political career, but in this he had only limited success, being regarded by the Conservative Party, which he joined, as an outsider and an adventurer. In another field, however, Lord Beaverbrook, as he soon became, was to have notable success. For in 1916 he obtained the controlling interest in the *Daily Express*, at that time a

---

[1] Size of circulation was not, however, the only thing that mattered. Quality was also important, as many advertisers sought newspapers which were read by top spenders.

Lord Beaverbrook.

daily paper struggling to keep afloat. He then devoted his tremendous energy and wizardry into creating a new type of newspaper. The *Daily Express* became unique in British journalism as a newspaper which appealed to all classes of reader, and this without undue reliance on violence and scandal. Always readable and entertaining, often infuriating and irresponsible, it was seldom boring and reflected the dynamism of its proprietor. And yet in his main purpose Beaverbrook failed, for in entering the newspaper business his main object had been not to make money but to influence public opinion which, he thought, would lead to political power. He wanted to make his newspapers[1] a successful instrument of propaganda, and this they never became. Although millions read and enjoyed them, it seemed that people did not take his political views to heart. None of his political campaigns was successful. It was Beaverbrook's hope that his newspapers would bring him power and influence, and for the sake of this he had been prepared to lose a lot of money. But in the event power and influence eluded him, but he made more and more money.

At times the struggle between newspapers for larger circulations became intense, notably in the so-called 'newspaper war' of the 1930s when free gifts were distributed on a large scale to attract new readers. But it was soon found that such methods, besides being extremely expensive, had only temporary effect. The only lasting way of building up circulation was to give the readers as much as possible of what they

---

[1] Later he acquired the *Sunday Express* and the *Evening Standard*.

wanted, and in this the newspaper which had most success at that time was the *Daily Mirror*. The *Daily Mirror* had been founded originally by Lord Northcliffe as a newspaper for women, but this had been a failure. Subsequently, however, it was to have great success as a halfpenny newspaper printing photographs by a special new method on high speed rotary presses. But by 1930 it had again hit hard times and seemed to be heading for extinction when it was rescued and transformed into the daily paper with the largest circulation in the world. This was, to a large extent, the work of H. G. Bartholomew who had joined the picture department of the *Daily Mirror* as a young man and had worked his way up from the bottom. In 1934 he was appointed editorial director and changed the character of the paper entirely. He knew that British working people liked to be entertained rather than informed by their newspapers and did not want to do too much reading. And so in the new *Daily Mirror* news stories were crisp and full of punch and there were a lot of skilfully presented photographs. It also contained large and dramatic headlines, numerous strip cartoons and extensive sports coverage. There were, inevitably, many critics of the *Daily Mirror*, who thought it was vulgar and pornographic and pandered to people's less creditable tastes. If there is some truth in this it is also true that the *Daily Mirror* was a paper with a conscience. It was authentically working class; the interests of working people were its concern.

Broadcasting

First Beginnings

At the same time as newspapers were spreading all over the country a new and even more powerful means of mass communication was being developed. At the end of the First World War broadcasting was still in its infancy, confined to the armed services, a few commercial firms and a number of amateurs who looked on it as a hobby. By the outbreak of the Second World War, twenty years later, broadcasting was bringing news, information, music and entertainment into millions of homes.

The way for broadcasting had been opened up by the work of Guglielmo Marconi who showed that electric signals (Morse Code) could be transmitted without wires; and later (1912) by the invention of the thermionic valve which made it possible to send music and the spoken word to anyone who had the appropriate receiving apparatus. It is, perhaps, surprising that organised broadcasting did not come to Britain sooner, but it was not until 1920 that there was the first demand for it. This came from the manufacturers of radio sets who saw from the example of the United States that large-scale broadcasting could bring a wide demand for their products. Accordingly they approached the

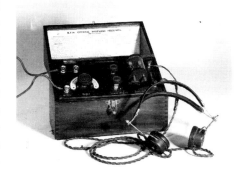

A crystal set of the early 1920s.

Postmaster General, who controlled all wireless communications in the country, and asked to be allowed to establish broadcasting stations. To this there was some opposition, as there were only a limited number of wavelengths available in Britain, and the experience of the United States, where several hundred broadcasting stations had been set up, all encroaching on each other's wavelengths, showed the danger of the air becoming overcrowded. Because of this and because he did not want the invidious task of deciding which firm should have which wavelength, the Postmaster General took an important decision: all the radio companies (some 20 in number) should join together to form one broadcasting organisation to be known as the British Broadcasting Company; and this company was to be financed not, as in America, by advertising revenue, but by a tax on the sale of radio sets. For three years, until the end of 1924, the Company was to have a monopoly of all broadcasting in Britain, and in return for this was required to establish broadcasting stations which could cover most of the country.

The British Broadcasting Company

It is probable that in the normal course of events the monopoly given to the British Broadcasting Company would not have been permanent, but in the time allotted to it it was to have an outstanding success. At first broadcasting had been of interest only to a small number of amateur operators ('hams' as they were called) who were more concerned with the number of stations they could pick up rather than with the actual matter which was broadcast. But broadcasting soon became more than a hobby; it spread all over the country and became extremely popular. And it was not confined to the well-to-do, for crystal sets could be bought for less than a pound.

Inevitably the new Company encountered opposition. Newspaper owners thought that people would listen to the news on the radio rather than read it in the press; theatre owners thought that broadcasting would take away their business, as also did concert agencies and sports promoters. For a time these people organised a boycott of the Company; but they soon came to realise that broadcasting, far from harming their businesses, actually assisted them by the publicity it gave them. During the five years of its existence the British Broadcasting Company showed great initiative and imagination; it broadcast whole plays and operas, took over the Promenade Concerts,[1] and introduced *Children's Hour* and programmes for schools. Especially popular were the running commentaries on sporting events.

The success of the Company during these first years was due in large measure to its managing director, John Reith who, by his strength of character, energy and ruthlessness, was to determine the nature of broadcasting in Britain for many years. When he joined the Company in 1920 Reith had never heard of broadcasting, but he soon learned. The son of a Scottish Presbyterian minister, he had strong religious convictions and was adamant that in this new and vital means of communication the highest moral standards should be maintained at all times. Sunday programmes were to be quiet and decorous; religious programmes were to be given proper prominence; and the general tone of broadcasting was to be improving and educational. Entertainment there could be, but there was to be no pandering to vulgarity. To some extent people were to be given what they wanted, but they were also to have a certain amount of what was considered good for them.

There was, of course, much criticism of Reith's regime. Many complained that it was bad enough for all broadcasting to be in the hands of one company only, and this was made worse when that company was dominated by one man. Opponents maintained that the Company was too orthodox and conventional and that programmes were stereotyped and lacking in spontaneity. There were some too who felt that the

---

[1] These had been started in 1895 by Sir Henry Wood in the Queen's Hall; but in recent years they had run into financial difficulties.

Company was too middle class in tone and did not adequately take into consideration the wishes and tastes of the workers. There was a strong belief that it was wrong for one body to decide what listeners should or should not hear, and that what the Company needed was competition. So long as it had broadcasting to itself there was liable to be complacency and narrow-mindedness, and the growth of broadcasting in Britain would be stunted. To all these arguments Reith was inflexibly opposed. He believed devoutly that broadcasting must remain a monopoly as only in this way could high moral standards be maintained. If the right to broadcast was extended to others it would have to be paid for by advertising, and this would mean that advertisers would be able to exercise some control over programmes, and they would only be concerned to attract the largest possible audiences. They would have little interest in serious programmes and would not give due weight to religion and education.

The Company's licence was due to come to an end in 1926, and in the previous year there was a long public enquiry which heard both sides of the argument. But in the end Reith's view prevailed and the monopoly was maintained. At the same time the British Broadcasting Company was brought to an end and was replaced by the British Broadcasting Corporation, ever since known as the BBC. The new Corporation, partly business firm and partly government department, was something new in Britain. It was intended that it would be non-profit making and that its funds should be raised by the sale of radio licences. It was also to be free of government interference. Broadcasting was to remain a monopoly in Britain for twenty-five years.

The Cinema

Of all forms of entertainment in the inter-war years, and there were more of these than ever before, the most popular was the cinema.

The cinema had been evolving slowly since the end of the last century. When they first appeared in public 'moving pictures' or 'movies' were no more than a peepshow in a Penny Arcade. One put a penny in a slot, looked in the opening, wound a handle and saw some simple scene – perhaps of people bathing or animals feeding. The next stage came when it was discovered how to project moving pictures on to a screen; and this led to 'movies' being shown as a turn in a music hall or as a sideshow in a fair, and in time to the first motion picture houses. At first these were very rough and ready – a back room in a shop or a barn in a back yard. But as more and more people began to 'go to the pictures', grander and plusher buildings became necessary.

In a short time the cinema became so popular that it was difficult for film makers to keep pace with demand. More and more films were being demanded and especially films with a difference. Gradually new techniques were developed and films aimed to do more than just photograph scenes from life. Film studios were set up (at first very rugged – hardly more than a large shed) and the cinema came to tell a story, at first only a short one and a simple one – perhaps a chase by the famous Keystone Cops or the rescue of a beautiful maiden from the clutches of a monstrous villain. But in those early days it was quantity that was needed rather than quality. Little interest was taken then in films as an art form; the main consideration was to turn them out as quickly and cheaply as possible.

In the struggle to satisfy the ever-growing cinema craze it became evident to film makers that audiences were more interested in film actors and actresses than in the film itself. At first these 'picture players', as they were called, were anonymous, but later, when it became apparent that the public would go to any film, however bad, provided certain players were in it, it became good business to build them up into great 'stars'. In this way some picture players suddenly found themselves with worldwide reputations.

The Americans had been first in the field in film making and then, partly because the First World War had brought film making to a halt in Europe, they were to establish in the post-war

Charlie Chaplin in The Gold Rush.

years a near monopoly. The British film industry took a long time to get off the ground, and many talented British players were lured away to Hollywood where opportunities were much greater. These were to contribute much to the 'Golden Age of Hollywood' and they included the greatest star of all – Charlie Chaplin. One of the great clowns of all times, he had made his way from a desperate childhood in South London into the music halls and then into films which were ideally suited to his genius. In his prime his output of films was incredible – in one year he made no less than thirty-five all phenomenally popular. For a time he must have been the most famous man in the world.

In the late 1920s other great developments came to the cinema notably the 'talkies', as they were first called, and then the musical. In the hard times of the Great Depression and then in the war years the cinema played a major role in people's lives. It was cheap, readily available entertainment which everyone could understand. More than any other form of entertainment it provided an escape from reality into a world of fantasy. More than any other form of entertainment too it accelerated the trend of people depending on others for amusement rather than creating it for themselves.

The Theatre

It might have been expected that with the coming of radio and the cinema the live theatre would have fallen on hard times. But this was not the case. Audiences continued to come and British achievements in this field were much more notable than in the cinema.

There had been a great surge of theatre going at the end of the nineteenth century. This was partly due to improved public transport, which brought theatres into the range of people living in the suburbs, but mainly to the appearance of a new type of drama. Until then most plays had been stereotyped and unreal; good characters and bad had been all too obvious, and when they came into conflict, the former always prevailed. There was no discussion of what was good or bad, no bandying of ideas and no references to subjects considered improper or unpleasant. The new plays had much more power and realism and were about ordinary people and their problems, sordid and painful as these often were. In particular they questioned present day morality and put forward new ideas on subjects to which for a long time people's minds had been closed. The first person to write plays of this sort was the Norwegian, Henrik Ibsen. At first his works had been received with horror, but they made a great impact and had the effect of causing people unease and making them think. Ibsen had an enthusiastic disciple in the Irish playwright, George Bernard Shaw who once declared: 'The theatre should be a factory of thought. It ought to raise problems of conduct and character, to stimulate discussion and make people see other points of view.' Altogether he was to write some sixty plays in which he expounded wittily and trenchantly the ideas that occurred to him, however shocking or controversial these might be. Later he described himself as 'a specialist in immoral and heretical plays'.

The inter-war years were not a great age of British theatre, although they did include some of Shaw's best plays and there were many outstanding performers. The most gifted and successful man of the theatre of that period was Noel Coward who, like Shaw, first made his name by shocking people with plays on dangerous subjects such as drug taking. Later, being a man of great versatility, he became a master of the art of comedy besides writing highly successful revues and musicals.

Although in general the live theatre stood up well to competition from the cinema, there was one part of it which went into a decline, the Music Halls. In the last century these had been the main form of entertainment for the less well off, and hundreds of them had cropped up all over the country. Now they began to disappear. Big names, however, could still pull in the crowds and of these much the most popular was Gracie Fields, the Lancashire mill girl. With an exceptionally fine voice which could have brought her a career in opera, she preferred with her great comic talents to stay in Variety where at one moment she might be giving a virtuoso performance of a song or aria and the next be croaking out a ditty about her bleeding heart or the biggest aspidistra in the world. Audiences adored her and when in 1939 she was operated on for cancer (successfully) there was universal consternation; prayers were offered for her in churches all over the country, people kept vigils outside her hospital and over half a million get-well cards were sent to her.

Perhaps the most important feature of the British theatre between the wars was the preparatory work that was being done for the future. It was at that time that the Old Vic[1] was established as 'the home of Shakespeare in London', and the Sadlers Wells theatre[2] was rebuilt as a base for opera and ballet. Until then ballet had been a virtual monopoly of the Russians, but in the 1930s under the leadership of Ninette de Valois and Marie Rambert British ballet came more and more on to the scene.

---

[1] The Old Vic, or Victoria Theatre, had been a rather low class music hall-cum-drinking bar when it was taken over in 1880 by Miss Emma Cons and set up as the Royal Victoria Coffee Music Hall. Miss Cons' purposes were philanthropic – to provide wholesome entertainment without alcohol for the poor. It was Miss Cons' niece, Lilian Baylis, who took the theatre over in 1912 and gave the Old Vic a national reputation.

[2] So called because in the seventeenth century a certain Sadler had built a place of amusement there on the site of a holy well with healing properties.

Chapter 7

THE BRITISH EMPIRE – TOWARDS THE COMMONWEALTH

The Statute of Westminster

During the inter-war years the British Empire continued to evolve into the Commonwealth. Basically this meant that Britain, the mother country, with colonies under her rule changed into being a member of a group of countries which were equal and independent partners and connected of their own free will.

By 1919 Canada, Australia, New Zealand and South Africa, once colonies, had been granted Dominion Status, that is they had responsible government which meant one elected by their own peoples rather than one imposed on them from London. However, these countries were still regarded by many as appendages of Britain and, indeed, their independence was not complete. The British monarch, advised by his ministers, still appointed each Dominion's governor-general. The Dominions' foreign affairs were to a large extent left to the British government and it was unusual for Dominions to have their own embassies abroad.[1] Also in law it was possible for any Dominion citizen to appeal from the highest court of his own country to the British Privy Council.

Since the First World War the status of the Dominions had changed considerably. The distinguished record of their armed forces during the war, their separate representation at the Peace Conference and their individual status in the League of Nations did much to establish them as countries in their own right. However, it was felt that something was needed to define the new relationship between Britain and the Dominions. At the Imperial Conference of 1926 this was provided in memorable words:

They are autonomous communities within the British Empire, equal

---

[1] This first occurred in 1918.

in status, in no way subordinate one to another in any aspect of their domestic or internal affairs, though united by a common allegiance to the Crown, and freely associated as members of the British Commonwealth of Nations.

Although relations between Britain and the first Dominions were thus amicably arranged, there were other parts of the Empire where changes went much less smoothly.

Ireland

'The Troubles'

When the First World War broke out Ireland had been on the verge of a civil war. Home Rule was in the process of being granted by the Liberal government, and the people of Ulster were arming themselves to resist by force any attempt to compel them to belong to an independent Ireland. During the first years of the war there had been an uneasy truce, but this had come to an end with the Easter Rising of 1916. By the end of the war the Home Rule Bill had been passed but this had not satisfied everyone in Ireland. Recently the party of Sinn Fein[1] had been gaining strength, and in the general election of 1918 it had won 73 of the 105 Irish seats – nearly all the seats outside Ulster. At the time 40 of the Sinn Fein candidates elected were in prison or had been deported, but the remainder proceeded to act as if Ireland were already independent. They proclaimed a Republic and set up an Irish parliament (Dail Eirann); Eamon de Valera[2] was elected president and an Irish delegation was sent to attempt (in the event unsuccessfully) to obtain a hearing at the Peace Conference.

The original intention of the Sinn Fein leaders had been to avoid violence and to act as if the British government in Ireland no longer existed. But they were unable to control the members of the Irish Republican Brotherhood which emerged as the Irish Republican Army

---

[1] Sinn Fein means 'Ourselves'. The object of the society was to 'de-Anglicise' Ireland and establish her as a distinct and separate nation.

[2] De Valera had been born in New York. His father, a Spanish artist, had died when he was a baby and his Irish mother had then sent him to Ireland where he was brought up by his grandmother.

(IRA) and embarked on a campaign of terror and violence. The British government of the time, the coalition under Lloyd George, decided that force should be met with force. However, this was not easily done. For the IRA had the support of the majority of the Irish people. Moreover they were able to obtain a plentiful supply of arms and became highly skilled guerrilla fighters. Their tactics were to assemble suddenly, attack a police station or army supply depot and then disappear back into civilian life. At that time the British army in Ireland amounted to some 50,000 men with a police force of about 10,000, but they found themselves unable to suppress the IRA whose forces seldom amounted to more than 5,000. The government therefore decided to reinforce the police with specially recruited ex-servicemen known officially as the Auxiliary Division but who soon, by reason of their khaki uniforms and black hats and armbands, came to be known as 'The Black and Tans'. These new forces soon began to take the law into their own hands and to use drastic and brutal methods. Terror was met by terror, and many innocent people suffered. A military commander arriving in Ireland at that time described these methods as 'to murder, rob, loot and burn up the innocent, because they could not catch the few guilty on the run.' In England there was widespread horror at these methods. King George V was greatly disturbed, and Mr Asquith, the ex-prime minister, declared that 'things are being done in Ireland which would disgrace the blackest annals of the lowest despotism in Europe.'

Establishment of the Irish Free State

The British government, however, was not relying on force alone. In 1920 a Government of Ireland Act had been passed. This provided for two parliaments, one for Ulster and one for the rest of Ireland with a Council of Ireland to be drawn from both. This arrangement was accepted by Ulster but rejected by Sinn Fein. But by 1921 desire for peace in Ireland was growing, and in July of that year a truce was called and an Irish delegation, headed by De Valera, came to London to negotiate. The main point at issue was whether Ireland (apart from Ulster) should be an entirely independent republic or remain in the British Empire as a Dominion with the same status as other Dominions. At first no agreement could be reached on this matter, and after ten days the Irish delegation returned home. However, the movement for peace continued to grow and a few months later another Irish delegation came to London, this time headed by Arthur Griffith, the founder of Sinn Fein. This conference lasted for two months and in the end an agreement was hammered out by which The Irish Free State was established as a Dominion in the British Commonwealth. But Irish opinion was furiously divided over this treaty; De Valera was totally opposed to it and resigned, and the Dail confirmed it by a majority of only seven votes. For another year 'the troubles' returned to Ireland in the form of a bitter and bloody civil war.[1]

India

Towards Self-government

Ever since Britain had united the whole of the Indian sub-continent under her rule, there were people who realised that this situation would not last; the time would inevitably come when Britain, having prepared the way, would hand over the government of the country to the Indians themselves. In the twentieth century there was little disagreement about this. The only question was when and how. Would Britain choose the right moment and bequeath to the Indians a workable constitution? Or would she delay too long so that the Indians became resentful and rebellious and came to look on Britain as a tyrant and oppressor?

With Britain's other Dominions the timing of self-government had been comparatively easy, and the transfer of power had been smooth and without rancour. In India this was not possible, as the circumstances there were very different and the difficulties overwhelming. India did not, like the other Dominions, consist mainly of Britons who had settled abroad. Indians were of an entirely different race and civilisation – a much older one than that of Britain. Mutual understanding was difficult, especially as for the last 200 years the Indians had been in the position of a subject race and the consequence of this had been that Britons in India had often become imperious and overbearing and the Indians obsequious. In the twentieth century the two peoples were supposed to be coming together as equals, but there were still many Britons who were patron-

---

[1] In which Michael Collins, a leader of the Easter Rising and later commander of the IRA was killed. A charismatic figure, known as 'The Big Fellow', he had become something of a legend.

As Emperor of India King George V receives the homage of the Nizam of Hyderabad.

ising and condescending and some Indians who were edgy and, in their hurry to obtain self-government, unrealistic about the difficulties.

There were two main problems. In the first place there was the position of the Indian hereditary rulers or 'princes' who at that time ruled about two-fifths of India. Their states, as they were called, were scattered haphazardly over the country, and in all local matters the rulers, perhaps a Nizam or a Maharajah, had almost total authority.

Officially they were under British 'suzerainty' which meant that Britain kept control of all matters of defence and foreign policy, and could intervene in local affairs if it was considered necessary. Many of these princes had enormous wealth and power and it was unlikely that they would welcome the setting up of a central Indian government based on democratic principles.

The second and much greater problem was that of the religious divisions in India. The majority of Indians (about two-thirds) were Hindu, but about a quarter were Moslem, and there was a deep and historic division between them. The religious practices of one often infringed on those of the other,[1] and Moslems, although in a minority, remembered that at the time of the Mogul Empire in the sixteenth century they had been the ruling race. The inability of Hindus and Moslems to reach agreement was the greatest stumbling block to self-government and resulted eventually (in 1946) in Pakistan being set up as a separate Moslem state. (See p. 291.)

With the coming of the twentieth century the movement towards Indian self-government gained momentum, and the feeling grew that Britain's task in India had now been completed. That this task had had some success was recognised by some Indians. At the first National Congress in 1885 the first speaker had declared:

> By a merciful dispensation of providence Britain had rescued India from centuries of external aggression and internal strife ... For the first time in the history of the Indian population there is to be beheld the phenomenon of national unity among them, of a sense of national existence.

Britain had derived great wealth from India and British rule had not been perfect, but much had been accomplished. The unification of the country was a historic achievement. The opening up of communications by road, rail and telegraph, the establishment of law and order and the introduction of one common language (English) in which all Indians could communicate[2] had meant that for the first time the whole sub-continent could be effectively controlled by a central government. For

---

[1] As for example when the music of a Hindu marriage procession disturbed the peace of a Moslem Mosque, and when Moslems sacrificed cows which were sacred to Hindus.
[2] Altogether there were some 200 different languages in India.

the first time too the Indian people had a security they had never known before, not only from lawlessness and violence and foreign invasion but also, if as yet in a small degree, from famine and disease. There was something else too which Britain had brought to India with crucial consequences – British-style education. It could, of course, be foreseen that in time British ideas about freedom, equality and democracy would have a profound effect on educated Indians. Inevitably they would demand these rights for themselves. Education more than anything hastened the day when Britain would relinquish her control of India.

In the early years of the twentieth century a number of measures were taken to give to Indians a greater share in the government of the country, but to many Indians these had not been enough. In consequence there was considerable unrest and many disturbances. One of these had tragic and far-reaching consequences. In 1919 a large crowd gathered unlawfully at Amritsar and the British military commander ordered his troops to open fire on the unarmed crowd. Altogether 379 people were killed and many more wounded. The military commander had hoped that this would shock the Indian population into submission, but it had the opposite effect; people were outraged and all the more determined to be rid of British rule.

Mahatma Gandhi

On one person in particular the Amritsar shootings had a profound effect. This was an Indian lawyer, Mohandas Gandhi who came to be known as 'Mahatma' or 'Great Soul'. Gandhi had qualified as a lawyer in London and had afterwards spent a number of years in South Africa where he had taken a leading part in the struggle against racial discrimination in that country. When Gandhi returned to India he was not particularly anti-British and during the First World War gave Britain wholehearted support. Later, however, his views changed. It seemed to him that the British still looked on Indians as a subject race and were in no hurry to grant them self-government. He believed strongly that until this happened India as a country would have no self-respect and would not command the respect of the rest of the world. He also believed that spiritually India was more developed than Europe and he did not want to see her corrupted by foreign ideas. In particular he distrusted all machinery and thought it a great evil when it deprived poor people of their livelihood. The poor of India were his great con-

Gandhi aged twenty – the law student in London.

Forty years later – the Mahatma on the steps of 10 Downing Street.

cern. One of his declared objectives was 'the awakening of the poorest of the poor' by which he meant in particular the lowest caste of Hindus or 'untouchables' as they were called. It was with these people that he associated himself and their simple way of life which he adopted for himself, including the replacement of European dress by the peasant's loin cloth and shawl.

In time Gandhi came to have a unique influence over the people of India. In appearance he was, according to the British viceroy, Lord Irwin, 'small, wizened, rather emaciated and with no front teeth'. But his spiritual force was phenomenal and had been intensified by rigorous fasting and penances, regular days of total silence and, above all, readiness to accept suffering. He taught his followers that there was nothing they could not achieve if they too were willing to endure suffering and to abstain from all forms of violence. In this way Britain could be made to feel ashamed and embarrassed, her self-confidence would be undermined, and she would lose the will to carry on the struggle.

Soon after the Amritsar shootings Gandhi called on his followers to adopt a policy of passive resistance or 'civil disobedience'. He urged them to give up their titles and offices and to boycott British goods. Repeatedly he emphasised the importance of avoiding all forms of violence; but this was not achieved. He found that he had stirred up forces which he could not control and, in spite of everything he could do, violence kept on breaking out; and because of this he called off his campaign. In 1922 Gandhi was sentenced to six years imprisonment for incitement to rebellion, but was released after two years following the breakdown of his health. It was not until 1930 that he resumed his campaign for ending British rule in India. The opening of this he marked with a dramatic gesture. Accompanied by a large following of supporters and pressmen, he walked 60 miles to the sea where he ceremonially filled a pan with salt water and waited until it had evaporated and there were only a few grains of salt left. Officially this was illegal as the government had a monopoly of salt making. Once again civil disobedience was proclaimed, but once again violence broke out and in some areas hostility between Hindu and Moslem became intense.

After 1930 the British government made attempts to come to terms with Indian nationalists. Two Round Table Conferences were held in London, the second of which Gandhi attended after being specially released from prison.[1] However, little was achieved. Gandhi wanted independence for the whole of India; millions of Moslems refused to belong to a Hindu-dominated India; and there was still in England a powerful group of Conservatives, led by Winston Churchill,[2] which was totally opposed to Indian self-government. The Government of India Act of 1935 made some concessions and gave Indians more power in local affairs, but by the outbreak of the Second World War self-government still seemed far off.

---

[1] In London Gandhi insisted on living among the poor in the East End. He caused his hosts a problem by requiring a regular supply of goat's milk. Later in shawl and loin cloth he attended a garden party at Buckingham Palace.

[2] Winston Churchill described India as 'the brightest jewel in the British crown'. To him Gandhi was 'a seditious Middle Temple lawyer posing as a half-naked fakir'.

Egypt

A British Protectorate

When in 1881 Britain had become involved in Egyptian affairs and had invaded the country, it was not her intention to stay there for long. Mr Gladstone, prime minister at the time, said that British forces would be withdrawn 'as soon as they had converted the present state of Egypt from anarchy and conflict to peace and order.' But this was not easily achieved and British rule in Egypt was to last for some seventy years.

During this time Egypt was never formally annexed by Britain and was not officially part of the British Empire. At first she remained in law a province of the Sultan of Turkey, but when in 1914 Turkey entered the war on Germany's side, this was changed and a British 'Protectorate' was proclaimed. During the war Egyptians, who had no love for Turkish rule, remained loyal to the Allies, but soon afterwards there was a strong demand for independence. Several British statesmen were sympathetic to this demand, but there were two main stumbling blocks. In the first place Britain was vitally concerned with the security of the Suez Canal of which at that time she was part-owner, and insisted that British troops should be stationed in the area. Secondly Egypt was insisting that the Sudan, once an Egyptian province but for the last thirty years ruled by Britain, should be returned to Egyptian rule. But the Sudanese did not want this and the British were unwilling to coerce them.

'Qualified Independence'

Despite these difficulties Britain issued a declaration in 1922 by which the Protectorate was ended and Egypt became an independent sovereign state. But this independence was qualified: a British army was to remain in the country for the time being, and the matters of the Sudan and the Suez Canal were to be settled later. At the same time a son of the old Egyptian Khedive Ismail was set up as King Fuad I and parliamentary institutions were introduced.

The years that followed were uneasy. The king, who had spent most of his life in Italy and spoke little Arabic, was often at loggerheads with the Egyptian parliament, and the position of Britain was awkward; as the ex-ruler of the country with troops still stationed there, she had considerable influence but little legal authority. In 1936 the situation improved when King Fuad died and was succeeded by his sixteen-year-old son, Farouk who had more modern ideas than his father. Also in that year some Egyptians became seriously alarmed by the Italian invasion of Abyssinia (see p. 116) and the declared intention of the Italian dictator, Mussolini, to create a new Roman empire. In these circumstances pressure for British troops in Egypt to be withdrawn became less insistent. Soon afterwards a new treaty was signed which gave Egypt more, but still not complete, independence. One of the clauses of the treaty was that in the event of war Britain should reoccupy the country, and three years later this was to occur.

Palestine

A Turbulent History

When at the Paris Peace Conference Britain was granted a mandate to govern Palestine (see p. 53) there were those who thought that this was another example of British imperialism on the march. Britain's only interest, they contended, was to strengthen her position in the Middle East. If this was true, Britain was to pay a heavy price for it, for nowhere in the Empire, apart from India, was she to be confronted with such apparently insoluble problems. Basically her role was to act as arbiter and peacemaker between two violent and highly emotional forces – those of Jewish and Arab nationalism. On the one hand the Jews, after centuries of being scattered in foreign countries, thought they saw an opportunity at last of establishing a homeland for themselves in the land of their forefathers. On the other were the Arabs who had been living in the country for over a thousand years and were determined not to be dispossessed.

The history of Palestine has been a turbulent one. Its capital, Jerusalem, is a city sacred to three of the world's great religions. To Jews it is their historic home and the site of the great temple of Solomon. To Christians it is the place of the death and resurrection of Jesus Christ. And to Mohammedans it is the site of the great mosque, known as The Dome of the Rock, where Mohammed took flight into Heaven.

In 1918 Palestine, a country hardly larger than Wales, was a poor, thinly populated province of the Turkish Empire. It had known no independence since being conquered by the Roman general, Pompey, in 63 BC. Palestine had been a province of the Roman Empire for 500 years, and during that time had given her rulers incessant trouble, so much so that in AD 135 Jerusalem was razed to the ground and most of the Jewish people driven into exile. In the seventh century AD the country was overrun by the Mohammedan Arabs who rebuilt Jerusalem. And then, some 400 years later came the Turks who, despite a number of Crusades to expel them, occupied the country until 1918.

History of the Jews – The Diaspora

The period since AD 135 is known to the Jews as the Diaspora (Dispersal). During that time there were few Jews living in Palestine, the great majority being scattered over the countries of Europe and the Middle East. Here their treatment was often brutal. In Mohammedan countries, although considered inferior, they were usually accepted and tolerated. But in European countries they encountered great hostility; they were regarded as strangers and heretics and condemned as members of the race which had crucified Christ. It was made very difficult for them to earn a livelihood: they were not allowed to own land which prevented them from becoming farmers and they were not allowed to join Guilds which prevented them from becoming tradesmen. It was necessary for them, therefore, to become some sort of middleman, such as a pedlar or money-lender, an occupation forbidden to Christians at that time.

At the time of the Crusades the Jews, along with all non-Christians (as well as some Christians suspected of heresy) suffered great persecution, and this culminated in their being expelled from England (1290) and other countries of Western Europe. From here some took refuge in the Turkish Empire, while others made their way into Eastern Europe where they lived a precarious life – herded into ghettos, marked with a special yellow badge, and with the threat of pogroms (semi-official massacres) never far away. And yet in spite of heavy persecution the Jewish race did not die out, nor were they assimilated into other races. It seemed that the more they were persecuted, the more intensely did Jews cling to their religion and their belief that they were a people set apart by God. Paradoxically a greater danger to the Jewish religion came when Jews were tolerated and treated as equals, as then many of them did intermarry and become Christians and were absorbed into their countries of adoption.

With the coming, in the latter part of the eighteenth century, of the 'Age of Revolution' with its ideas of brotherhood and equality, life for European Jews became more settled and secure. They were allowed more freedom and many of them rose to prominent positions. But anti-Semitism had not disappeared, and towards the end of the nineteenth century it became stronger, particularly in Germany and Russia. It is estimated that between 1880 and 1910 some three million Jews fled from Eastern Europe. Of these the great majority went to America, while others settled in Western Europe. But there were a few who made their way to Palestine. There they had to struggle hard for an existence, but help was forthcoming from the wealthy Jewish banker, Lord Rothschild, and they managed to survive, and the number of Jewish settlers began to increase.

Zionism

It was at this time that the feeling began to grow among Jews that it was essential for them to have a national home. For centuries they had been scattered and 'a stranger in a strange land'. Miraculously the Jewish religion and culture had survived, but if these were to be truly valued and the Jewish people accorded a proper dignity, they must have a country which they could call their own and in which any Jew could settle 'as of right and not on sufferance'. And to most Jews such a national home could only be Palestine.

For centuries Jews had dreamed of a great return to the land of their forefathers where they would await the coming of the great Messiah promised to them by their prophets of old. But for over a thousand years Palestine had been occupied by Mohammedan Arabs, and while these might look tolerantly on the establishment of a few Jewish settlements, they would feel very differently about a mass immigration of Jews and the setting up of a Jewish national state. Also until 1918 Palestine was part of the Turkish Empire and the Turks were strongly opposed to any such idea.

The Balfour Declaration

Even before the end of Turkish rule in Palestine Britain had pledged her support for a Jewish national home there. This occurred in 1917 when Britain was hard pressed in the First World War, and desperately needed the support of world Jewry, particularly of the rich and powerful Jews in America. The pledge was given in the Balfour Declaration, named after the Foreign Secretary of the time, which stated that 'His Majesty's government view with favour the establishment in Palestine of a national home for Jewish people.' Accordingly at the end of the war Palestine was hived off from Syria to which she had previously been attached and placed under a British mandate. The way was then open for Jewish immigration, and Jews from all over the world began to arrive. In theory their number was restricted, but in practice it was found difficult to keep out illegal immigrants who were determined to get in.

The Arabs

Inevitably the Arabs in Palestine became alarmed at this great influx of foreigners into their country. At first they had not been unduly apprehensive. They outnumbered the Jews by ten to one and the Balfour Declaration had stated clearly that 'nothing shall be done which may prejudice the civil and religious rights of existing non-Jewish communities in Palestine.' Later Lord Balfour had asked the Arabs not to grudge the Jews 'a small notch' of their country, and if it had remained at that there might have been little friction. Gradually, however, the 'small notch' began to assume larger and larger proportions.

The problem was made more difficult by the fact that the Jewish immigrants were a different type of people from the Arabs. The majority of the Arabs were Fellahin, that is they were peasant farmers who scraped a living from tiny plots of land; their way of life was simple and had not changed for centuries. The Jews, on the other hand, were much more sophisticated; many of them had come from Europe and included distinguished artists, scientists and technicians. They arrived in the country with a passionate enthusiasm to establish the Jewish national home and were eager to get started on schemes for reclaiming desert lands, harnessing the waters of the Jordan, and setting up new industries. And so whenever they could they bought up the lands of the Fellahin and applied to them new and intensive methods of agriculture.

More and more the Arabs found themselves being excluded from the country they regarded as their own, and it was not long before they resorted to violence. The first uprisings occurred in 1920, and in 1929 there was a major clash. The situation became even more critical in 1933 when Hitler came to power in Germany and began the persecution of the Jews. The inevitable consequence of this was that the number of Jewish immigrants into Palestine began to soar. In 1933 it rose from 9,550 to 30,327, and in 1935 to over 60,000. By then the Arabs, who still comprised 70 per cent of the total population, were becoming desperate. Power fell more and more into the hands of the extremists and in 1936 there was an open rebellion; a general strike was called and guerrilla bands roamed the country taking life and destroying property.

The responsibility for maintaining order in the country rested with the British government which found itself being tugged violently in opposite directions. On the one hand was Jewish nationalism, rapidly growing and with powerful backing in many countries, particularly America. On the other was Arab nationalism, also growing and with great support for Palestinian Arabs in their fight not to be dispossessed. British statesmen tried hard to conciliate and find a settlement acceptable to both sides, but this was, perhaps, impossible. In their efforts they incurred at one time or other the fury of both Arabs and Jews. Soon after the end of the Second World War (1948) they relinquished their mandate and handed the problem over to the United Nations.

Timescale

1917	Balfour Declaration concerning Jewish national home in Palestine.
1919	British mandate to govern Palestine. Amritsar shootings. Gandhi starts campaign of non-resistance.
1921	Irish Free State established.
1926	The Statute of Westminster.
1930	Gandhi renews campaign to end British rule.
1935	Government of India Act.

Chapter 8

KEEPING THE PEACE IN EUROPE 1919–1931

War Between Greece and Turkey

At the Paris Peace Conference Turkey was made to pay heavily for taking the side of Germany in the war. She was deprived of her provinces of Iraq, Syria and Palestine in the Middle East and of all her territory in Europe except Constantinople. In addition she also had to cede to Greece parts of Anatolia, the old Turkish homeland in Asia Minor where there was a large Greek population. Although this had been agreed by the Sultan, there were many in Turkey who resented it bitterly. Revolutionary forces were gaining ground at that time and a new government took over in Ankara under Mustapha Kemal,[1] the man who during the war had saved the day for Turkey at Gallipoli (see p. 25).

In 1919 fighting broke out in Anatolia between Greece and Turkey. At first the Greeks had some success, but in 1922 they were heavily defeated and not only the Greek army but the whole Greek population of the area were either put to death or expelled. The army of Mustapha Kemal then advanced to the Dardanelles (see map on p. xxx) where a small British force was guarding Constantinople at Chanak. For a time it looked as if it might be attacked and war break out between the two countries, but in the end a conference was held and a new treaty drawn up by which Turkey retained all of Anatolia and sovereignty over the Dardanelles.

There were fears at the time about the future intentions of Mustapha Kemal, but these proved unnecessary as he was to turn his attention to the modernisation of Turkey where he introduced Western ideas and institutions including the Latin alphabet and European-style dress.

---

[1] He later adopted the title of Attaturk meaning 'Chief Turk'.

Russia at the End of the War

When Russia made peace with Germany at Brest-Litovsk in 1918 (see p. 38), she had been forced to concede vast areas of territory. In the following year at the Paris Peace Conference these territories were put at the disposal of the Allied Powers to do with them as they thought fit. At the time Russia was still in the throes of civil war and was regarded with suspicion and hostility by the rest of Europe because of the Bolshevik[1] takeover and the declared intention of the Bolshevik leaders to spread Communism into other countries. And so the lost territories were not restored to Russia but were divided up into a number of new states to form a cordon separating Russia from the rest of Europe. In this way the country of Poland was re-established and the countries of Latvia, Lithuania and Estonia were created.

In 1919 the Russian civil war came to an end with the defeat of the anti-Communists or 'White' Russians, but the Bolsheviks then had to face a threat from the new Poland where there was a strong feeling that the country had not been assigned enough territory by the Treaty of Versailles. Recklessly the Poles invaded Russia in an attempt to take the lands which they regarded as being historically Polish. In due course they were defeated and the Russians then invaded Poland. This caused great alarm in Europe as the Russians soon reached Warsaw and there seemed to be nothing to stop them from advancing as far as they wanted. However, there then occurred 'the miracle of the Vistula' when the Polish army under its leader, Joseph Pilsudsky, with help from the French Marshal Weygand, defeated the Russians and drove them back. The Battle of the Vistula is regarded by many as one of the decisive battles of history; for the time being it stemmed the advance of Communism.

In the years that followed Russia's relations with the rest of Europe have been described as 'suspended war'. In 1924 the Bolshevik government was officially recognised by Britain and France, and subsequently some efforts were made to bring Russia into the community of nations. Occasionally it seemed that progress was being made, as when Russia

---

[1] Bolshevik was the name taken by the Russian Communists. It means 'majority'.

joined the League of Nations in 1934. But the doctrines of Communism and the threat they posed caused great mistrust and hostility.

Russia and Communism

The doctrines of Communism as propounded by Karl Marx in his monumental work, *Capital*, laid down that the fundamental conflict in the world was not between different nations but between different classes – the 'bourgeoisie' and the 'proletariat' or, put simply, the 'haves' and the 'have nots'. Marx also stated that the needs of the workers were wholly material and that moral values were of no significance. Any kind of religion he abhorred, regarding it as 'the opiate[1] of the people'. All-important was the state, and to this man's conscience and natural rights must be subjected. Ultimately a perfect Communistic society would be created with liberty and equality for all, but in the meanwhile there must be a dictatorship of the proletariat to safeguard the interests of the workers against the bourgeoisie.

Communism was to prevail in Russia for the next seventy years, but during that time there were few signs of the emergence of a perfect Communistic society. As in other so-called Communist countries there was no progress beyond the stage of dictatorship. In its early days Communism had great attractions for idealists all over the world and many of them worked openly and conspired secretly to bring about a Communist millennium.[2] At times, particularly during the Great Depression of the 1930s it seemed possible that Marx's prediction of the collapse of capitalism and its replacement by Communism might be fulfilled. But in the event this did not happen and eventually it was Communism that collapsed. In Britain Communism never posed a serious threat. The British Communist Party was founded in 1920, but it made little headway; it was seldom able to obtain the election of a representative either in Parliament or in local councils, and the British Labour Party always kept it at a distance.

Many reasons have been given for the failure of Communism. In the first place the workers of the world did not unite. Marx was wrong in his supposition that class divisions were stronger than racial divisions.

---

[1] A soothing drug that induces contentment and sleep.
[2] A period of perfect peace and happiness.

Whenever wars broke out, notably the two world wars, the workers always rallied behind their governments and not with foreign workers in a class war against the bourgeoisie. Workers generally have had little interest in establishing Communistic societies. More attractive to them has been the prospect of joining the ranks of the bourgeoisie. Marx was also totally mistaken about the role of the bourgeoisie in an advanced industrial society. He looked on it as a small, narrow group which before the Industrial Revolution it was, but since then its ranks had been swollen by millions of managers, clerks, technicians and other skilled workers without whom an industrial society could not exist. But the fundamental error of Marxism lay in its devaluation of moral values. Surely no perfect society can be created without these.

The Problem of Germany

In the years following the Peace Conference the basic problem of Europe continued to be the future of Germany. As has been seen, the Germans bitterly resented the Treaty of Versailles, regarding it as 'a slave treaty', and all German statesmen, either secretly or openly, were determined to overturn it and restore Germany to her rightful position in Europe. At the same time the French were determined that Germany should remain weak and insisted that the Treaty of Versailles be carried out to the letter. More and more the French were feeling that they had been cheated at the Peace Conference. There they had given up their claim to extend their frontier to the Rhine in return for an Anglo–American guarantee of their new frontier; but with the American withdrawal from Europe this guarantee had become worthless. France felt that she had been abandoned and left alone to confront a rapidly recovering Germany with a population of 65 million as against her own of 40 million.

In the conflict between the two countries Germany had great advantages. In the first place, as Allied armies in Europe became smaller, the Treaty of Versailles became increasingly difficult to enforce. Without a large army of occupation Germany could not be compelled to disarm and pay large sums in reparations; this could only be done if Germany herself was willing to cooperate. But Germany's greatest advantage was that in the hour of defeat she had remained a united country; the empire created by Bismarck had not fallen apart. This meant that time was on her side; with her greater population, bounding birth rate and dynamic energy she would inevitably become again the strongest power in Europe.

Keeping the Peace

In the years between the two world wars great efforts were made by European statesmen both to calm the fears of France and to satisfy the grievances of Germany. The period may be divided into three parts: the first from 1919 to 1923 was dismal and embittered; the second from 1924 to 1931 was brighter and more hopeful; and the third from 1931 to 1939 saw the slide with gathering momentum into another world war.

1919–23

This was a dark period in Europe: in the east there were wars between Russia and Poland and Greece and Turkey; in the west Anglo–French relations became very strained and all international relations were bedeviled by disagreements on the subject of German reparations. At the Peace Conference the actual figure for these had been left open, but in due course a sum of £11 billion had been demanded from Germany to be paid over forty-two years. The Germans were aghast at this figure which was considerably more than the cost of war damage which was what they had agreed to pay in the Armistice terms. They declared flatly that it was impossible for them to pay such a sum and delayed handing over the first instalment. The consequence of this was that the French proceeded to occupy the Ruhr, Germany's industrial heartland, and attempted to extract the reparations by force. This was followed by the German workers in the Ruhr coming out on strike; and so a deadlock was reached. Soon afterwards there was a total collapse of the German monetary system. Suddenly everyone took fright that German paper money was worthless and tried to get rid of it. And the more this occurred the more valueless the German mark became, so that in the end a ten million mark note could be bought in the streets of London for two pence. This was an appalling catastrophe for Germany and caused tremendous hardship and suffering, particularly among the middle classes who saw the overnight disappearance of their life savings. However, it did have a sobering effect on European statesmen in their demands for reparations. It was in no-one's interest that Germany should be in a permanent state of bankruptcy.

1924–31

This was a period of hope for Europe. The collapse of the German mark not only brought about a more reasonable attitude among Europeans; it also brought America back on to the scene. America might opt out of Europe's politics, but she remained heavily involved in her finances, not only in the matter of trade but also as regards war debts which were considerable. It had been unfortunate that America had been absent from the first reparations conferences where she might have exercised a moderating influence. But in 1924 the American General Dawes presided over a conference which produced a settlement acceptable to both France and Germany. With this knotty problem out of the way the situation in Europe became brighter, and in the following year (1925) a new atmosphere was created by the Treaty of Locarno. This was signed by Great Britain, France, Italy and Belgium, and the main provision was the guarantee of Germany's western frontier. Also Germany renounced for ever all claims to Alsace–Lorraine, and France agreed to the evacuation of Allied troops from the Rhineland; and both countries were to be guaranteed against the aggression of the other by Great Britain and Italy. In the following year (1926) the spirit of reconciliation was carried a stage further when Germany was at last admitted into the League of Nations. And in 1928 the United States made her contribution when her Secretary of State, Frank B. Kellogg, induced all the leading countries of Europe, including Russia, to sign a pact renouncing war altogether except for self-defence. However, as countries going to war invariably claim that they are acting in self-defence, the pact was to be of no great value.

In 1929 the Great Depression broke on the world (see p. 66) and this presaged the end of Europe's years of hope. In 1931 Japan invaded China, and the final tragic inter-war period began (see chapter 10).

The League of Nations

Besides making treaties and redrawing the map of Europe the delegates at the Paris Peace Conference were also responsible for setting up an international organisation which, it was hoped, would bring an end to

war. At first eighteen countries joined the League of Nations but in time
it was to contain fifty-nine. The ideal of the League was a noble one:
to preserve the peace of the world by conciliation and consent rather
than by compulsion and force. Each member-state was to guarantee the
territory of other member-states and all disputes between countries were
to be submitted to arbitration. It was also provided that the League
would take instant action against any country failing to keep this undertaking either by imposing sanctions (cutting off foreign trade) or by
force. Great were the hopes at the time that the League would prevent
future wars. One of the great tragedies of the twentieth century was that
it failed to do so.

Certainly the League had great weaknesses. Of these perhaps the
most serious was its incompleteness of membership; there were some
crucial omissions. It has already been seen that the United States Senate
would not ratify the peace treaties and insisted on a complete American
withdrawal from European affairs. Also, on French insistence, Germany
and the other defeated countries were not allowed to join for the time
being; and Russia, in bad odour with the rest of Europe because of
Bolshevism, was another non-member. This meant that at first the
League of Nations was in fact a league of victors, dominated by Britain
and France with a number of smaller neutral countries joining in.

Another great weakness of the League was that it lacked any effective means of taking action against aggressors and states who violated
their undertakings. It could ask its members to apply sanctions or even
force, but it had no power to compel them to do so, and they were
entitled to refuse. And sanctions to be effective must be universal; if
only a few countries maintain their trade, the effect will be lost.

Perhaps the failure of the League was inevitable because of the spirit
of the times. This was dominated by an overwhelming war-weariness
and an intense desire for peace at any price. This was so great that
people deluded themselves into thinking that the League had no need
to use force, for no country would dare to defy the judgement of the
rest of the world. But sadly this was not the case; the League needed
power to enforce its decisions, and power needed armaments. Pacifists
all over the world were to discover that it was not consistent to be
supporters of the League and at the same time to clamour for disarmament. Statesmen of countries which had disarmed too quickly, notably
Britain, found themselves obliged to condone flagrant violations of the

League of Nations Covenant. And statesmen from democracies were prevented by public opinion from going to war on behalf of countries situated, perhaps, on the other side of the world. Thus in 1931 public opinion in Britain was appalled at the thought of going to war with Japan on behalf of China.[1] The record of these years then was a sorry story of avoidance of responsibility, non-fulfilment of pledges and compromises with wrongdoing.

In its early years the League had some success; disputes were brought before it and conciliation of a sort was effected. Its first real test, however, was when Japanese forces invaded Manchuria, and China appealed to the League for help. Immediately its ineffectiveness became apparent. The only member state which could have taken any action was Britain which at that time was in the throes of the Great Depression. In the end a commission of investigation was appointed which accepted most of the Japanese reasons for their action but blamed Japan for resorting to force before all peaceful means had been attempted. The result of this was that Japan remained in Manchuria and withdrew angrily from the League.

Although the League was weakened by the Manchurian affair it was not until the Italian invasion of Abyssinia that it received a fatal blow (see p. 116). This was a clear-cut case of aggression. Without any justification the Italian dictator, Mussolini, decided in 1935 to attack Abyssinia which (with Liberia) was one of the remaining independent African states. The Abyssinian emperor, Haile Selassie, immediately brought the matter before the League which declared Italy an aggressor and imposed sanctions, prohibiting the export to that country of all war materials. But the one vital commodity, oil, was not included, and Italy was able to obtain most of her other needs from countries outside the League. In the end Italian rule in Abyssinia was established and recognised and sanctions withdrawn. The effect of this on the authority and reputation of the League was devastating. It was clear for all to see that the authority of the League could be defied with impunity. One person to note this was the new German dictator, Adolf Hitler.

---

[1] Except for a left wing group which until that time had been clamouring for greater disarmament.

Timescale

1919	End of Russian civil war.
1919–22	War between Greece and Turkey.
1920	Russians driven back at battle of Vistula.
1923	French occupy the Ruhr.
1925	Treaty of Locarno.
1926	Germany admitted to League of Nations.
1929	Great Depression begins.
1934	Russia joins League of Nations.

Chapter 9

THE RISE OF THE DICTATORS
(Part One)

Italy under Mussolini

Post-War Chaos

One of the tragedies of post-war Europe was the way in which democracy in Italy collapsed, and the country succumbed to a dictator.

Italy had suffered heavily during the war. For most of the time her armies had been hard-pressed and at the battle of Caporetto heavily defeated. But Italians felt they had made a worthy contribution to victory. Had they not tied down large enemy forces which were badly needed elsewhere? And had not half a million Italians lost their lives? At the Peace Conference Italy expected to be treated by the Allies as an equal and to be granted, as a matter of right, all the territory she had been promised by the Treaty of London (see p. 26). However, as has already been seen, the terms of this treaty were not in accordance with President Wilson's Fourteen Points, and at the Paris Peace Conference Italy was denied those parts of Yugoslavia where Italians were in a minority. This caused great resentment to Italians who felt they had been defrauded; their great war effort was being ignored and they were being treated as a second-class power.

As well as this blow to their national pride Italians had other troubles at that time. For Italy had never been a rich country and the huge cost of the war had devastated her economy. Returning ex-servicemen found widespread unemployment, rising food prices and high taxes. Everywhere there was great poverty and great anger – anger with Italy's one time allies for having let her down and anger with their rulers for having failed her. In this mood many Italians were ready to listen to the doctrines of Communism. Many too were organising strikes and riots, and some were forming themselves into brigand bands which roamed

the country, looting and terrorising as they went. There were many
bitter divisions in Italy at that time, but at heart all Italians longed for
a powerful and united country with strong and dynamic leadership.

Benito Mussolini

The political scene in Italy after the war was confused. There were
many small political parties, some law-abiding and respectable, but
others noisy and violent and quite ready to resort to strong-arm methods. Of these the most notorious was the Fascist Party of Benito Mussolini.

Mussolini was the son of a blacksmith and in his young days had
been a violent revolutionary with strong Communist views. As such he
had been imprisoned on eleven occasions, and had gone into exile in
Switzerland rather than be conscripted into the Italian army. At the time
he was absorbed in the class struggle, and patriotism to him meant
nothing. But then came the First World War and Mussolini, like many
Communists, found that, when it came to the crunch, love of country
was greater than love of class. All talk of a 'capitalist war' was put
aside and Mussolini lost no time in joining the army. During the war
years Mussolini gained a good reputation as a soldier and seems to have
stood up well to the appalling conditions in the trenches; but in 1917 he
was injured in an accident and discharged. By then he had completely
shed his Communist views and in 1919, when he was a newspaper
editor, he founded his own party, the Fascists, with the main object of
combating Communism.

In the post-war years conditions in Italy grew ever worse; no government lasted long, lawlessness and violence increased and efforts were
being made to organise a general strike. In this situation there were
many Italians, usually of moderate political beliefs, who thought that
Communism would soon gain the upper hand and that the only party
which could prevent this was the Fascists. This feeling spread to the
highest in the land, even to King Victor Emmanuel himself. In 1921
Mussolini and some of his followers were elected to parliament and
soon afterwards organised a march on Rome in order to demand that
Fascists be included in the next government. But the king anticipated
them. Fearing that civil war was imminent, he sent a message to
Mussolini inviting him to form a government. A few days later
Mussolini was prime minister.

Mussolini (centre) with his henchmen at the time of the March on Rome.

It was not at once that he became dictator. At first he aimed to work within the constitution and made no move to abolish either parliament or the monarchy. During his first years his achievements seemed to be considerable. Italy was revived; in place of fatigue and despair came vitality and enthusiasm. The threat of anarchy and civil war receded and Italians became more united and more ready to make sacrifices for their country. Some people abroad were amazed at the change, so much so that Fascist parties began to appear in other countries, including England.

But to some Italians and outside observers it soon became evident that all was not well; great as Mussolini's achievements seemed to be, Italy was paying a high price for them, in particular a price which Italians had treasured for centuries – their freedom. In the years following the so-called March on Rome Mussolini gradually built up his own power and cut down that of everyone else. Parliament was packed with his supporters and agreed to everything he decreed. Criticisms of his regime were silenced ruthlessly, and roaming squads of Blackshirts used brutal and humiliating methods on political opponents.[1] All the usual trappings of dictatorship soon appeared: secret police, censorship, racism, glorification of war and, above all, a tremendous build-up of the dictator himself. It was certainly this which interested Mussolini most, and he spent long hours creating for himself an image of a superman. All press reports and photographs were carefully censored and doctored. On public occasions he was to be seen unsmiling and purposeful, his jaw thrust well out, marching, running or goosestepping.[2] Off duty he was shown in some manly pursuit – riding, fencing, flying, motor racing – and always doing it supremely well. At all times he sought to give the impression of a strong and vigorous man of action, a perfect leader who was always right.

Although today such a propaganda campaign might seem absurd, at the time it had considerable success; it sustained Mussolini in power for over twenty years. But that his regime would collapse eventually was certain. For it was based on a myth: Mussolini was no superman. Outwardly he might be all vigour and drive, but below the surface were inefficiency, timidity and endless chopping and changing. Everything he did was for show; projects were judged not by their intrinsic value but by the effect they would have on his image. Thus factories were built and then not used, contradictory orders were frequently issued, and the army was provided with many gaudy uniforms but not many modern weapons. Mussolini might brag noisily that Italy was 'a master race with breasts of steel' and that 'better one day as a lion than 100 years as a sheep', but when war came the Italian armed forces were unprepared and half-hearted.

Inevitably in time Mussolini fell a victim to his own propaganda and really believed it to be true. Having reiterated it repeatedly he became genuinely convinced that Italy was the greatest nation on earth and that he was the greatest leader since Napoleon. It was these illusions which prompted the mistakes which led to his downfall. And of these the greatest and most fatal was his decision to invade Abyssinia and found a new Roman Empire overseas. This was an out-of-date concept; by that time colonialism was on the decline, and this act of unprovoked

---

[1] Sometimes they were beaten up, sometimes they were forced to swallow large quantities of castor oil and even live frogs. One leading opponent was murdered; but this caused a great outcry and nearly brought about the downfall of Mussolini.

[2] A high-stepping march much favoured by dictators.

aggression brought Italy many enemies. Also it threw him more and more into the clutches of his fellow dictator, Adolf Hitler.

Eventually Mussolini's rule was to end in complete ignominy and disaster with Italy a defeated and humiliated nation and himself shot by his fellow countrymen and his body strung up outside a petrol station. During his twenty years of power he had achieved little of lasting value, and today his doctrine of Fascism is the most hated of all political creeds. Deriving its name from the *fasces*, a bunch of rods and an axe carried by magistrates in ancient Rome, its emphasis is on conformity, and acceptance of authority. For freedom and democracy it has no use. Unthinking obedience is required from all its followers, and for those who dissent and go their own way there is brute force and 'the rule of the rubber truncheon'. Fascism contained no new idea or principle; it was a doctrine for thugs. Also its insistence on a fierce and hysterical patriotism led inevitably to racism and war.

Russia under Stalin

The Long Suffering of the Russian People

At the time of the Russian Revolution there was great hope among the Russian people that a new age was dawning for them. After the afflictions and injustices of life under the tsars and then the disasters and defeats of the First World War the government of the country was in the hands of the Bolshevik Party which promised peace and the establishment of a workers' paradise based on Communism. Few then can have guessed at the horrors and miseries that lay ahead. Peace with Germany had been made on very humiliating terms but this had been followed by two years of civil war in which perhaps as many as seven million people lost their lives.[1] Then with the country in chaos and agriculture upset by disastrous Communist reforms (see p. 118) came years of famine with millions dying of starvation. At the same time, with the country in the grips of a dictator more terrible than any tsar, millions more were liquidated in political purges or sent to labour camps in Siberia. And then came the Second World War with all the agony of a foreign invasion and further immense losses of life.

---

[1] This brought the total of Russian dead since 1914 to some 28 million.

When the Bolsheviks first came to power their leader, Vladimir Lenin, did not attempt to set up a Communist state immediately; he realised that Russia was not yet ready for this. In any case he was preoccupied first with making peace with Germany and then with the struggle to hold on to the power he and his party had just won. However, far-reaching changes were made: factories, shops and businesses were taken over, and land was taken away from large landowners and distributed in smallholdings to the peasants. At first reasonable freedom was allowed to the Russian people: the press was not censored; opposition parties were tolerated and a free election was held. However, when the Bolsheviks did badly in this election, obtaining only about a quarter of the votes cast, there was a change of attitude and the Constituent Assembly was dispersed by force. Soon afterwards the civil war broke out and the Bolshevik leaders became ever more dictatorial; censorship was introduced as also was conscription, and strikes were prohibited. These changes were supposed to be temporary, but they had come to stay.

The Civil War

Of course the Bolsheviks had many enemies inside Russia. The dispossessed landowners and businessmen were ready to fight them to the death. The Russian Orthodox Church was strongly hostile, its land and riches having been confiscated and its priests persecuted. To these were added later the democrats and idealists who believed in freedom of speech, free parliaments and the rule of law.

In 1918 a number of anti-Bolshevik groups were formed and the civil war broke out soon afterwards. At first the 'White' Russians had some success with the whole of Siberia coming under their control, but it was never likely that they would prevail in the end. They lacked unity; there was little mutual sympathy between the ex-landlords who wanted to restore the tsars and the democrats who wanted rule by a freely elected parliament. Also some White Russian leaders openly declared that it was their intention to restore all land and factories to the previous owners, and this brought great support to the Bolsheviks, as the peasants were willing to fight for their smallholdings,[1] as were the factory

---

[1] If they had but known it the peasants were, in due course, to be deprived of their smallholdings by Stalin (see p. 125).

workers to keep control of their factories. Another factor which weighed heavily against the Whites was the amount of foreign support they received. Great Britain, France, Japan and the United States all sent aid of some sort, and this interference was greatly resented by many Russians and led them to give support to the Bolsheviks for whom, at heart, they had little sympathy.

In the event the civil war dragged on for three years. The ultimate victory of the Bolsheviks was in part due to the organising ability of Lenin's chief lieutenant, Leon Trotsky,[1] who has been called the creator of the Red Army. When the civil war was over the Bolsheviks took the offensive and invaded some of those parts of Russia which had been lost at the Treaty of Brest-Litovsk. Georgia and the Ukraine were regained but, as has been seen, when the Red Army invaded Poland it was driven back.

Reconstruction and Retreat from Communism

After the civil war conditions in Russia were desperate. In some towns people lay dying of hunger in the streets; there were outbreaks of typhus; and medical supplies were often unobtainable. Many townspeople fled to the country in search of food which meant that factories were having to close because of shortage of labour. In the country too conditions were grim. The peasants had been driven to despair by the pillaging of their crops by the Red and White armies and at the end of the war were sullen and resentful that they were not allowed to sell their surplus grain at whatever prices they could obtain. Accordingly they were growing only enough for themselves. In 1921 the area of land put down to crops was about one half of that in 1913; also the number of livestock reared was much smaller. In these circumstances Lenin realised that emergency measures were needed which were not in accordance with the doctrines of Communism. And so the New Economic Policy of 1921 gave more freedom to private enterprise. Peasants were allowed to sell more of their surplus produce, more scope was given to shopkeepers and small traders, and factory workers were motivated into higher production by bonuses and piece-work. To some this represented a shocking retreat from Communism, but to Lenin it was unavoidable.

---

[1] Trotsky was of Jewish origin. His real name was Lev Davidovich Bronstein.

Pure Communism he did not expect to be established in his generation. For the time being the workers' slogan must be: 'From each according to his ability; to each according to his work.' Later Lenin hoped that this would change to: 'From each according to his ability; to each according to his need.'

Lenin was the one man who might have led Russia out of chaos; he alone had the courage, the commonsense and the personal authority. But in 1922 he had the first of a series of strokes and in 1924 he died. Just as he was about to build on the ruins he had created he was removed from the scene. It was a tragedy for Russia and for the world.

Vladimir Lenin (1870–1924)

Lenin[1] is perhaps the best known and most successful of all revolutionaries. Yet there was nothing in his origins which might have pointed him in this direction; his family background was middle class, Christian and happy. His father was an inspector of schools and the family had a comfortable home in the small, quiet town of Simbirsk on the banks of the river Volga. Lenin was one of six children, all but one of whom became in time revolutionaries. His elder brother, Alexander, was an early casualty, being executed for subversive activities when he was only twenty-one. Lenin himself was soon in trouble with the police, constantly being harassed by them because of the association with his brother. Although expelled from university, he was able in time to qualify as a lawyer and for a time this was his profession. However, he had little interest or success in legal work. More and more he became preoccupied with politics and drawn into revolutionary activities. In 1895 he was arrested and spent a year in prison in St Petersburg.[2] Later he was sent into exile in Siberia, but not in a slave labour camp; he was allowed to live in a house of his own where he had some freedom and where he was later joined by his wife.

In 1900 Lenin was set free, but it was evident there was little safety for him in Russia, so he and his wife went into exile abroad and he devoted himself to editing a Communist newspaper which he called

---

[1] His real name was Vladimir Ulyanov, the name Lenin being a code name he later adopted in the underground revolutionary movement.

[2] Then capital of Russia. Later for some seventy years it was known as Leningrad.

Lenin, the leader of the Bolshevik Revolution and founder of the Russian Communist state.

Iskra ('The Spark'). There were many Russian revolutionaries living abroad at that time and with these Lenin became associated, although he was soon to find that with some of them he was in strong disagreement. For they were mainly interested in increasing the size of the Communist Party, whereas Lenin was convinced that a revolutionary party, to be effective, should be small, united and totally dedicated. And so in time Lenin broke away from the main body and formed his own party which became known as the Bolsheviks.

On the outbreak of the First World War there was a great surge of patriotism in Russia and nearly the whole country was united in the war against Germany. Lenin was one of the few people who denounced the war, declaring that there was no good reason for it and that the only people who would gain from it were the capitalist arms manufacturers. For the first years of the war he lived in Switzerland, but, as has been seen (p. 38), in 1917 the Germans arranged special transport to take him back to Russia when the first revolution broke out. However, Lenin gave this no support. He bided his time, waited until the new leaders were in difficulties and then staged his own revolution. Although this was successful and Lenin was to have as much power as the tsars, he found it impossible to fulfil the promises he had made to the Russian people. When he died they were still hungry, had little freedom and no political rights; also the great majority of industry and agriculture were still in the hands of private enterprise. Lenin's achievement will always be a matter of controversy. To some he merely replaced one tyranny with a much greater one; and the methods he employed to achieve his revolution inevitably wrecked the ideals for which it stood. But to others he is the great hero of the poor and underprivileged, the man who upset the old social order and paved the way for a new one.

The Rise of Stalin

With the death of Lenin a power struggle among Bolshevik leaders was inevitable. The man whom most people expected to succeed him was Leon Trotsky who had been his right-hand man and who had won a great reputation for himself during the civil war (see p. 119). In the event, however, the man who did emerge as Russia's new ruler was the Communist Party's General Secretary, Josef Stalin,[1] who up to that time had been content to remain in the background, biding his time and stealthily building up his power.

Stalin was a different man from Lenin. He lacked his culture and had none of his warmth and love of people. Whereas Lenin had been the intellectual force behind the Russian Revolution, Stalin had been one of the principal terrorists, staging hold-ups and murders and organising blackmail and 'protection' payments. Cunning, suspicious and completely ruthless, he was to be one of Russia's most powerful and terrifying rulers; it was he who, regardless of human suffering and loss of life, was to make Russia a great world power.

Stalin was born in Georgia, a district in the south which had only become part of Russia in the nineteenth century and where anti-Russian feeling was still strong. His parents were very poor. His father, an ex-serf, earned a precarious livelihood as a cobbler, most of which he spent on drink; he had no love for his son and treated him brutally. His mother, a deeply religious woman, took in sewing and washing and worked as hard as she could to support her only surviving child. Her great ambition was that he should become a priest. Stalin was not a robust child; he had been born slightly deformed with a shortened left arm and some of his toes joined together; and this, together with his unhappy family background, led to his becoming an 'outsider', keeping apart from other children.

By dint of hard work and great self-sacrifice Stalin's mother was able in time to scrape together enough money for him to go to a theological college; but it became clear soon that Stalin was not cut out for the

---

[1] Another code name. His real name was Josef Djugashvili.

Stalin, Lenin's successor. His power ranged from Korea to Eastern Europe.

priesthood, and after a short time he was expelled. From then on he became more and more involved in revolutionary movements. On several occasions he was sent to prison, and the outbreak of the First World War found him in Siberia. Although he escaped from there in 1917, he does not seem to have played a leading part in the revolutions of that year. But he was by then sufficiently well known in the Bolshevik Party for Lenin to give him an important post in the revolutionary government. Later he gained the key post of General Secretary of the Party and it was from there that he was able to manoeuvre himself into the chief position of power after Lenin's death. Before he died Lenin had foreseen that this might happen and had tried to prevent it. He wrote: 'Stalin, having become General Secretary, has concentrated enormous power in his hands. I am not sure he knows how to use that power with sufficient caution ... Stalin is too rude. I propose that the comrades find a way to remove Stalin from the position and appoint another man.' But, incapacitated as he was by then, Lenin was unable to check Stalin, and once in power he could not be shifted.

Stalin and Reconstruction

It was never likely that Stalin and Trotsky would be able to work together; their temperaments clashed violently and they disagreed on one fundamental matter: Trotsky was convinced that the Communist revolution should be spread into other countries, and that only thus would it be successful in Russia. Stalin on the other hand maintained strongly that other countries were not their concern and that it was the duty of Russian Communists to build up Russian strength and make the country a great world power. In time it was Stalin who was to prevail and Trotsky was driven into exile, denounced as the greatest traitor of all, and later murdered in Mexico.

Once installed in power, Stalin soon realised that, if he was to achieve his object of creating a powerful Russia, there would have to be a further retreat from Communism. Strength meant greater production, and if this could only be achieved by such un-communistic methods as financial incentives and higher pay for skilled workers, then this would have to be. Inevitably this led to a new class system in which the top people were no longer aristocrats or landowners but technicians, teachers, doctors and administrators. These people were allowed great privileges: not only did they have their own cars, large flats and villas in the country, but they were allowed to bequeath their wealth to their heirs and were even allowed, although only for a time, to send their children to special fee-paying schools.

In agriculture too Stalin was not in a hurry to introduce Communism. At first he was content that peasants should be left in possession of their smallholdings and that there should be a gradual introduction of collective farms, that is those where peasants pooled their lands and resources and worked cooperatively, each being paid a wage and profits being invested in farm improvements. However, this attitude was to change suddenly and completely. For it soon became evident that an agricultural system based on peasants' smallholdings was inefficient and incapable of providing enough food for the growing population of the towns. Peasants were inclined to produce only slightly more than their own needs and were unable and unwilling to introduce new machinery and scientific methods.

Once convinced of the need for collectivisation, Stalin was ruthless. The process was forced through regardless of human suffering and loss of life. The first to be expropriated were the Kulaks, the peasants with larger holdings. As these were prepared to resist collectivisation to the death, Stalin decided that they should be exterminated. Accordingly they were driven from their farms, some were shot, some sent to Siberia and left to die, a few lucky ones were able to escape abroad. The Kulaks, numbering some six million people, simply disappeared from the country.

Stalin hoped that the poorer peasants could be induced to join collectives by the lure of more land and better animals and equipment taken from the Kulaks, but here too he met with sullen resistance. Rather than be collectivised the peasants slaughtered their animals and left their land uncultivated; they thought that the famine conditions which resulted would force the government to relent, but they were mistaken. The government reacted with savagery: opposition was crushed ruthlessly, whole villages being destroyed and their inhabitants killed or left to starve. The total death roll will never be known for certain, but it is believed to have been many millions. In the end some concessions were forced from the government, and peasants were allowed to own 'gardens' of up to two and a half acres and to own a cow and be allowed to sell their surplus produce.

During the years 1928–33 all the farming land of Russia was collectivised, some 25 million holdings having been taken over. In the years that followed agricultural production did increase, but the cost of this in human terms was incalculable.

Meanwhile in the cities Stalin was forging ahead with plans to make Russia an industrial country. A series of five-year plans was introduced which were always fulfilled well in advance. The rate of development was, indeed, extraordinary, but here too it was achieved with little regard to human life and suffering, large numbers of workers dying from accidents, exposure and starvation.

Years of Terror (1936–38)

It was, of course, inevitable that the immense power Stalin achieved would in time affect his character. He had always been cold and hard and suspicious by nature, but in his later years he became obsessed with fears and distrust and devoid of all human feelings. He suspected everyone and thought he saw plots and disloyalty on every side. Partly because of this and partly because he knew that with the rise of Hitler he would soon have to fight a major war and could not afford to have traitors in his ranks, Stalin initiated in 1936 a series of political purges.

For two years the Russian people were submitted to the most terrifying and inhuman reign of terror. Everyone suspected of opposition, especially Troskyites, were mercilessly exterminated; nearly half the officers of the army were purged; ordinary citizens too lived in terror of their lives and millions were taken from their homes either to the firing squad or to the forced labour camp. Stalin's object was to terrify the people of Russia into total submission to his will. At the same time any remaining freedom of speech was stamped out, vitriolic propaganda was directed against all real and imagined enemies, and history books were rewritten to show that Stalin had always been right. For the time being his power was absolute.

The Coming of War

It has been seen that at first Stalin had little interest in foreign countries; all he wanted was that Russia should be left alone to build up her strength and develop her resources. But with the coming of Hitler as dictator of Germany it became clear that Russia was not going to be left alone. For Hitler had loudly proclaimed his intention of seizing the Ukraine and obliterating Communism. For a time Stalin was inclined to form an alliance with Britain and France and other opponents of Germany, but then, following the Anglo–French climb-down at Munich (see p. 143), he became convinced that he must operate on his own. His great need was for time in which to build up the Russian fighting forces, and it was with this in mind that in August 1939 he made a treaty of friendship with Germany. This treaty between deadly enemies caused amazement and

'Someone is taking someone for a walk.' Cartoon by David Low in the Evening Standard *at the time of the Nazi-Soviet pact.*

horror, and both dictators must have known that it would not last and that war between them would come in time. But for each there were short-term advantages; for Hitler it meant that it was then safe for him to proceed with his invasion of Poland;[1] for Stalin it meant a few more years of peace which would enable him to be ready for war when it came. Both these calculations were to prove woefully mistaken.

Civil War in Spain

A Revolt of the Generals

In 1936 Europe was already on its way towards the Second World War. Three years remained before it actually broke out, but during that time there occurred a prologue to it in Spain. The Spanish Civil War started as an exclusively Spanish affair, but it was not long before most of the leading countries of Europe became involved, and it has been described as 'a European war in miniature'.

An explosive situation had been building up in Spain for some time. For in the twentieth century the country was still an old-fashioned aristocracy with most power and wealth in the hands of the very few. However, the winds of change were blowing. Movements for reform and a new order were becoming stronger, and in 1931 the Spanish king had been forced to abdicate, and the country became a republic. Since then the clamour for change had grown louder. In 1936 a general election was held in which power was gained by an alliance of left-wing parties (Liberals, Socialists and Communists) known as the Popular Front. At this the forces of conservatism in the country became alarmed and there was a revolt, mainly of Fascists and Monarchists, headed by the leaders of the army. At first the attitude of the government to this revolt was weak and hesitant; for a time it even tried to pretend that it had not happened. But to the workers it was a signal for a general uprising. Everywhere trade unionists and peasants formed themselves into workers' militias and demanded that the government should give them arms. At first the government held back, but when it became clear that it was being deserted by most of the army and police, it agreed.

---

[1] The treaty provided that Poland would be invaded by both Germany and Russia and divided between them.

Suddenly all Spain was in turmoil. Many of the militias were dominated by revolutionary parties and many revolutionary acts occurred: factories were taken over by their workers and agricultural land was confiscated and distributed to the peasants. Particular fury was vented on the Church as it was believed that it had always been on the side of the old order and strongly opposed to change, and there were many instances of priests being murdered and churches being desecrated and destroyed. For a time the country was in chaos, as in every city and province it was uncertain who was on the side of the government (Republicans) and who supported the rebels (Nationalists).

At first it seemed likely that the Nationalists would gain a quick victory. Their commander-in-chief, General Franco, had come from North Africa with the Spanish Foreign Legion, the crack troops of the Spanish army and, with German and Italian air support, was advancing on Madrid. However, the government forces, although ill-armed and disorganised, were larger in numbers and were fired with great enthusiasm. Also they too were beginning to receive help from abroad. In the end Madrid was to endure a siege of twenty-eight months and the war was to drag on for three years.

Foreign Intervention

Foreign countries had not been slow to intervene in Spain's civil war; the clash between the liberal forces of the Popular Front and the army-dominated forces of the old regime aroused strong passions throughout Europe. The Fascist dictators, Hitler and Mussolini, had no hesitation in supporting Franco and sent him considerable help, particularly in aircraft. France on the other hand, ruled at that time by a Popular Front government, had great sympathy for the Republicans and sent them some assistance, as also on their own terms did the Russians. The British government was ambivalent; it had no wish to see a Fascist dictatorship set up in Spain, but was also anxious that the civil war should not escalate into a full-scale European war. And so it adopted a policy of non-intervention. If all other countries had done the same, the civil war would have come to an end much sooner, but there was never much likelihood of this happening, even though most countries agreed to it in theory. In the event the policy of non-intervention worked out to the great benefit of the Nationalists because the agreement was broken more blatantly by the Germans and Italians than by the French and Russians.

Although European leaders gained scant credit for their attitudes and conduct, there were thousands of European individuals who showed great heroism and selflessness. To many the rising of the Spanish workers was a moment of truth; their struggle was the struggle of all workers; they were fighting for those things held dear by workers everywhere – liberty, democracy and the right of ordinary people to a decent life. Above all a stand was at last being made against the forces of Fascism. From all over Europe volunteers made their way to Spain to join in the fight.[1] An International Brigade was formed and this took a leading part in the defence of Madrid.

Quarrels among the Republicans

The attitude of Russia to the Spanish Civil War was cautious and devious. On the face of it there should have been no hesitation; Stalin should have been ready to send help to the enemies of Fascism and to give support to those revolutionary militias whose aim it was to bring Communism to Spain. But this is not what happened. Stalin sent no help at first and when he did, it was sparing and on stringent terms. In the first place the Spanish government was compelled to send to Russia all its reserves of gold. But more important was the treatment meted out to the Spanish workers' militias; those dominated by Communists not only received no support from Russia but were suppressed on Stalin's orders. There were various reasons for this. In the first place, as has been seen, Stalin's policy had always been one of Russia first and Communism second; and his main concern at that time was to avoid a war with Germany for which Russia was not yet ready. Also he had no wish to upset France with whom he had just made an alliance, and this was likely to happen if he started fomenting Communist revolution in France's southern neighbour. There was too another reason for Stalin's hostile attitude to workers' militias: for some of these were not Russian-style Communists; some were Trotskyites, Stalin's arch enemies, and some were anarchists,[2] and Stalin had no love for rival brands of Communism. And so it came about that of the different groups which made up the Popular Front the Russians and their supporters were the most

---

[1] About 2,500 Britons fought in Spain of whom about 400 were killed.

[2] Anarchists were different from Communists in that they hated all forms of central authority. They wanted all decisions to be taken by local committees of workers.

conservative. And their intervention altered the whole nature of the Republican forces; at their instigation the workers' militias – with their free and easy discipline, comradeship and common sharing by all ranks of pay, clothing and food – were disbanded and their members forced to join the Popular Army which was run on conventional military lines.

The Spanish Civil War was a nasty and savage affair, generating great anger and hatred. Of the 600,000 who were killed only about a half were killed in action; the remainder were slaughtered behind the lines. It also gave rise to much bitter and fraudulent propaganda with each side blaring out scurrilous and often ridiculous abuse not only about its enemies but also sometimes about its allies. Thus the Russian Communists felt no reluctance in describing the Trotskyites, some of whom had been in the front line for months, as traitors in Fascist pay. If there was little heroism among the leaders of both sides, there was, as is often the case, plenty among the rank and file, those in the firing line who endured for long periods the horrors of mud, stench, rats, vile food and the prospect of a horrible wound or an agonising death.

The Spanish Civil War had started off as a kind of Crusade with men from all over the world coming to strike their blows for freedom and democracy. But all too soon the idealism faded and it became a sordid wrangle between factions, ending up with the setting up of another Fascist dictatorship.

Timescale

1919	Mussolini founds Italian Fascist party.
1921	Mussolini's 'March on Rome'.
1924	Death of Lenin.
1928	Farm collectivisation in Russia begins.
1929	Trotsky expelled from Russia.
1931	Japan invades Manchuria.
1935	Italy invades Abyssinia.
1936–49	Spanish Civil War.
1939	Russian–German treaty.

Chapter 10

THE RISE OF THE DICTATORS
(Part Two)

Germany – A Nation Enslaved

End of Democracy in Germany

Following the general election of 1932 the Nazis, led by Adolf Hitler, became the largest party in the German parliament (Reichstag). This foreshadowed the end of democracy in Germany. In the next year Hitler became Chancellor and in less than a year had made himself dictator of the country, overruling Parliament and the law as it suited him. At the time he was forty-four, the youngest head of state in the world; he was not by origin a German citizen, having been born in Austria; and only fourteen years before he had been an unknown lance-corporal in the German army. For a brief time he was to be the most powerful man in Europe since Napoleon.

Adolf Hitler – The Early Years

Hitler was born near Vienna in 1889. His father was a customs officer and reasonably well off. As a boy Hitler showed no great promise and at school gained the reputation of being lazy and ineffective. At first his ambition was to be an artist, but he had only limited talent and failed to get into the Academy of Fine Arts – the history of Europe might have been different if he had. However, he refused to accept any other kind of work except of an artistic nature, even if this meant living near to starvation in sordid hostels and men's homes.

In 1913 Hitler left Austria and settled in Germany. Here too he led an aimless, drifting life, occasionally earning a little money painting post-cards and posters. But this form of existence came to an end with the outbreak of the First World War. This was a milestone in Hitler's life, for he suddenly discovered something about which he cared passionately;

he felt a surge of patriotism for his newly adopted country and at once joined the army.[1] For the next four years Hitler fought in the trenches on the Western Front, and it seems that he was an exemplary soldier. He twice won the Iron Cross, he was twice wounded and once gassed, but never complained or shirked or had thoughts of defeat. It is an extraordinary fact that the man who in the Second World War was to be commander-in-chief of the German armies and was to mastermind some of its most successful operations, in the First World War never rose above the rank of lance-corporal.

The end of the war marked another milestone in Hitler's life. It is said that when he heard the news of Germany's surrender he burst into tears; he could not believe that the German army, which he considered undefeated, was being let down by the politicians. Later it was to become an obsession with him that the army had been 'stabbed in the back' by cowards and traitors, and it was this, more than anything, which brought him into politics.

Rise of the Nazi Party

It has been seen that in the post-war years in Germany there was fearful hardship and distress. The Allied blockade, which continued until the signing of the peace treaty in June 1919, brought starvation to German cities and there was great disorder and unrest; strikes and riots were frequent as also were violent clashes between rival political groups. Such conditions were a breeding ground for Communism, and there was a strong possibility of a Communist revolution similar to the one in Russia. It was in these bitter, violent, chaotic times that Hitler first appeared on the political scene.

Hitler remained in the army for two years after the end of the war, employed as an 'Instruction Officer'. Part of his duties was to attend political meetings and speak out against Communism and other revolutionary ideas; and it was then, when he was over thirty, that he discovered for the first time his extraordinary and terrible powers as a public speaker. In spite of a poor speaking voice and an unimpressive personal appearance he found he could hold and enthral an audience for

---

[1] All the more surprising as one of his reasons for leaving Austria had been to avoid military service.

hours, working himself and his listeners into a frenzy. He seemed to know by instinct their fears and their hates, and he told them what they wanted to hear – that the misfortunes of the German people were not their fault, but were due to others – the Communists, the Jews and those politicians who had signed the Versailles Treaty.

In 1919 in the course of his military duties Hitler attended a meeting of the German Workers' Party, at that time about forty strong. Soon afterwards he enrolled as a member and became the party's main attraction. In the following year he left the army and devoted himself full time to politics. The German Workers' Party was renamed the National Socialist German Workers' Party (later abbreviated to Nazi), and from that time it began to grow rapidly as people from all over the country flocked to hear Hitler speak. With his violent, aggressive views he inevitably stirred up strong opposition and to protect him and other party members a strong-arm squad was formed known as the 'Storm Detachment' (SA for short); its members wore brown uniforms and jackboots, and in time it was used not only for defence but also for breaking up the meetings of hostile parties.

In 1923 Hitler and the other Nazi leaders thought that they were strong enough to seize power by force, and this they attempted to do in what became known as 'The Beer Hall Putsch'.[1] But the operation was a total failure, and Hitler was convicted of treason and sentenced to five years imprisonment. In the event he was only to serve nine months of this term which he spent writing *Mein Kampf* (My Struggle) which was partly the story of his life and partly an exposition of his political ideas. Apart from the usual rantings against Jews and Communists *Mein Kampf* set out the doctrine that the Germans were a master race, that all Germans must be reunited with the Fatherland, and in time must seek extra 'living room' in Eastern Europe, particularly in Russia.

The Nazis Gain Power

When Hitler came out of prison the fortunes of the Nazi Party were at a low ebb, but he at once set about reorganising and revitalising it. On one point he had come to a firm decision: never again would he attempt to gain power by unlawful means. At first the Nazis made little head-

---

[1] So called because it began in a Munich beer cellar.

The old Germany meets the new.
Field Marshal Hindenburg and
lance-corporal Hitler.

way; during the years 1925–29 Germany was showing signs of an economic recovery, and in these better times the German people were less inclined to listen to political extremists. However, in 1930 came the Great Depression and mass unemployment. This was Hitler's opportunity. In their despair the German people became bemused by his promises to find work for all and to restore Germany as Europe's foremost power. In a general election in 1930 the Nazis increased the number of their seats in the Reichstag from 12 to 107, and became the second largest party in the country; and in the following year there were more elections and the Nazis made further gains. In 1933 Hitler was able to gain the support of other parties so that together they had a majority in the Reichstag, and the elderly President of the Republic, Marshal Hindenburg, felt obliged to make him Chancellor. The parties who had given Hitler their support were soon to realise they had made a terrible mistake. It seems that they had completely underestimated him, regarding him as 'a useful tool' to be discarded in case of success and disowned in case of failure. But it was not Hitler who was to be discarded.

Hitler's Tyranny

In 1933 Hitler was the legally appointed Chancellor of Germany. He at once set about establishing himself as dictator. An Enabling Act was passed giving his government the right to pass laws without reference to the Reichstag; other political parties were suppressed so that Germany became a one party state; and when Hindenburg died in 1934 Hitler took the office of President by his own decree. At the same time the trade unions were crushed and replaced by the Nazi-dominated Labour Front, the middle classes were overawed, and religious leaders with a few exceptions silenced. It seemed that the whole of Germany had come under Hitler's spell. Only one group retained any independence – the leaders of the army; Hitler dared not attack them; he needed them too badly.

In imposing his tyranny on Germany Hitler owed much to his spell-binding oratory and political cunning, but he also had good luck. In 1933 a near-mad Dutchman set fire to the Reichstag building and Hitler was quick to put the blame on to Jews and Communists and start a scare that the country was in great danger from them and could only be saved by his taking greater powers. For the most part the German people acquiesced in this. Not only were they bemused by his oratory but they were delighted by the success of his economic policy. Here too Hitler had luck as the German economy was on the mend before he came to power, but he and his advisers gave it a boost by embarking on a programme of public works including roads and buildings and, more especially, on armaments. This policy appeared to be brilliantly successful; between 1933 and 1937

The oratory which held millions spellbound. Hitler in full spate.

When the oratory was over. A dejected and crumpled figure.

unemployment dropped from six million to one million. Of course
Hitler claimed the credit for this and his prestige soared. More and more
Germans came to regard him as a wonder worker.

But at the same time as Hitler seemed to be working an economic
miracle there was a much darker side to his rule. He had shown from
an early stage that he was ready to make ruthless use of terror as an
instrument of government. Thousands of people, particularly political
opponents but including also Jews and so-called 'inadequates' were
rounded up and imprisoned without trial. So many of these were there
that special concentration camps had to be set up to contain them where
brutalities were perpetrated such as Europe had not known before. Hitler
showed particular ruthlessness towards his own followers. When the leaders of the SA showed signs of rebelliousness he had over eighty of them
put to death in 'the night of the long knives'.[1] As these men had been

---

[1] Also murdered on this occasion were a number of political opponents not connected
with the SA. Altogether some 150 people were put to death.

convicted of no crime Hitler and his henchmen were by law murderers; but it had become evident that rule of law in Germany had been replaced by the will of Hitler.

The 'night of the long knives' was a clear indication to the rest of the world that democracy in Germany had broken down and had been replaced by a brutal and vicious dictatorship; but compared with the cold-blooded, long drawn-out political purges of Stalin (see p. 125) it was a minor affair. A far greater crime and one that appalled the civilised world was Hitler's persecution of the Jews. In Germany, as in other countries, there had been anti-Semitism for centuries, but in Germany in the 1930s there were few who had thoughts of active and merciless persecution. But on this subject Hitler was deranged; a blind and unreasoning hatred obsessed him, and as he became more and more corrupted by power and more and more bereft of human compassion, he showed that he meant it literally when he said that he would rid Germany of the Jews. There were, in fact, not a large number of Jews in Germany itself (about half a million out of a population of 62 million), but later, when Austria, Czechoslovakia and Poland were annexed, the number increased considerably. It was not until the war years that 'the final solution' was put into practice when perhaps as many as six million Jews were systematically put to death.

The Rhineland and Austria

It has been seen that what brought Hitler into politics and changed him from a dreamy, artistic drifter into a fanatical firebrand was his anger at Germany's surrender in the First World War and the terms imposed on her by the Versailles Treaty. His obsessive ambition had become to revoke the peace treaty, to restore Germany to a dominant position in Europe and then to expand her frontiers into Eastern Europe with Germans of Aryan descent as the 'master race'. He lost little time in setting about this. In 1934 he asserted German independence by withdrawing from the League of Nations. In the following year there occurred the Abyssinian crisis (see p. 116), and Hitler saw that the League was prepared to talk rather than to act. This led him in 1936 to his first open defiance of the rest of Europe when he sent German troops into that part of the Rhineland which, according to the Treaty of Versailles, should remain demilitarised. This was a foolhardy undertaking as at the time Germany had only a tiny army, and if France had taken action,

German troops march into Austria as the frontier barrier is raised.

Inmates of concentration camp line up for food – just enough to keep them alive.

it would have been necessary to withdraw at once with loss of face that might have brought about his downfall. But Hitler knew instinctively that neither France nor Britain would make a move, and he was proved right.

Having thus tested the nerve of European statesmen and found it wanting, Hitler was encouraged to proceed with his design of uniting all German people into one nation. There were at that time about six million Germans in Austria, three million in Czechoslovakia and 350,000 in Poland. Hitler took it for granted that in time there would be some sort of union between Germany and Austria, and on this point some foreign statesmen agreed with him. The question was how it was to be achieved. At first Hitler favoured a policy of gradual and peaceful absorption, but then he changed his mind and, when it happened, the union of the two countries was brought about by a combination of terrorism, military force and broken faith. It was a significant step towards world war.

The Nazi Party in Austria had been active for some time. In 1934 it had attempted an uprising in which the Austrian Chancellor, Engelbert Dolfuss, had been murdered. But the movement had failed mainly because Mussolini at that time had no wish to see Austria taken over by Germany and moved Italian troops to the frontier. In the following years, however, the Austrian Nazis continued to make trouble and in 1937 they stirred up great disorder in the country. It happened that at that time Hitler was having political difficulties at home and a diversion abroad was what he needed. He, therefore, decided to intervene in Austrian domestic affairs, and a meeting was arranged between himself and the Austrian Chancellor, von Schuschnigg. In the course of this the latter was ruthlessly browbeaten and compelled to agree to Hitler's terms: prominent Nazis were to be given places in his government, and economic and military ties between the two countries were to be strengthened. In return Hitler was to use his influence with the Austrian Nazis to call off their subversive activities.

Here the matter might have rested, but a month later (March 1938) Schuschnigg suddenly decided to hold a plebiscite to decide whether or not Austria should remain independent. This sent Hitler into a fury. He said that he had been tricked and ordered the German army to prepare for an invasion. At the same time he made a number of demands on the Austrian government including the dismissal of Schuschnigg and the cancellation of the plebiscite. In the end all these demands were met, but the invasion went ahead all the same (12th March), the official reason given being that it was necessary in order to help restore order in Austria. The German troops met no resistance;[1] they were, indeed,

---

[1] The only trouble they had was from their own vehicles; it was estimated that 70 per cent of these broke down.

given a rapturous welcome by some Austrians, as also was Hitler himself. It was, perhaps, because of this and the news that Mussolini would make no objection that caused Hitler to make a sudden change of plan. On the spur of the moment he decided that he would not be content with the setting up of a National Socialist government in Austria but that, despite previous pledges, Austria would be incorporated into Germany. Subsequently a plebiscite was held which claimed to show that 99 per cent of the Austrian people were in favour of this union with Germany or *Anschluss* as it was called.

The annexation of Austria was a notable coup for Hitler. His reputation in Germany was greatly enhanced by it, but in foreign countries there was great anger. People were shocked by the methods Hitler had employed and by his breach of faith, and later they were horrified by the introduction of concentration camps into Austria and the brutal and inhuman treatment meted out to Austrian Jews. Many who had felt hitherto that they could trust Hitler and were in favour of a policy of 'appeasement' (see p. 140) began to change their minds. As for Hitler himself he came to be more rash and violent and more determined than ever to get his way by any means.

Czechoslovakia and the Munich Settlement

After the *Anschluss* it was not long before Hitler proceeded to the next stage of his grand design of creating a greater Germany. Czechoslovakia had been set up as a new sovereign state in 1918 by the Paris peace treaties. Although to some extent it had flourished since then, it had one basic weakness: it was made up of a number of different racial groups. Of these the Germans (known as Sudetens), numbering about three million out of a total population of fourteen million, were a turbulent and powerful minority. For some time their leaders had been alleging that they were being badly treated by the Czechs and demanding that they be reunited with Germany. After the *Anschluss* this campaign was intensified and received much encouragement from Hitler. Hitler had always regarded Czechoslovakia as a thorn in the flesh; not only did the country protrude deep into Germany (see map on p. 48) but the Czech leaders were hostile and had made alliances with Germany's two main enemies, France and Russia. In view of this and in view of the fact that Czechoslovakia had a well-trained and well-equipped army Hitler did not intend at first to invade the country. He hoped that by

At the Munich conference. From left to right: Mr Chamberlain, Mr Daladier (prime minister of France), Hitler, Mussolini and Count Ciano (Italian foreign minister).

threats of war and the creation of tension Czechoslovakia would fall apart of its own accord. Accordingly the Sudeten Germans were urged to 'make such demands that they can never be satisfied', and Hitler himself made hysterical speeches about the treatment of German people by the Czechs.

In the crisis which ensued the two countries which should have been foremost in protecting Czechoslovakia remained in the background – France because her government was weak and divided, and Russia because no-one, including the Czechs, was willing to invoke her help, it being felt that once Russian troops were in Czechoslovakia, it might be difficult to get them out again. And so it fell to Britain to take the lead.

The British prime minister at the time, Neville Chamberlain,[1] was a believer in the policy of Appeasement. Like some other Britons he felt that the Treaty of Versailles had been unfair and that Germany had

---

[1] He replaced Stanley Baldwin in 1937.

*Czech women weep as they make the Nazi salute when
German forces enter Prague (March 1939).*

some justifiable grievances. He also believed, in spite of what had
happened in Austria and the Rhineland, that if these grievances were
removed Hitler would become peaceful and contented. And so, when
Europe seemed to be heading for war over the Czech problem, he
suddenly took it upon himself to fly to Germany for a personal meeting
with Hitler. The two men met at Berchtesgaden, Hitler's mountain
retreat, and despite some noisy ranting from Hitler, reached general
agreement that the Sudentenlands were to be ceded to Germany. Chamberlain then left in order to obtain the agreement of his own government
and that of the French. A week later he returned to Germany and had
another meeting with Hitler at Bad Godesburg. He brought with him a
plan agreed to by both the French and the Czechs whereby the actual
territory to be handed over to Germany would be decided not by a
plebiscite (to which Hitler had objected) but by a commission of three
(one German, one Czech and one neutral). To Chamberlain's dismay
Hitler dismissed the plan out of hand. Since the first meeting he had
been developing plans for a military invasion and he now stated that,

unless the areas which he wanted were handed over in nine days, war would be declared. He seemed to be near to madness and hell-bent on war; but then he subsided somewhat. Mussolini, his only ally in Europe, suggested a four-power conference to settle the Czech problem, and to this he agreed. This was held in Munich and here Hitler obtained all the territory he wanted, Britain and France compelling the Czechs to agree. Chamberlain then returned home in triumph, claiming that he had won peace with honour. Perhaps he genuinely believed Hitler when he said that he had no further territorial demands in Europe. He certainly believed that Britain was unready for war at that time.

Once again Hitler had imposed his will on European statesmen and had shown, at least to his own satisfaction, that in a crisis his nerve was stronger than theirs. More and more he became convinced that he had a 'divine mission' and there was nothing he could not achieve if he put his mind to it.

Within six months of Munich it was shown how much value could be given to Hitler's pledged word. By then it had become clear that what was left of Czechoslovakia could not survive as a nation; the different national groups were quarrelling among themselves and the country was falling apart. The Poles and Hungarians took over those parts which contained their nationals, but most of the country, including Prague, was seized by Hitler. This had profound effect on British public opinion and in particular on Neville Chamberlain. It had become evident that Appeasement was not working, that Hitler could not be trusted to keep any agreement he made and that he was a permanent danger to peace. This change of attitude led to a new departure in British policy: a firm guarantee of support was given to Poland where Hitler was already stirring up trouble.

Poland and the Danzig Corridor

In Poland, as in Czechoslovakia, Germany did have a reasonable case, although this became obscured by Hitler's wild ranting and unscrupulous methods. As has been seen (p. 55) the Treaty of Versailles in re-establishing Poland as a country had provided her with the port of Danzig (present day Gdynia), which was almost entirely German, and with a 'corridor' through Germany by which it might be reached. It had also given Poland part of Silesia, although the inhabitants had voted overwhelmingly in a plebiscite in favour of remaining part of Germany.

The Danzig Corridor was an awkward arrangement; it meant that part of Prussia was cut off from the rest of Germany. It was not unreasonable that there should be a revision of this settlement. At first Hitler was inclined to be moderate. He did not have the same hatred for the Poles as he did for the Czechs, and was anxious to obtain their support in Germany's eventual war with Russia. Accordingly he tried to come to an agreement with them, but the Polish government refused to discuss the matter.

The British government was in a difficult position. It believed that Poland should negotiate the Danzig question with Germany, but could not force her to do so, and was in honour bound to come to her help if, as a result of her refusal, the country was invaded by Germany. Moreover it was realised that in the event of invasion there was little that Britain could do to prevent it. It was almost certain that Britain would be supported by France, who also had treaty obligations to Poland, but the French too were unready for war, and the two countries between them could do little more than create a diversion on Germany's western frontier. The one country which could have given effective help to Poland was Russia, and during the summer months of 1939 the British and French governments did make tentative efforts to draw Russia into their alliance, but, largely because of their dread of Communism, these were half-hearted and came to nothing. In the end it was not with Britain and France but with Germany that Russia made a treaty (see p.126).

With the signing of this treaty Hitler felt he was in a position to proceed with his plans regardless of Britain and France. He thought too that by blustering and bullying he could again force them to cave in as they had done at Munich. In any case he was ready to go to war; and in order to stabilise his position in Germany he needed a quick, dramatic victory.

At the last moment there were frantic efforts to avoid war, but they all foundered on Poland's adamant refusal to negotiate about Danzig and Hitler's insistence that the question must be settled at once. There was some talk among British and French politicians of backing out of their treaty obligations, but by that time public opinion, particularly in Britain, was strongly against Hitler. There was much shame about the Munich settlement and much anger about the way it had been broken. There was also apprehension about the Italian invasion of Albania, which had occurred in the spring of 1939, and it was felt that the Axis powers (as Germany and her allies came to be called) were out to dominate Europe and perhaps the world. There was too mounting anger and disgust at the treatment of the Jews and the horrors of the concentration camps.

And so events moved swiftly to a head. There were no negotiations, as over Czechoslovakia. On 1st September Germany invaded Poland; an ultimatum was then issued by Britain and France demanding the immediate withdrawal of German forces from Poland, and when this was ignored war was formally declared.

Timescale

1919	Hitler joins German Workers' Party.
1923	'Beer Hall Putsch' in Munich.
1932	Nazi Party largest in Germany after election.
1933	Hitler becomes Chancellor.
1934	'Night of Long Knives'.
	Germany withdraws from United Nations.
1936	German troops occupy Rhineland.
1938	
March	German invasion of Austria followed by *Anschluss*.
September	Munich settlement.
1939	
March	Break-up of Czechoslovakia. Germany seizes more territory.
	British guarantee of support for Poland.
April	Italy invades Abyssinia.
September	Germany invades Poland.

Chapter 11

THE SECOND WORLD WAR
(Part One)
Europe Overrun

The Invasion of Poland

It has been seen that in the land fighting in the First World War advantage almost always lay with the side on the defensive. Thanks to a combination of machine guns, barbed wire and dug-out trenches the defenders were able to take a fearful toll of those attacking them. But in the final stages of the war there were signs that this situation was beginning to change, and that with the development of tanks and aeroplanes the advantage was passing to the attackers.

This advantage was demonstrated dramatically by the German invasion of Poland. In this the Polish armed forces, amounting to over two million men, were totally defeated in just over a month for the loss of about 10,000 Germans. Certainly the Germans had every advantage: the Polish frontier, protruding far into Germany, was difficult to defend; also Polish armaments were, for the most part, out of date; but above all the Germans struck the first blow, a blow so heavy that the Poles never recovered.

The German attack had been planned with great care. The first stage was for the German air force, the Luftwaffe, to devastate all Polish airfields so that no aircraft left the ground. Then, with complete command of the air, the Luftwaffe would bomb all rail centres, bridges, road junctions and other vital communications points. Then German armoured forces would move in. In most other armies at that time tanks were distributed so as to give support to the infantry, but in the German army they were concentrated into armoured divisions, known as Panzers, which operated independently. Their function was to make deep thrusts into Polish territory and then turn and carry out encircling movements of the opposing forces (pincer movements, as they came to be called); in this they would be closely supported by the Luftwaffe, and infantry would follow to mop up pockets of resistance. In face of these tactics, which came to be known as the blitzkrieg, the Poles were helpless. Against the six German armoured divisions they could put into the field two motorised brigades and eleven brigades of horse-mounted cavalry which were, of course, helpless against tanks. Speed, mobility, surprise and the application of force at the most vulnerable points – these were the main elements of the blitzkrieg, and in Poland they carried all before them. In just over a week (9th September) the Panzers were in Warsaw. Soon afterwards Polish resistance had been paralysed, and any chance there might have been of prolonging the conflict vanished when, on 18th September, the Russians invaded from the east to make sure of obtaining that part of Poland which had been allotted to them in their treaty with Germany. By 6th October all fighting had come to an end.

Once again, as had happened on previous occasions in her history, Poland was partitioned among her conquerors. Once again too after a period of time she was to be reconstituted. In the meanwhile about 90,000 Poles escaped from the country to carry on the fight in other parts of the world.

The Phoney War

In her hour of need Poland had little help from her allies in the West. At the time the German position on her western frontier was weak – no more than 23 divisions against 85 of France; but the French made no serious attempt to take advantage of the situation; there was only minor activity and no major offensive. In the years between the wars the French had constructed a strong line of fortification along their eastern frontier known as the Maginot Line. This, in spite of the fact that it came to an end at the Belgian frontier, they believed to be impregnable, and all they aimed to do at present was to remain inside it and wait to be attacked. This static, defensive attitude was to have fatal results later on.

The British too showed reluctance to start fighting in earnest. On the Western Front the newly arrived British Expeditionary Force (BEF) engaged in patrol activity, and the Royal Air Force showered Germany with propaganda leaflets, but nothing more was attempted. At sea the

Royal Navy set about hunting down U-boats which, nevertheless, claimed some notable victims,[1] and protecting shipping from a new menace, the magnetic mine. There was no question, as there had been in the First World War, of a German battlefleet putting to sea; it would soon have been outnumbered and outgunned. However, the Germans did have some formidable pocket-battleships which, operating on their own, had the ability to inflict great damage on Allied shipping. The hunting down of one of these, the *Graf Spee*, was one of the most dramatic events of the Phoney War.

The *Graf Spee* had been operating in the South Atlantic and Indian Oceans where it had sunk nine British merchant ships. On 13th December she came into contact with three British cruisers off the coast of South America. In the action which followed the *Graf Spee* had the advantage – her guns had a longer range than those of the British ships, which as a result suffered great damage, and one of them was put out of action altogether. Damage to the *Graf Spee* was slight but the captain decided he must put into port for repairs before setting out on the return voyage to Germany. Accordingly he made for Montevideo – with two of the British ships following him. It would have taken some time for British warships, large enough to sink the *Graf Spee*, to arrive on the scene, but in Montevideo British intelligence put it about that they had already done so, and word of this came to the captain of the *Graf Spee* who became convinced that his ship was doomed. He therefore ordered it to be scuttled, and soon afterwards took his own life.

The Home Front

On the home front too the war started in a low key. Everyone had been expecting heavy air raids at once, but these did not occur. However, great precautions were taken: air-raid shelters were constructed in back gardens, millions of sandbags were filled and, for a time, gas masks were carried everywhere. More inconvenient and dangerous was the imposition of the blackout;[2] an elaborate combination of curtains, blinds and shutters had to be devised so that no chink of light could be seen outside. But perhaps the most important precaution was the evacuation

---

[1] Notably the aircraft carrier *Courageous* and the battleship *Royal Oak*.
[2] In the first months of the blackout deaths from road accidents increased sharply.

Children trying on their gas masks.

of women and children out of the big cities into the countryside. This did not take place without difficulty and some friction; townspeople were ill at ease in remote country areas, far from shops and buses and forced to rely on paraffin lamps and water which had to be fetched from a village pump. The country people for their part were shocked by the health and habits of some of the children from slum areas and their infestation by vermin. It was not long before many evacuees were longing to go home and, when air raids still did not occur, this is what many of them did.

The other major interruption of normal life was the introduction of rationing. Petrol, butter, bacon and sugar were the first to be restricted with meat following soon afterwards. In time jam, milk, eggs, cooking fats, tinned foods, sweets and clothing were also to be included. Many common foods, such as oranges and bananas, disappeared from the shops, while newcomers like dried milk, spam and powdered eggs made their appearance. Rationing did much to ensure fair shares for all, but well-off people were able to escape the worst effects by buying expensive unrationed foods, such as fish and poultry, and by eating in restaurants.[1]

During the war most British people were eager to 'do their bit' in helping the war effort, but at first there were few outlets for them. Some enrolled as air-raid wardens or took courses in first aid or fire fighting; some again responded to the government's call to 'dig for victory' or knitted woollen comforts for the troops. It was not until later in the war that great sacrifices were to be demanded from the British people.

---

[1] It was not only the well-to-do who were able to supplement their diet by eating out. A number of 'British Restaurants' or 'Communal Feeding Centres' were set up where cheap, simple meals could be obtained.

Evacuees. Mothers and children arrive at their destination
to be billeted on unfamiliar homes.

Invasion of Norway

During the 'Phoney War' Britain's main hope of putting pressure on Germany had been to make use of her sea power to cut off Germany's supplies of vital raw materials from abroad. Similarly Germany hoped to do the same thing to Britain by U-boat attacks on merchant shipping. Of vital importance to both sides was the coastline of Norway. For the Germans it would provide valuable bases for U-boats. For the British it would provide bases from which they could interfere with Germany's supplies of iron ore from northern Sweden, for ships carrying these were using Norwegian territorial waters. In April 1940 the British government, at the instigation of Winston Churchill, then First Lord of the Admiralty, gave orders for these Norwegian waters to be mined – a flagrant breach of Norwegian neutrality. At exactly the same time

Hitler, who had long suspected that something was up in this area,[1] ordered an invasion of Norway.

At the time it seemed almost impossible that Germany should be able to carry out a seaborne invasion of Norway. But Hitler, overruling his generals, reckoned that both Britain and Norway would be taken by surprise, as indeed they were; he also thought that German air power would offset Britain's command of the seas.

In the event the operation was soon over. First Denmark was occupied without a shot being fired and then, with the use of Danish air bases, the attack on Norway was launched. This too was completely successful. British naval forces were largely avoided, and once the Germans had gained control of the Norwegian airfields, the issue was no longer in doubt. On land German losses were small, but at sea they were more considerable, including three cruisers and ten destroyers sunk, and two heavy cruisers and a pocket-battleship put out of action.

The Norwegian campaign was a heavy setback for Britain. It had made clear how unready the country was for war. Particularly brought into focus was the inadequacy of British air forces and the lack of cooperation between the fighting services.

Invasion of the Low Countries

Ever since the defeat of Poland Hitler had been urging his generals to carry out a full-scale invasion of France, but for one reason or another, principally the weather, this had been put off. However on 10th May an attack was launched in force.

The original German plan of campaign had been similar to the Schlieffen Plan of 1914 (see p. 4) by which the main attack was to be made through Belgium, while fighting only containing actions on other fronts. But in the course of the winter a new plan, the Manstein Plan, had been adopted. Like the Schlieffen Plan this included an invasion of Holland and Belgium, but this was not to be the main attack; its purpose was only to lure the British and French forces out of their prepared

---

[1] On 30th November 1939 Russia, then an ally of Germany, had invaded Finland which had resisted heroically. There was a loud outcry for help to be sent to the Finns, which would have had to go across Norway, and plans to do so were drawn up, but were found to be impracticable.

positions on the frontier into Belgium; the main attack would then be delivered in the Ardennes (see map on p. 14). It was intended that when German armoured forces had broken through here they would then wheel to the right and make for the coast, thus cutting off and trapping the Allied forces in Belgium.

At first this plan went like clockwork. The whole of the BEF and some French forces advanced into Belgium, as required, while the German Panzers in the Ardennes made a quick breakthrough at Sedan some distance from where the Maginot Line came to an end. The French had not expected an attack here as the country was wooded and hilly and believed to be impassable; but the Panzers of Generals Guderian and Rommel were hardly held up at all. By 12th May they had reached the Meuse which was expected to be a formidable obstacle, but bridgeheads across the river were achieved the following day, and by the 15th the Panzers had broken right through, had wheeled to the right and begun their drive to the coast. French forces appeared to have been dazed by the speed of the advance and resistance was very weak. By 18th May the Panzers had reached St Quentin and on the 20th they were on the coast at Abbeville. The trap had been closed.

The Allied army was now divided in two. But the German position was insecure: the long and rapid advance of the Panzers had meant that their supply lines were over-extended and weak, and supporting infantry had not been able to keep up with them. A determined attack from the north or south should have been able to break through and so cut off the leading Panzers from their base, but French leadership was hesitant and ineffective, and the opportunity was missed.[1]

Meanwhile in Belgium the BEF, along with the French and Belgian forces, had been falling back before another German army. Their position was critical. Before the German invasion the Belgians, for fear of provoking Hitler, had given the Allies no cooperation; so there had been no planning and there was much confusion. Also Holland had collapsed at once and, following a devastating air raid on Rotterdam, had asked for an armistice five days after the invasion. Then came the news that the Panzers had got round behind the Allied forces and cut them off from the rest of France, and soon after word came that the Panzers were

---

[1] At a crucial moment the commander-in-chief, General Gamelin (aged sixty-eight) was replaced by General Weygand (aged seventy-three).

on the move again, driving up the coast to capture the Channel ports, so making it impossible for the trapped armies to escape by sea. By 24th May they had already invested Boulogne and Calais and had driven on to within eighteen miles of Dunkirk, the last remaining port from which the BEF could escape.

Dunkirk

There can be little doubt that, if they had been allowed to, the Panzers could have captured Dunkirk, and so sealed the trap completely; but on the 24th an order came from Hitler halting their advance. The reasons for this are not clear. It may be he thought the Panzers had advanced as far as was safe and it was time they consolidated their position. It may be that he was persuaded by Goering[1] that the Luftwaffe could prevent the BEF from escaping through Dunkirk. It may be that he was looking ahead to the next phase of the campaign, the drive on Paris, and wanted the Panzers to prepare for this. But whatever the reasons, the BEF was allowed to slip through the net and the retreat to Dunkirk was allowed to proceed.

The difficulties of the operation were formidable. The roads were crammed with millions of refugees – terrified, despairing people with a few possessions piled into prams and wheelbarrows; overhead there were constant attacks from dive bombers; and on either side of the BEF the French and Belgian forces were crumbling rapidly. On arrival at Dunkirk came the equally difficult and dangerous task of getting the troops on to the boats. The docks were soon put out of action by enemy bombers and it was necessary to use the beaches. This meant that a large number of small boats was needed to ferry the men from the beaches out to the large ships which could not come in close. In England an appeal went out for every available small craft to come to the rescue, and the response was immediate: hundreds of boats of all descriptions – ferryboats, fishing boats, tugs, lifeboats – came out to play their part.[2] The dangers were great, mainly from the Luftwaffe

---

[1] Hermann Goering, one time SS commander and then commander of the Luftwaffe. After Hitler perhaps the most powerful man in Germany.

[2] Altogether some 860 ships took part. The whole operation was superbly organised by Admiral Bertram Ramsay, commander-in-chief at Dover.

British soldiers on the beach at Dunkirk waiting for ships to take them back to England.

which made continuous attacks, but also from U-boats, mines, underwater wrecks and German shore batteries. But by a miracle the operation succeeded and before the Germans finally closed in on Dunkirk more than 338,000 men had been taken off of whom 224,000 were British. Inevitably losses had been heavy, including some 68,000 men, 243 ships, 106 fighter aircraft and all the army's guns, tanks and equipment. But the nucleus of the army had been saved and, provided time was afforded to reconstruct it, would live to fight another day.

The Fall of France

After Dunkirk it was only a matter of time before the final defeat of France. On 11th June Hitler's ally, Mussolini, at last considered it safe to declare war on Britain and France, not wanting to be left out of any peace treaty, and invaded from the south. On 14th June Paris fell and two days later the eighty-four-year-old Marshal Pétain, the man who had defended Verdun so heroically in the First World War (see p. 29) became prime minister and immediately asked the Germans for an armistice. This was signed on 22nd June, on Hitler's orders in the same railway coach in which the armistice had been signed at the end of the First World War.

Once again the Germans had won an overwhelming victory. Their success stunned everyone including themselves. For their armies had been no larger than those of the Allies; the French, in fact, had more tanks and more guns and in the Maginot Line the strongest fortification in the world. Why then was the campaign so one-sided? There were perhaps three main reasons. In the first place the Germans had decisive superiority in the air; they had more aircraft than the Allies and, apart from the Spitfire, better ones. Particularly effective were their dive bombers, not so much from the damage they inflicted as from the terror they struck as, with deafening screech, they swooped on their targets. Also the German army was better led. Whereas French leaders were elderly and still geared to the trench warfare of the First World War, putting their trust in impregnable lines of defence, the German commanders believed in speed and mobility. The German army was altogether more modern and dynamic and there was close cooperation between air and ground forces, unlike among the Allies where there was separation and jealousy. Also German tanks were organised into hard-hitting, far-ranging armoured divisions, whereas in the French army their main purpose was still thought to be to give support to the infantry. Finally, and most important of all, was the matter of morale. In the German army, after the Polish and Norwegian campaigns, this was soaring; there was great patriotism and devotion to their leaders, particularly Hitler, and complete confidence in victory. In the French army, on the other hand, there was hatred of the war, little trust in their leaders and little will to win.

The terms of the armistice were not as harsh as they might have been. Principal matters were left to a final treaty to be drawn up later; but in the meanwhile France was to be divided in two; the larger part, which included Paris and all the Atlantic coastline, was to be under German control; the remainder was not to be occupied by the German army and was nominally to be under the rule of the French government with its capital at Vichy.

From the point of view of Britain the most important parts of the armistice were those dealing with the French fleet and colonies. Hitler had not demanded these as to do so would probably have meant that they would at once have joined forces with Britain. Accordingly the colonies were left under the control of Vichy and the fleet was to be disarmed in French ports under German or Italian supervision. In agreeing to this the French government had issued a secret order that, if there was ever any question of warships being taken over by the Germans, they were to be scuttled at once. However, the British government did not know of this and thought they only had the word of Hitler that the warships would not one day be used against them. And so they insisted that all French warships be disarmed in British or neutral ports. This led to one of the most tragic incidents in the war when the French battlefleet at Oran in West Africa refused to accede to this demand, and the Royal Navy then opened fire, sinking two battleships and one battle-cruiser and causing great loss of life. Inevitably the French felt bitterly angry at this, and these feelings were to last throughout the war and long after. At the time it nearly caused the Vichy government to declare war on Britain. However, when France made peace not all Frenchmen supported the Vichy government; there were many who felt deep shame that it should have come to terms with Germany, and at the time of the signing of the armistice a young and comparatively junior French general, Charles de Gaulle, arrived in London and set up the standard of the Free French. In stirring tones he declared that France had lost a battle but not the war, and called on all Frenchmen to continue the fight. Many responded to the call and for the rest of the war, as underground fighters in France or alongside their allies in other parts of the world, they fought with great heroism.

Timescale

1939

September	1	Germany invades Poland.
	3	Great Britain and France declare war on Germany.
	9	Germans capture Warsaw.
	18	Russia invades Poland.
November	30	Russia invades Finland.

1940

| April | 8 | Germany invades Denmark and Norway. |

May 10   Germany invades Holland, Belgium and France.
20   Panzers reach coast. BEF cut off.
24   Panzers halted by Hitler.
27   Dunkirk evacuation begins.
June 11   Italy declares war on Great Britain and France.
14   Germans enter Paris.
22   French sign armistice.

Chapter 12

THE SECOND WORLD WAR
(Part Two)
Britain Stands Alone

The Home Front

Political Parties Unite

After the fall of France there were few people in the world who gave
Britain much chance of survival. The odds against her seemed overwhelming. She stood alone against the combined forces of Germany and Italy,
and it seemed possible that these might soon be joined by Japan, Fascist
Spain and even, after the action against the French fleet at Oran, Vichy
France. Russia too was still an ally of Hitler, and although the alliance was
beginning to show signs of strain, it was to last for another year yet. It is
true the countries of the Commonwealth stood staunchly behind Britain
and some help was forthcoming from the free forces of France, Holland,
Belgium, Norway, Poland and Czechoslovakia. Also more help was beginning to come from the United States, although the majority of the American
people were still strongly determined not to become involved in the war.

At no time in her history has Britain been in such danger. But, as in
the past, danger was to bring out the best qualities of the British people.
In particular it gave them a unity they had not had for many years. Old
quarrels and rivalries were put aside in the determination to save the
country at all costs from Nazi Germany. Already before Dunkirk the
three main political parties – Conservative, Labour and Liberal[1] – had

[1] But not by the Communist Party which continued to oppose the war until the German
invasion of Russia in 1941.

agree to coalesce to form a National Government under Winston Churchill. Here the country was fortunate: Churchill was the one man who had the courage and the leadership to see Britain through the years ahead.

Winston Churchill (1874–1965)

Winston Churchill was a descendant of the first Duke of Marlborough, one of England's greatest soldiers. His father, Lord Randolph Churchill, was a brilliant but erratic politician whose career, after a spectacular start, had then faded out. His mother, Jennie Jerome, was an American lady of great strength of character in whose veins was said to run in small measure blood of the Iroquois Indians. After leaving school, where he was not highly regarded, Churchill joined the army and saw service in Cuba and India and took part in the last great cavalry charge at the battle of Omdurman in the Sudan. Soon afterwards he left the army in order to devote himself to politics and writing, but in his first parliamentary election he was defeated. When the Boer War broke out he was sent to South Africa as a war correspondent, where he was taken prisoner by the Boers, but had an exciting and well-publicised escape and returned to England a popular hero. In 1900 he fought another election and was returned as Conservative member for Oldham.

Churchill's political career was to be unorthodox. A mixture of conservatism and rebelliousness, he was not at heart a party politician. He began as a Conservative, but four years later he 'crossed the floor of the House' and joined the Liberals. Soon afterwards he was given his first post in the government and promotion came quickly. In 1910, when he was only thirty-six, he became Home Secretary and a year later First Lord of the Admiralty where he was to play a vital role in bringing the fleet to a state of readiness for the First World War. During the early years of the war he was one of the most aggressive and imaginative members of the government but he came to grief when the expedition to the Dardanelles failed (see p. 24) and he was held mainly responsible. It became necessary for him to resign from the government and for a time he resumed his old career as a soldier and commanded a battalion on the Western Front. In 1917, however, he was brought back into the government by Lloyd George as Minister of Munitions where he took a leading part in the development of the new tanks.

With the coming of peace Churchill became Secretary for War in Lloyd George's coalition government (see p. 58). Here he displayed great belligerence towards the Communist revolutionaries in Russia and was a strong supporter of the White Russians (see p. 118). With the ending of Lloyd George's government and a decline in the fortunes of the Liberal Party, Churchill suddenly found himself in 1922 not only out of office but also out of Parliament. However, two years later he was back, having rejoined the Conservative Party. There was little sympathy between Churchill and the Conservative leader, Stanley Baldwin, but, to general surprise, he was given the key post of Chancellor of the Exchequer in Baldwin's second government (1924). Finance was not Churchill's strong suit, and his decision to bring England back on to the Gold Standard (see p. 67) caused great controversy and is said by some to have had disastrous consequences.

It was always unlikely that Churchill and the other Conservative leaders would remain for long in harmony. They had little in common. The break actually came in 1930 when Baldwin supported the Labour government's proposals to give some responsible government to India (see p. 97). This upset Churchill greatly. He saw in it the beginning of the end of the British Commonwealth (or Empire as he still liked to call it). He thought it would lead to India gaining full dominion status and then seceding from the Commonwealth altogether. He attacked the proposals violently but had little support except among right-wing Conservatives. For the next eight years Churchill was out of office, a lone voice in the 'political wilderness'. During this time he became seriously alarmed by the rise of Fascism in Europe and German rearmament. Often he warned the government in ringing tones that it must stand up to Hitler before it was too late. For the policy of Appeasement he had nothing but contempt, declaring that concessions to Hitler would merely whet his appetite for more; the Munich settlement he described as 'a total and unmitigated defeat'. But at the time Churchill's prestige was not high; many regarded him as wild and irresponsible and 'a political has-been'; and his warnings were not heeded. It was not until the outbreak of war, and he was shown to have been right, that he made his comeback to government as First Lord of the Admiralty once more. He was sixty-four, but the greatest and most momentous years of his life lay ahead.

During his political career, with his chopping and changing and extremist political views, Churchill had made enemies in all parties but with his resilience, humour and magnanimity enmity seldom lasted long. Sworn foes usually found themselves relenting. And so in 1940 at the moment of crisis people forgot old scores and turned to him. Certainly he had the qualities of a great war leader – tremendous courage, pugnacity and a ringing oratory which excited people and gave them hope. To him Britain's crisis was wonderfully exhilarating, indeed 'her finest hour'. 'And now,' he declared, 'it has come to us to stand alone in the breach, and face the worst that the tyrant's might and enmity can do.'

Britain's Situation

At the end of June Britain's military situation was desperate. Of the 400,000 men of the BEF in France about 360,000 had been brought home, but these were unequipped and, for the most part, untrained. Nearly all their tanks, guns, transport and ammunition had had to be abandoned. At most there were no more than two fully trained and equipped divisions at that time, as against 130 armed and victorious divisions of the Germans. At least two months would be needed before the British army could be brought to anything near a state of readiness.

Everything depended on the ability of the Royal Navy to prevent a seaborne invasion. But the Royal Navy had suffered heavily in the operations off Norway and France; at the end of June nearly half the destroyers in home waters were out of action. In capital ships Britain still had a great preponderance, but it had been seen how vulnerable these were to attacks from the air, and so they could not be used in the English Channel where they were most needed. As well as protecting Britain from invasion, the Royal Navy also had to contend with a considerable Italian fleet in the Mediterranean and keep guard against a Japanese attack in the Far East.

During the fighting in France and the evacuation at Dunkirk the RAF had more than held its own against the Luftwaffe, but their losses had been crippling. Between 10th May and 10th June 463 fighter planes had been lost with 284 pilots. This left fighter command dangerously depleted with only 42 squadrons instead of 60 considered the minimum needed for the defence of the country. In the immediate future everything was going to depend on them. Air power would be vital.

All three fighting services then desperately needed time to lick their wounds and build up their strength. Mercifully time in some measure was to be granted them.

The Threat of Invasion

With the defeat of France and the expulsion of the British army from Europe, Hitler seems to have thought for a time that the war was over. He was sure that Britain would not fight on alone and was anxious to make peace. At that time it seems that all his ambitions lay in Eastern Europe and he had no great wish to destroy the British Empire. Accordingly for the time being he showed little interest in plans for invading Britain and set about putting out peace feelers. There were not even heavy air raids on England, the Luftwaffe doing little more than dropping pamphlets urging peace.[1]

This lull, so valuable to Britain, was not to last long. It soon became clear that the British government was not interested in peace talks, and on 16th July Hitler gave orders that an invasion of Britain was to take place in the second half of September, although he continued to hope for some time that it would not be necessary. The difficulties of the operation (to be known as 'Sea Lion') were considerable. There was a major difference of opinion between German army chiefs who wanted the invading force to land on a broad front (between Ramsgate and Lyme Regis) and the naval chiefs who insisted that only a narrow front (between Folkestone and Eastbourne) would be possible. On one point, however, they both agreed – that nothing could be achieved without complete mastery in the air. An essential preliminary, therefore, was to drive the RAF from the skies, a task which Goering had every confidence could be achieved in four days.

Meanwhile in Britain frenzied preparations were being made to defend the country. Coastal defences were being installed, road blocks constructed, and sign posts, milestones, road signs – anything which might help invading forces – removed. The army was being organised to repel an invasion and was reinforced by over a million part-time volunteers in the Home Guard. In factories and dockyards men and

---

[1] These were treasured as curios in England and some of them were subsequently sold in aid of the Red Cross.

women worked seven days a week to produce the munitions and equipment that were so desperately needed. Everywhere people prepared to sell their lives dearly, but for the present all depended on the fighter aircraft of the RAF. If they could keep the Luftwaffe at bay all might be well. If they were overwhelmed it would be the end; an invasion then might not even be necessary.

The Battle of Britain

Fortunately Fighter command of the RAF was well prepared for the great battle. By the beginning of August it was once again up to strength thanks to a tremendous drive to increase aircraft production. The RAF was, of course, still heavily outnumbered by the Luftwaffe, but it had important advantages. In the fighting over France it had been demonstrated that Spitfires and Hurricanes were superior to any fighter plane of the Germans. Luftwaffe losses had been more than twice those of the RAF, and over British territory they were liable to be even greater. For at home British fighters were supported by a highly efficient air defence system including Observer Corps posts, control rooms, carefully sited airfields and, above all, radar stations.

Radar was to play a crucial part in the Battle of Britain. It had been invented by a Scottish scientist, Robert Watson-Watt, and its importance was quickly realised by the Air Ministry,[1] for it gave advance warning of enemy aircraft approaching when they were more than 75 miles away and established their range, direction and height. Later a VHF (very high frequency) telephone was developed which enabled ground control to communicate with aircraft in the sky. This meant that it was unnecessary for RAF fighters to go on patrol; they could wait until warned that enemy aircraft were approaching and, once in the air, could be guided to their targets. In the Battle of Britain this system was to be the salvation of the country, and great credit is due to the Air Ministry for its foresight in setting it up and to no-one more than the commander-in-chief of Fighter Command, Air Marshal Sir Hugh Dowding. Dowding had had to fight hard to obtain both the system and the number of aircraft he needed. Later

---

[1] Unlike the Luftwaffe commanders who persistently underrated it.

The victors of the Battle of Britain. Spitfires and their pilots.

he had had another hard struggle to prevent too many aircraft being lost during the fighting in France.[1] Taciturn and reserved (with a nickname of 'Stuffy'), he was an unlikely leader of the dashing young pilots who won the Battle of Britain; but they were infinitely better served by this dedicated professional than were the Luftwaffe by the flamboyant and garrulous Goering.

The Battle of Britain began in earnest on 12th August when the Luftwaffe made a massive attack on airfields and radar stations in the south of England. These attacks were repeated in the following days, and great damage was done. However, the defence system held together and British fighter planes took a heavy toll on the attackers. On 15th August, the day on which Goering had hoped to finish off the RAF, 76 German planes were shot down. It was not long before German pilots realised at what a disadvantage they were; with no help from radar and with no VHF communications to control centres, they lacked the flexi-

---

[1] In this he clashed with Churchill which may have been one of the reasons why he was dismissed a few months later.

Mr Churchill meets the civil defence workers after an air raid on Birmingham.

bility of the RAF and could only persevere with the operation to which they had been assigned before they left. In brief it was being borne in on them that 'in comparison with their opponents they were blind, deaf and dumb.'[1]

However, German raids were to continue over the next weeks and fighter escorts for the bombers were increased. For a time German losses compared with those of the RAF began to level off. Between 8th and 18th August these had been 363–181, but between 23rd August and 6th September they were 378–277. Moreover German bombers were reaching their targets and inflicting serious damage on airfields and installations. By 6th September the situation had become critical; the defence system was near to breaking point, reserves of fighter planes were dangerously low, and there was a grave shortage of trained pilots. But a respite was at hand, for on 27th August the RAF dropped bombs

---

[1] C. Wilmot, *The Struggle for Europe* (Collins, 1952).

on Berlin, and this so enraged Hitler that he ordered mass raids on London, and Goering agreed, thinking that Fighter Command was at the end of its resources and would finally be destroyed in attempting to defend London. He also hoped that the raids on London would break the spirit of Londoners.

And so on 7th September the Luftwaffe attacks were switched from the airfields to London. This was a major error on the part of the Germans and one that saved Britain. Fighter Command was given a respite to repair and reorganise, while the raids on London, although causing widespread damage to property, had no serious effect on the British war machine and were not to cause panic or defeatism.

Meanwhile on 1st September Germany's invasion fleet began to assemble in the Channel ports, and Hitler fixed the 21st as the provisional date for the invasion. But it soon became clear that the RAF was still very much a fighting force as the ships and barges, which had been collected with such difficulty, came under attack from British bombers. On 10th September Hitler ordered a postponement of three days and then, a week later, the invasion was put off indefinitely, and the invasion fleet began to disperse. For during that time the Luftwaffe had had a setback over London. Here German bombers were being closely escorted by up to five times as many fighters, but in spite of this their losses continued to be very heavy while those of the RAF decreased. Between 7th and 30th September 435 German planes were shot down as against 164 of the RAF. It was now becoming clear to Goering that he was not going to be able to eliminate the RAF, and that in future it would only be safe for his bombers to operate at night when accurate and strategic bombing would be impossible. He must also have known, like the other German war leaders, that every day that passed made an invasion of Britain more difficult and unlikely.

St Paul's Cathedral during the Blitz.

The 'Blitz'

For eight weeks London was bombed every night. Then, in the course of the winter, came the turn of other cities – Birmingham, Manchester, Glasgow, Cardiff, Coventry. London too was revisited many times until, after the heaviest raid of all on 16th May, the attacks were called off. By then Hitler needed all his resources for his forthcoming invasion of Russia.

During these grim months only limited defence against the raiders was possible; fighter aircraft could achieve little at night and anti-aircraft guns had no great effect. The Germans could make no attempt at precision bombing of military targets and usually dropped their bombs at random.

Widespread and terrible damage was done. In some cities, like Coventry and Plymouth, whole areas were flattened. More than three and a half million houses were destroyed or damaged, as also were a number of famous buildings including the Houses of Parliament and

Londoners seek refuge from the Blitz in Aldwych tube station.

Coventry after an air raid. November 1940.

Buckingham Palace. Sometimes life in a city became totally disrupted with no water, gas or electricity and public transport at a standstill. The people in the cities took refuge from the bombs as best they could – sometimes in air-raid shelters, sometimes on subway platforms and sometimes just crouching in cellars or under the stairs. It is estimated that about 30,000 people were killed in air raids – about half in London – but when the Blitz came to an end it was evident that the Germans had failed in their main purpose – to terrorise the civilian population and break its spirit. Later in the war, when the British and US air forces made much heavier raids on Germany, they too were to discover that bombing alone could not win the war.

War in the Mediterranean

A Desperate Situation

In the early part of the war there was no anxiety about the situation in the Mediterranean. The combined fleets of Britain and France with bases throughout were in complete control; but the position changed abruptly when France dropped out of the war and Italy came in. Britain was then left alone with such forces as she could muster to confront the entire armed forces of Italy.

The situation appeared desperate. A large Italian army in Libya, then an Italian colony, was poised to invade Egypt; and in East Africa in the Italian colonies of Eritrea, Italian Somaliland and Abyssinia further armies, again with a heavy preponderance in numbers, seemed about to invade British Somaliland, Kenya and the Sudan. At sea the Italians had one less battleship than the British and, a more serious matter, no aircraft carriers; but of cruisers, destroyers and submarines they had many more; and in the air they had some 2,000 planes as against Britain's 200.

Besides much larger forces the Italians also had a great strategic advantage: because of their central position they were able, to a large extent, to divide the Mediterranean into two parts. From their bases in Sicily and the island of Pantelleria they could make the passage through the Sicilian straits almost impassable. One consequence of this was that British ships going to Egypt had to make the long journey round the Cape of Good Hope, as also did ships going to India and the Far East. Strongly protected convoys occasionally passed through the Mediterranean but losses were always heavy. Another consequence was that the British Mediterranean fleet had to be divided, with one part in the west based on Gibraltar and the other in the east based on Alexandria. In the central Mediterranean the only British base was the island of Malta, of crucial importance as the only base from where the Italian, and later German, supply line to North Africa could be threatened. Because of this in the years ahead Malta was to be heavily bombed by German and Italian aircraft.

In theory, then, the British position in the Mediterranean looked hopeless, and there were those who thought it should be abandoned; but Churchill would have none of this. Apart from the shattering blow to British prestige, it would leave exposed Britain's vital oilfields in the Middle East. Also, always a telling point with Churchill, it would deprive Britain of an area where hard and telling blows might be delivered against the Axis powers. And so on 15th August, when the invasion threat at home was at its height, the courageous decision was taken to reinforce the British armies in the Mediterranean and send out there the tanks and guns which were so desperately needed at home.

Disasters for Italy

Soon after coming into the war a series of disasters befell Italy. Mussolini had waited until France was on her last legs before declaring war, but even then the 32 divisions he sent against her made little impression on the eight which confronted them. In Libya the Italian forces made no move against Egypt until 13th September when they advanced some sixty miles as far as Mersa Matruh, but this success was to be short-lived. For the time being the only notable Italian achievement was to occupy an almost undefended British Somaliland, but here too it was not to be for long.

Later in 1940 Mussolini made a reckless move when, without a word to Hitler, he undertook an invasion of Greece; but victory eluded him. The Greeks resisted stubbornly and drove the Italians back into Albania,[1] and throughout the winter, even though they had much larger forces and complete air superiority, the Italians were hard pressed to hold their ground.

Then came further setbacks. On 11th November aircraft from a British aircraft carrier made a well-planned attack on the Italian battle-fleet in Taranto. For the loss of two British aircraft three Italian battle-ships were put out of action and the rest of the fleet forced to withdraw to the west coast of Italy where they would be out of danger. And then on 8th December the British struck in Egypt. The British commander-in-chief in the Middle East, General Wavell, had entrusted this operation to General O'Connor. So great was the disparity between the English and Italian armies (two divisions against ten) that it was considered at first the attack could be no more than a heavy raid. But then, when Italian resistance crumbled, the possibility arose of defeating the whole Italian army, and this opportunity was taken with brilliant success. In the next two months O'Connor's force of about 31,000 men, which included forces from Australia and India, was to advance about 500 miles and take some 130,000 prisoners; British losses were about 2,000. It was indeed a spectacular victory. It seemed that the Italians had no stomach for the fight and their leaders were half-hearted and incompetent, having been appointed for their political attitudes rather

---

[1] Invaded by Italy in 1938 (see p. 144).

Italian prisoners pour in. No guard in sight.

than their military abilities. It was evident that, in spite of all Mussolini's bragging, the Italian army was totally unready for war. This was also demonstrated in East Africa when an attack was made on Italian Somaliland from Kenya in February 1941. As in Egypt it had been expected that this would be no more than a raid, but once again Italian resistance collapsed, and it became possible to occupy the whole country. In the next three months British and Commonwealth forces under General Cunningham reoccupied British Somaliland and then drove the Italians out of Abyssinia and Eritrea. On 5th May the Emperor Haile Selassie, the first victim of the Fascist dictators, returned to Addis Ababa.

German Intervention

These outstanding successes gave a much needed boost to British morale and British prestige in the rest of the world. However, they had another consequence: they induced Hitler to come to Mussolini's help. At first he had been content to leave the war in the Mediterranean to Italy, but when everything began to go wrong, he decided he must intervene. At the beginning of January 1941 squadrons of the Luftwaffe arrived in Sicily and soon afterwards made a heavy and successful attack on a British convoy sailing to Malta. A month later units of the German army began to arrive in North Africa, and it was becoming evident that the Germans were also about to intervene in Greece.

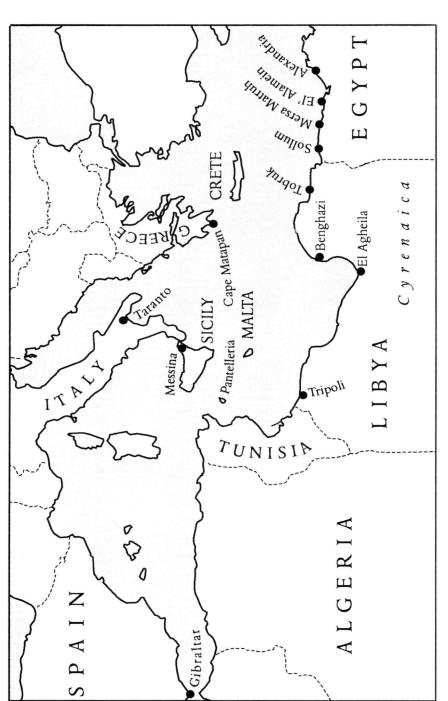

The Mediterranean – Second World War.

Directly after the Italian invasion Britain had offered Greece all possible aid, but the Greeks had been unwilling to accept too much because they feared it might provoke Hitler. Help had therefore been confined to arms and a few units of the Royal Air Force. However, when it became likely that the Germans were going to invade in any case, the attitude of the Greeks changed and they became ready to accept any aid that was going. This posed a difficult question for the British high command. Would they be able to send enough troops to make any difference to the final outcome? In doing so they would have to take forces badly needed on other battle fronts which might lead to disaster there. On the other hand to leave Greece to her fate without any significant help would be a great blow to British prestige and might induce other Balkan countries, like Yugoslavia and Turkey, to come to terms with Hitler rather than resist him. Anxiously British war leaders pondered the problem. Finally it was decided that British troops should be sent to Greece; and from then on the tide turned, and once again, as a year earlier, Britain had to face up to a series of defeats and disasters.

British Defeats

In scraping together a force to send to Greece it was necessary for General Wavell to draw heavily on the troops in Libya. Here a halt was called to the pursuit of the Italians; the most seasoned troops were withdrawn, and only a skeleton force was left to defend the newly won gains. Wavell reckoned that it would be several months before the Italians, even with German help, would be in a position to mount an offensive. But this calculation was upset by the arrival on the scene of a remarkable German general – Erwin Rommel. As soon as he reached Tripoli in the middle of February Rommel galvanised everyone into activity, and only a month later began his offensive against the remnants of the British army in Libya. These were taken by surprise; their forces were depleted and disorganised and very deficient in tanks. They fell back and then, as Rommel kept pushing forward, continued to fall back. In a few weeks Rommel's forces had regained all of Cyrenaica and crossed the border into Egypt before being halted at last near Sollum. The only place where strong resistance had been offered was at Tobruk by Australian forces. During the following months, while they were besieged, they held out heroically – ' a constant threat to Rommel's supply line.

Meanwhile disaster had overtaken the British expeditionary force in Greece. On 6th April, only ten days after the first British troops had reached the front line, the Germans invaded both Greece and Yugoslavia. Once again they gained a blitzkrieg victory. On 17th April, after a devastating air raid on Belgrade, Yugoslavia surrendered, and a week later Greece did the same. During this time the British forces had been engaged in a long and difficult retreat followed by an evacuation – on a smaller scale than Dunkirk but no less hazardous. In the end 50,000 of the 62,000 troops were taken off, but all heavy arms and equipment had to be left behind.

With Rommel advancing into Egypt and Greece overrun, still further defeats were in store for Britain. It had been hoped that with command of the seas it would be possible to defend the large and strategically important island of Crete. However, as had already been demonstrated on several occasions, sea power could not be effective without air support, and this could not be provided over Crete; from their bases in Greece the Luftwaffe dominated the area completely. The British Mediterranean Fleet was under great strain at the time. It had undertaken the transport of the British Expeditionary Force to Greece; then when the Italian fleet, goaded on by Hitler, attempted to intervene, had inflicted on it a heavy defeat off Cape Matapan; then with no air cover it had had to evacuate the British forces from Greece, and at the same time keep guard on Crete.

The invasion of Crete began on 20th May. After a heavy bombardment from the air the Germans dropped parachutists who managed to gain control of an airfield where further troops were landed. The Germans also tried to land forces by sea, but these were intercepted and suffered heavy losses. The defence of Crete was being undertaken mainly by New Zealand forces under General Freyberg; these fought heroically and were well matched with the crack troops of the German airborne division, but they were at a great disadvantage: most of them had been landed from Greece recently and were short of arms and equipment, particularly tanks and heavy guns; more important they had no air support and were bombed incessantly. After a week it became evident that another evacuation was going to be necessary. Once again the Royal Navy carried it out but with heavy losses; and some 12,000 troops had to be left behind to become prisoners of war. The battle of Crete was not, however, an unmitigated disaster. Heavy losses had been inflicted on Germany's best troops – so heavy that airborne forces were not used again by the Germans for the rest of the war.

While the battle of Crete had been raging General Wavell had had plenty to occupy him elsewhere. A new government had recently been set up in Iraq and it was believed to be having secret negotiations with the Germans; it was also believed that German aircraft were being allowed to use airfields in Syria, then under the rule of Vichy France. Under incessant pressure from Churchill Wavell somehow managed to scrape together enough forces to occupy these countries where, fortunately, resistance was light. At the same time Wavell was also being pressed to mount an offensive against Rommel in Egypt. This he did on 15th June before he was ready, and partly because of this and partly because of the superiority of German tanks it proved a failure. Shortly afterwards General Wavell was transferred to India and was replaced by General Auchinleck.

And so in June 1941 Britain was back in the same position in which she had been a year before – holding on desperately and stretched to her limits. At first sight it might seem that the Greek operation had been a total failure; but this may not have been so. On 22nd June Germany invaded Russia, five weeks later than had been intended. This delay was partly due to bad weather, but partly also to the campaign in Greece and Yugoslavia. Later in the year those lost five weeks were to prove vital to the Germans. If they were in some measure due to the British action in Greece, this was not in vain.

The War at Sea

A Constant Anxiety

Of all the cares weighing on British war leaders none bore so heavily or so persistently as the war at sea. On this everything depended. If Britain's supply lines were cut off all would be lost. The country would be starved into surrender.

At the beginning of the war the Germans were not ready for an all-out U-boat offensive. They had only about twenty ocean-going submarines, and for the first nine months of the war losses from these, although considerable, were not critical. But in June 1940 the position changed completely. By then the Germans occupied the whole western coastline of Europe from the North Cape in Norway to the Spanish frontier in the south of France. German U-boats and aircraft from bases in France could range far out into the Atlantic and down the west coast of Africa. German aircraft could also attack shipping in the English Channel and in the North Sea. It was at this time that the Germans began in earnest to impose a full blockade on Britain.

In this crucial struggle Britain was at first at a great disadvantage. With the south and east coasts unsafe for shipping – so much so that the Port of London became almost unusable – it was necessary to rely on the ports on the west coast (Glasgow, Liverpool, Cardiff, Bristol) and in due course these were to receive special attention from German bombers. The convoy system had been introduced at the beginning of the war, but there were far too few escort vessels,[1] and at that time the range of these was small – considerably smaller than that of the U-boats. This meant that it was possible for convoys to be escorted only about a hundred miles into the Atlantic. For the last part of their voyage they might be met by escort vessels based on Canadian ports, but in the middle there was a large gap of which U-boats took full advantage. For all too long U-boats had a happy hunting ground in the mid-Atlantic with numerous helpless targets. It would, of course, have made a great difference if the British had had the use of ports in Southern Ireland, but this was denied them by the government of Eire (as the country was then called) which remained neutral throughout the war.

It was not only from U-boats that losses were incurred. Aircraft too took a heavy toll as also did surface raiders. Germany had only a few battleships and heavy cruisers but these were modern and very powerful. It was difficult to prevent them slipping into the Atlantic where convoys might be at their mercy. It became necessary, therefore, to attach battleships to large convoys. Although surface raiders were a constant threat, they did less damage than might have been expected; this was partly because Hitler treated them as prize possessions and they were forbidden to engage British ships on anything like equal terms.

---

[1] Especially at the time of the Battle of Britain when destroyers had to be taken off convoy duties to meet the expected invasion.

The Sinking of the *Bismarck*

The most famous German battleship and the most powerful ship afloat at the time was the *Bismarck*. In May 1941, accompanied by the heavy cruiser *Prinz Eugen*, she set out on her first and only voyage. After making their way up the coast of Norway, the two ships entered the Atlantic through the Denmark Straits between Iceland and Greenland. Soon afterwards they were engaged by two heavy British ships – HMS *Hood* (a 25 year-old battlecruiser) and HMS *Prince of Wales* (a new battleship not yet in full commission). In the battle which followed the *Hood* which, like all battlecruisers, had only light armour, was sunk almost at once and *The Prince of Wales* forced to withdraw. However, the *Bismarck* herself had not survived unscathed, quite serious damage having been done to her fuel supply. Soon afterwards she parted company from the *Prinz Eugen* and, continuing her voyage southwards, gave the slip to the British cruisers who were shadowing her. For a time, to the great alarm of the British admiralty, she was at large in the Atlantic; but then she was discovered by an aircraft of Coastal Command. By then she was in a position to reach a French port before the Home Fleet could catch up with her from the north; but it was possible that she might be intercepted by a battlefleet coming up from the south from Gibraltar; and she was attacked immediately by aircraft from the carrier, HMS *Ark Royal*. This attack settled the fate of the *Bismarck*: she was struck by torpedoes, one of which wrecked her steering gear so that she could not sail in a straight line. The following day the heavy ships of the Home Fleet arrived on the scene and gave the *Bismarck* a tremendous battering; but she did not sink. It was necessary for a cruiser to close in and finish her off with torpedoes.

Perhaps the main importance of the sinking of the *Bismarck* was that it showed again that battleships were becoming out of date. Here, as at Taranto, it was carrier-based aircraft which struck the decisive blow.

Gleams of Hope

The sinking of the *Bismarck* was welcome news to the British people after all the setbacks of that time; but shipping losses continued to be alarmingly heavy. In the first half of 1941 average monthly losses were of the order of 470,000 tons which were far higher than the rate at which they could be replaced. This meant that Britain's shipping was being drained away; her imports were being heavily reduced; and it seemed that the noose was tightening around her neck. At that time the Germans had a total of 150 U-boats and were constructing new ones at the rate of eighteen a month. Also they were having great success by the employment of new tactics known as 'wolf packs'. This involved a large number of submarines – perhaps ten or twelve – making a surface attack together on a convoy at night. By this method they avoided asdic, the British submarine detector which would only pick them up when they were submerged.

In June 1941 the greatest shipping losses still lay in the future and it was to be another two years before U-boats were finally mastered. However, there were some gleams of hope. By then bases had been established in Iceland and Newfoundland so that the mid-Atlantic gap was being closed. Also more long-range escort vessels were coming into service and the crews of these were becoming increasingly skilful at tracking down the U-boats. Most important of all was that increasing help was coming from the United States. In September 1940 fifty long-service American destroyers had been traded to Britain and, even before America came into the war officially, the US Navy was taking a part in the Battle of the Atlantic.

Timescale

1940

May 10	Churchill becomes prime minister. Formation of National Government.
July 16	Hitler orders invasion of Britain in September.
August 12	Battle of Britain begins.
September 1	German invasion fleet begins to assemble in Channel ports.
7	First air raid on London.
17	Invasion of Britain called off.
October 28	Italy invades Greece.
November 11	Italian ships sunk at Taranto.
December 8	British forces attack Italians in Egypt.

1941

February	British forces invade Italian Somaliland and Abyssinia.
	German forces arrive in North Africa.
March	Axis forces under Rommel drive British back into Egypt.
27	Italian fleet defeated at Matapan.
April 6	Germany invades Greece and Yugoslavia.
24	Greece makes peace with Germany.
May 20	Germany invades Crete.
27	Sinking of *Bismarck*.
June 15	Unsuccessful British attack in Egypt.

Chapter 13

THE SECOND WORLD WAR
(Part Three)
The Grand Alliance

The Invasion of Russia

Hitler Turns East

Hitler's invasion of Russia came as no surprise to those who had studied closely his speeches and writings of the previous ten years. From these it was clear that he had an obsessive hatred of Bolshevism which he wished to stamp out; and he also had wild ideas of establishing 'living room' in Eastern Europe for the German 'master race' with the Slavs subservient and existing on sufferance.

This had always been Hitler's main design, but it had been necessary for him to digress from it when it seemed likely that German expansion eastwards would bring war with Britain and France. And so he made a treaty of friendship with Stalin which he hoped would keep him out of the war until the Western powers had been defeated. Stalin had been duped completely by this, and until the last moment, in spite of warnings from Britain and America and reports from his own agents that a vast German army was being amassed on the frontier, he had refused to believe that Hitler meant war, and had continued to appease him with economic aid and by deferring to his wishes. The Russian people were to pay a dreadful price for this misjudgment. It meant that they had to bear the full brunt of Nazi military might when they were unprepared for it. When invasion came at three o'clock in the morning of Sunday 22nd June the Russian army was off-guard and in the middle of a major reorganisation. The war against Finland in 1940 (see p. 151) had shown this to be urgently necessary. Not only was there a great shortage of armoured forces, with tanks still being treated as no more than a support to the infantry, but there were serious deficiencies in leadership. Most of the senior officers had been eliminated in Stalin's purges (see p. 125) and the new leaders had little knowledge of modern warfare and were so intimidated by Stalin and the political commissars that they dared not use their own initiative or voice their ideas.

Predictably then, Russia fell an easy victim to the blitzkrieg. Almost at once the Russian air force was grounded, some 1,200 planes being put out of action. Then, with complete command of the air, the German Panzers made deep thrusts into Russian territory, then turned to join up with each other, thus carrying out 'pincers' movements and encircling vast numbers of Russians. The tanks then advanced onwards, leaving these 'pockets' to be mopped up by the infantry coming up behind them. The main object of the Germans was to destroy the Russian armies on the spot and prevent them from withdrawing and fighting again deep in the heart of Russia.

The army which Hitler sent against Russia was the largest invading force in history – some 120 German divisions which were joined then or soon afterwards by 18 Finnish, 16 Rumanian, 3 Italian and 3 Slovakian – over three million men altogether. The operation, known as Barbarossa, had been planned with great thoroughness, and at first was completely successful. At the end of four weeks the Germans had shattered the Russian armies and advanced 300 miles. In the north one German army was approaching Leningrad; in the centre another, heading for Moscow, had encircled Smolensk and taken 300,000 prisoners; in the south German and Rumanian forces had driven deep into the Ukraine where many of the inhabitants, embittered by the collectivisation of agriculture (see p. 124) and the loss of their smallholdings, welcomed them as deliverers.

At the beginning of August German armoured forces in the centre seemed all set for the final drive on Moscow. But then came a fatal delay. For although most German generals thought that Moscow should be the main objective, Hitler disagreed. To him the wheatlands of the Ukraine and the industrial areas of the Don and the Dnieper were of greater importance. As always he got his way in the end, and the German Panzer group heading for Moscow was diverted southwards to meet up with another Panzer group coming northwards in the biggest 'pincer' movement yet. Whether or not this operation was the correct one in the long term, it was a complete success at the time. Four Russian

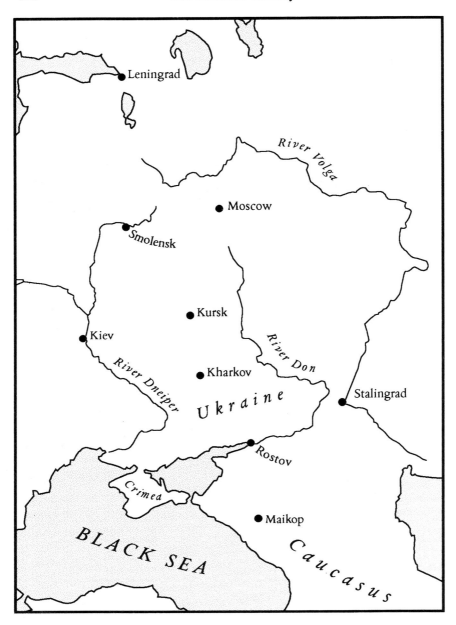

The Russian front.

A GERMAN PHOTOGRAPH, THE CAPTION OF WHICH SAYS: "NOTHING CAN HINDER THE GERMAN ADVANCE." YET HITLER IS TRYING TO EXPLAIN THE STANDSTILL.

German troops on their way to Moscow as winter sets in.

armies were trapped; a vast number of prisoners were taken;[1] Kiev and later Kharkov, the third and fourth cities of Russia, were captured; vital industrial areas were overrun; and the German army was in striking distance of the Caucasus with its desperately needed oilfields. This was, perhaps, Russia's heaviest defeat but, shattering as it was, it did mean that Moscow had been saved.

Failure of German Advance on Moscow

At the end of September the German generals at last obtained Hitler's permission to begin their drive on Moscow, but by the time the Panzers

---

[1] The actual number is uncertain as there is a discrepancy between German and Russian estimates, but it is likely to have been at least 500,000.

had returned from the south, it was not until 2nd October that the advance got under way; and by then Russia's greatest asset, her winter, was not far off. At first, however, the Germans again carried all before them. Another immense Russian force was caught in a 'pincer' movement, Moscow was three parts surrounded, and the Russian government had been compelled to leave the city. But then the weather intervened. First came heavy rains, turning Russian roads into a morass of mud. At the same time Russian resistance stiffened, and the German army was slowed down. The German commanders prayed for frost to harden the roads, and their prayers were answered with a vengeance. By the middle of November there were twenty degrees of frost. The Germans were quite unprepared for this; so confident had Hitler been that the war would be over before winter set in. Not only did the Germans have no winter clothing but their vehicles would not start, their guns would not fire and the batteries of their signalling equipment froze up. Even so they struggled on and by the end of November their advance guards were in the suburbs of Moscow; but this was as far as they could go, and on 5th December the attack on Moscow had to be abandoned. On the following day the Russians began their counter-attack.

The Turn of the Tide

The halting of the German advance and the counter-attack which followed was a prodigious feat. During the five months since the invasion began Russian losses had been colossal. The Germans had driven deep into the heart of the country and the territory which they occupied contained 40 per cent of the Russian population, all of their best wheat-lands and two thirds of their coal and heavy industry. The Russian army and air force had been overwhelmed, their losses in manpower amounting to as many as four million. No other country could have borne such losses, but the Russian people were fighting on and fighting back. Until the onset of winter little resistance had been possible to the Panzers. All the Russians could do was to fall back into the vastness of their country, destroying everything as they went,[1] and to keep going some-

---

[1] This was known as a policy of 'scorched earth'. Everything that could be of use to the enemy was destroyed including food, fuel, industrial equipment and even the newly built dam on the river Dnieper. Some industrial equipment was removed and set up again further east.

how until winter came and the German onslaught died down. In arms, equipment and leadership the Germans were greatly superior, but in the end it was the courage and powers of endurance of the ordinary Russian soldier which were to prevail.

By December many German military commanders were feeling that they had bitten off more than they could chew. It seemed that however much land they overran more stretched endlessly ahead of them. And however many Russians they killed or captured there were always more to take their place. Above all there were no signs of the Russians giving in. To the contrary their strength seemed to be reviving; the Russian air force was reappearing on the scene; fresh troops, specially trained and equipped for winter, were arriving from Siberia and Mongolia; and Russian leadership was improving. And so it was that when winter came the Germans found themselves thousands of miles from home with worn out vehicles, no warm clothing and an enemy all the time gaining in strength. Also their morale had taken a heavy blow; for the first time the German army had been checked and defeated; not only had it been forced back from Moscow but in the south too the German forces had over-extended themselves and been driven back from Rostov, the gateway to the Caucasus; and in the north Leningrad was still holding out.

Nothing shows more forcefully the Russian people's prodigious powers of endurance as the siege of Leningrad. It began in early September and was to last for 900 days. The city was not completely encircled, but only a trickle of supplies were able to get through. During this time the sufferings of the two and a half million inhabitants of the city were indescribable. There was no light, heat or transport and, for a time, thousands were dying every day of starvation. Everything possible was done to find food; after all dogs, cats and rats had been eaten, some kind of foodstuff was contrived from such things as cellulose, cotton-seed and seaweed; people even licked oil off the machines. It was reckoned that people were existing on one tenth of the normal number of calories. In the end perhaps as many as 665,000 people died.

The German Line Holds

There must have been many that winter who remembered Napoleon's retreat from Moscow 130 years before and wondered if the same fate was going to overtake Hitler's army. Certainly many German generals were wanting to make large-scale withdrawals; but Hitler was adamant that the armies should stand fast. At the time this policy caused great suffering and heavy losses, but it could be that it prevented a general rout of the German army. It was not to be this winter that it met with disaster. But the Russian counter-attacks from Moscow did have considerable success. Led by Marshal Zhukov, Russia's ablest soldier, the Germans were driven back 90 miles, but then their line held.

Hitler's disagreement with his generals was to have far-reaching effects. The relationship between them had never been an easy one, and after the setbacks of the winter Hitler dismissed thirty-five of them. He then made himself commander-in-chief of the army and took the whole direction of the war into his own hands. This meant that increasingly Hitler ignored the professional soldiers and relied on his own instincts; and although these were not always wrong, in the end they were to prove fatal.

War in the Far East – The Japanese Explosion

American Attitudes

At the end of 1941 Britain's fortunes had sunk to their lowest point. In the Mediterranean the British battlefleet had suffered crippling losses and there had been serious reverses in North Africa; in the Atlantic German U-boats, now numbering over 200, were taking an increasing toll of British shipping; and in the Far East the Japanese threat was growing. However, before the end of the year two things were to happen which made it virtually certain that, whatever disasters lay ahead (and these were to be considerable), Britain would eventually be on the winning side. In the first place, as has been seen, the German drive on Moscow was halted and driven back. Secondly, and even more important, America came into the war.

For the past twenty years the United States had been taking great care to avoid any foreign entanglements which might lead to war. Americans had been bitterly disappointed with the results of the First World War which they had hoped would indeed be 'a war to end wars'. Ever since 1920, therefore, when the US Congress refused to ratify American membership of the League of Nations, there had been a strong 'isolationist' feeling in the country, and when the Second World

War broke out the great majority of Americans were determined to have no part in it.

However, with the downfall of France in 1940 this attitude began to change. The prospect of the whole of Europe coming under Fascist domination caused great alarm, and the feeling began to grow that Great Britain in her lone stand must be kept going. Gradually more help was made available. At the beginning of the war it was remembered that it was trade with belligerent countries which had drawn America into the First World War, and so it was enacted that arms and other war materials would only be supplied on the basis of 'cash and carry'.[1] But from late 1940 important concessions were made. In September, as has been seen, fifty old but still serviceable US destroyers were handed over to Britain in return for the right to use bases in the Caribbean and Newfoundland. Then at the end of the year, when Britain's dollar resources had run out, Lend–Lease was introduced so that war materials could be provided without cash payments; and in time this led to America taking more responsibility for the transport of these goods. In July 1941 the United States took over from Britain the safeguarding of Iceland.[2] Also American warships undertook escort duties of ships carrying Lend–Lease materials, and this resulted inevitably in clashes with German U-boats. However, at the end of 1941 the American people were still firmly opposed to entry into the war, and President Roosevelt had to take great care about the measures he took to help Britain. The general feeling was clear: all aid short of war. However, events were soon to take place in another part of the world which left the United States with no option.

Japanese Dreams of Empire

For centuries Japan had kept aloof from the rest of the world. She had had little wish for outside contacts and had been unaffected by the Industrial Revolution and other changes that were occurring elsewhere. Then change came with a rush. In the space of about fifty years Japan was transformed from a medieval to an industrial society. She first

---

[1] This meant that no goods could be obtained on credit and American ships were not to be used for transporting them.

[2] Britain had occupied the country after the fall of Denmark of which Iceland was a part. Its importance in the Battle of the Atlantic was vital.

emerged on to the world scene when in 1904–5 she fought a victorious war against Russia. Soon afterwards she made an alliance with Great Britain and fought on the side of the Allies in the First World War. She continued to have close links with both Britain and the United States until 1931 when she occupied Manchuria which was officially part of China (see p. 111). From then on relations between Japan and the Western powers deteriorated. War with China broke out again in 1937, and by the outbreak of the Second World War Japan had occupied about half of China and built up strong naval and air forces.

For years many Japanese leaders had been dreaming of creating a large overseas empire in Asia. The seizure of Korea from the Russians and the invasion of China had been the first stages of this. In 1940 it seemed that great opportunities were occurring elsewhere. Two of the great colonial powers in Asia, France and Holland, had been conquered by Germany, and Britain was hard-pressed to survive. It appeared that the Dutch East Indies (Indonesia), French Indo–China (North and South Vietnam and Laos) and the British colonies of Malaya, Hong Kong, Burma and Borneo lay at Japan's mercy. Seizure of them would almost certainly mean war with the United States, but the Japanese government sought to avoid this by signing a Tripartite Pact with Germany and Italy by which each country would support the other if involved in war with America. This treaty was signed on 29th September 1940, and from then on events moved steadily towards war. In December the United States government banned all sales of raw materials, including oil, to Japan; and in April 1941 the decision was taken to supply China with arms on Lend–Lease. Then in July the Japanese induced the Vichy French government to allow them to occupy parts of South Indo–China.[1] Immediately afterwards the United States applied full economic sanctions against Japan, freezing all Japanese assets in America and persuading Holland and Britain to cooperate in cutting off all oil supplies. This drove Japan into a corner, as without oil she would be helpless; either she must give in to American demands to make peace with China, or she must go to war with the United States. If this happened Japan's principal objective would be the oilfields of the Dutch East Indies, but this would not be enough. In order to transport the oil safely back to Japan it would be necessary to occupy in addition

---

[1] They had been using air bases in North Indo–China since August 1940.

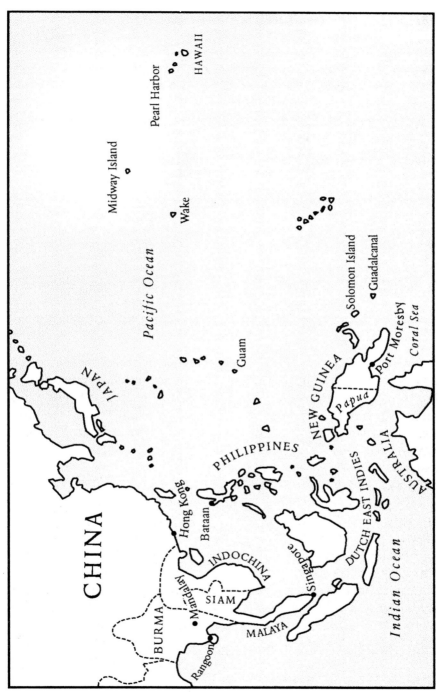

The Far East.

Thailand, Indo–China, Malaya and the Philippine Islands. If all of this was to be achieved it was essential for Japan to strike a devastating blow against the United States Pacific Fleet. For a time there was disagreement in Japan between the war party and the moderates; but by 16th October the former had gained the upper hand. By December Japan was ready to strike.

Pearl Harbour

Japanese war leaders had watched closely the course of the war in Europe and had seen how important it was in modern warfare to get in the first blow. They had also noticed how effective had been the attack by British naval aircraft on the Italian fleet at Taranto (see p. 170). They therefore planned to attack the American fleet at Pearl Harbour in Hawaii, before war had been declared, early on a Sunday morning with a large force of carrier-borne aircraft. They hoped the Americans would be taken completely by surprise and that at a stroke they would gain the mastery of the Pacific. The plan was prepared with great thoroughness. Up to a point it was highly successful.

Pearl Harbour. A small boat attempts to take off survivors
from a sinking US battleship.

On 8th December 360 aircraft from six large carriers launched the attack. First they bombed the airfields and put out of action the air force. After that the warships – nearly a hundred of them altogether – were sitting targets. The damage was devastating: four battleships were sunk and four put out of action; altogether eighteen warships were lost or damaged; 350 aircraft were destroyed, and total loss of life amounted to nearly 4,000. The Japanese lost 29 aircraft.

It was to take the Americans some time to recover from Pearl Harbour. The Japanese had seized the initiative and in the coming months were to make brilliant and successful use of it. However, the Japanese attack, shattering as it was, had not achieved enough. Certainly crippling losses had been inflicted on America's battleships, but it was already becoming evident that in modern naval warfare they were becoming out of date. Of far greater importance were the new aircraft carriers, and it so happened that all those of the US Pacific fleet were away from Pearl Harbour on 8th December, and survived to take a crucial part in later operations. The main result of Pearl Harbour, however, was that it brought a united and determined America into the war. All doubts were removed now about the need to crush Japan. For a time doubts still remained about the need to crush Germany, and President Roosevelt was uncertain that Congress would support him if he declared war. However, he was rescued from this predicament by Hitler who honoured his obligation under the Tripartite Pact and declared war on the United States.

And so the United States became fully committed. She was not ready for war, and it would take time for her tremendous resources to be brought to bear on her enemies. But there could be little doubt about the final outcome. Of the night of Pearl Harbour Churchill later wrote: 'I went to bed and slept the sleep of the saved and the thankful.'

Malaya – 'Britain's Greatest Military Disaster'

At the same time as the Japanese planes were delivering their attack on Pearl Harbour Japanese invasion forces were moving in on Hong Kong, Malaya and Thailand. In Hong Kong the defenders, beleaguered and outnumbered, put up a brief resistance for reasons of prestige before surrendering on Christmas Day.

In Malaya the British were woefully unprepared. Amid the crises and disasters of the war in Europe the Far East had until very recently been

Surrender of Singapore. 'Britain's greatest military disaster.'
General Percival goes off to seek terms from the Japanese.

neglected. The British, Australian and Indian troops in the country had had little training of any sort and none in jungle warfare; the air forces were inadequate and out of date; and there was no strong leadership. The Japanese on the other hand had had intensive training in jungle warfare, were fanatically determined and ready to fight to the death. From the beginning they carried all before them. They immediately gained control of the air and then, at a stroke, after only two days, gained command of the seas. When war was looming in the Far East the British government had sent out to Singapore Britain's newest battleship, *The Prince of Wales*, along with an old battlecruiser, *The Repulse*. But little heed was paid to the lesson, which should by now have been learned, that battleships without air cover were highly vulnerable, and when the two ships sailed north to intercept the Japanese invasion force they were attacked by Japanese aircraft and in the space of two hours both ships were sunk.[1]

---

[1] The British admiral realised the risk he was taking, but felt that it was impossible for his ships to stand by and do nothing. Of the loss of the two ships Churchill later wrote: 'In all the war I never received a more direct shock.'

Nothing could now stop the Japanese on land. The British high command had expected that they would be held up by the dense Malayan jungle and had based their plans on defending the roads, but the Japanese soldiers, tough and resourceful, forced their way through at bewildering speed. Repeatedly the British forces found that they had got round behind them. Under relentless pressure the morale of the British troops collapsed and nearly all resistance came to an end. Within 58 days the Japanese had overrun Malaya, and the British forces, what was left of them, had been driven back into the island of Singapore. Here it was hoped that a stand would be made. Singapore was Britain's greatest fortress in the Far East; large sums of money had been spent on its fortification and new troops had recently arrived there. But to no avail. The defences of the island had been directed against a seaborne attack and nearly all guns faced out to sea. And the newly arrived troops had had no time to acclimatise to the country after their long sea voyage, and the rapid Japanese advance through Malaya had caused panic and despondency. It was not long before the Japanese had crossed into the island and had closely invested the city of Singapore. By then the position was hopeless. With the city's water supply threatened, a large and terrified civilian population, and hopelessly dejected troops, it was necessary for the British commander to surrender.

The fall of Singapore has been described as 'the greatest disaster in British military history'; 60,000 men were captured; total losses in the whole campaign amounted to 130,000; of the Japanese force of 35,000 men less than 10,000 were lost.

Burma – The Longest Retreat

In Burma, as in Malaya, the British were unable to withstand the Japanese invasion. Here too untrained, ill-equipped British troops with little experience of the jungle and no air support were forced to fall back before the highly trained, ruthless, utterly dedicated Japanese who preferred death to capture and who needed only a handful of rice a day to keep them going.

Great importance was attached to Burma by the Americans as the Burma Road was the only way by which arms and supplies could be sent to the Chinese who were still holding down the majority of Japanese forces. Some help was, therefore, forthcoming both from the

Chinese and from American forces under General Stilwell, but the Japanese were not to be stopped, and the Burma Road was cut off in April 1942.

However, there was to be no major surrender in Burma as in Singapore. Under the fine leadership of two outstanding British generals, Harold Alexander and William Slim, the British army was extricated from Rangoon, and after the longest retreat in British history – some 1,000 miles – arrived exhausted and fever-ridden in India. By then the monsoons had brought the Japanese advance to a halt.

Certainly the British had suffered a humiliating defeat, but defeat can be a powerful medicine. Among the survivors of the British Fourteenth Army, and particularly its commander, General Slim, there grew a strong determination to avenge themselves and restore British prestige. But first they had to learn from their mistakes and defeats and so train and equip themselves that they would be on equal terms with the enemy. Among the Japanese, on the other hand, there were signs of 'victory disease' – over-confidence, arrogance and some loss of punch. And so it came about that three and a half years later the pathetic stragglers of the long retreat formed the nucleus of the army which reconquered Burma.

The Philippines, East Indies and the War at Sea

In addition to Malaya and Burma there were other parts of the Far East which were being overrun by the Japanese at that time. By Christmas Day (1941) the American-held islands of Wake and Guam had been captured, and by March the Dutch East Indies had been conquered, and Northern Australia was within bombing range.

The place where the Japanese encountered strongest resistance was the Philippines where there was a large army of Americans and Filipinos under America's distinguished general, Douglas MacArthur. Here again the Japanese struck the first blow when on the day after Pearl Harbour their bombers attacked American air bases and, catching their planes while refuelling, virtually eliminated American air power. Invasion came soon afterwards, and at first rapid progress was made, but then MacArthur withdrew to the Bataan Peninsula in the main island of Luzon, and for a time the Japanese were halted. However, the island was desperately overcrowded and food was extremely short. Soon afterwards the Japanese brought up reinforcements, and at the beginning of April the United States commander[1] was forced to surrender with 78,000 men who were treated by the Japanese with the greatest cruelty. For a time resistance continued on the tiny island of Corregidor, but a month later the forces here also surrendered.

By the beginning of May 1942 Japan had achieved all her principal objectives but then, instead of consolidating, she aimed to expand still further. In particular she resolved to invade New Guinea and the Solomon Islands, and thus cut off Australia from American protection. This led to the Battle of the Coral Seas and Japan's first defeat. The Battle of the Coral Seas was the first sea battle where the opposing forces were out of sight of each other, all the fighting being done by carrier-borne aircraft. The battle lasted three days and at the end of that time American losses were heavier than the Japanese,[2] but in that the Japanese were forced to abandon their main objective of capturing Port Moresby in Papua, and the life-line between America and Australia was kept open, it was an American victory. It was certainly the turn of the tide. Japanese victories were coming to an end.

A month later the Japanese were defeated much more decisively at the Battle of Midway. For some weeks the American commanders had come to know that a large-scale operation was about to take place in the North Pacific. Admiral Yamamoto, the Japanese commander-in-chief, had decided that the time had come for a final showdown with the US Pacific Fleet; he felt, with some reason, that he had overwhelmingly superior forces. His plan was to bring the American fleet to battle off Midway Island, lying some 1,000 miles north-east of Hawaii. The capture of Midway Island would mean that Hawaii, and Pearl Harbour in particular, would come within bombing range. Yamamoto reckoned that the Americans would bring into action their full forces to protect the island. He would, therefore, make use of his full forces to attack it. On paper the two fleets were uneven. Whereas Yamamoto had under his command four large aircraft carriers, three smaller ones, eleven battleships and fifteen cruisers, the Americans could muster only three aircraft carriers (one of which had been badly damaged in the Coral

---

[1] By then General MacArthur had been ordered to leave the Philippines to take up a new appointment as Supreme Commander in the Pacific.

[2] The Japanese lost one light aircraft carrier and some small craft and a heavy cruiser was badly damaged. The Americans lost a heavy carrier and two cruisers.

Seas), no battleships and eight cruisers. However, the Americans had two important advantages. In the first place they had support from aircraft based on Midway and, perhaps even more important, their intelligence had broken the Japanese naval code, and their commanders had knowledge of Japanese plans.

Yamamoto's plan was an elaborate one. His fleet was divided into two groups: one with all the aircraft carriers was to attack Midway; the other with most of the battleships was to create a diversion by attacking the Aleutian Islands in the north, but was to be ready to sail south and join in the main battle later on. However, the plan miscarried. With their superior intelligence and the cool judgement of their fleet commanders, Admirals Fletcher and Spruance, the Americans struck the first blow at the Japanese fleet off Midway. The first strike by American aircraft was beaten back with heavy losses, but this had diverted the Japanese fighter aircraft, and so when soon afterward thirty-five American dive bombers arrived on the scene they were unmolested and found an easy prey. In the course of the next five minutes three large Japanese aircraft carriers were sunk which meant that the whole balance of the war in the Pacific had been changed. Soon afterwards the fourth Japanese carrier was also sunk. The Americans lost one aircraft carrier.

For a time Yamamoto considered bringing down his battlefleet from the north for an all-out attack on Midway. He hoped that his huge battleships with their immense guns, thundering off into the horizon, might carry all before them. But then the thought of the two American aircraft carriers with their highly skilled flying crews made him change his mind.[1] The whole operation was called off and the Japanese fleet returned to home waters with the realisation that its mastery of the Pacific had been lost.

War in the Middle East and the Mediterranean

Heavy Naval Losses

It was not only in the Far East that disasters were befalling Britain in the last part of 1941. In the Mediterranean too the fortunes of war had swung heavily against her. In November German U-boats appeared on

---

[1] The range of naval aircraft was about thirty times longer than the largest gun.

the scene and soon reaped a rich harvest. Britain's newest aircraft carrier, *The Ark Royal*, was sunk, as also was the battleship *Barham*. Soon afterwards two cruisers were sunk by mines, and then Italian 'two-men torpedoes' penetrated into the harbour of Alexandria and two more battleships were put out of action. For the time being Britain's fleet in the Eastern Mediterranean was reduced to a skeleton.

At this time too a new Flying Corps of the Luftwaffe arrived in Sicily which meant that Malta came under heavy bombardment and became almost completely cut off. For a time the situation looked hopeless, but ultimately Malta was able to survive partly because convoys with arms and supplies forced their way through regardless of loss, and partly because of the heroism of the Maltese people. Partly too because the Axis missed the opportunity of capturing the island when, practically, it was theirs for the taking.

War in the Desert

For a time at the end of 1941 there was a gleam of hope in the desert war. On 18th November the new British commander-in-chief, General Auchlinleck, opened his offensive, and Rommel was caught by surprise and driven back into Libya as far as El Agheila (see map p. 172); but this success was short-lived. By the end of January 1942 Rommel had been reinforced and, catching the Eighth Army off balance, drove it back almost as far as Tobruk. This meant that the Libyan airfields, so important in the protection of convoys to Malta, were once again in Axis hands. At the end of May Rommel struck again, and was again successful. After a closely fought battle, so close that at one time even Rommel had thoughts of surrender, the British were forced to retreat in such a hurry that Axis forces swept into the fortress of Tobruk where they found quantities of supplies of all sorts, notably petrol.

The danger to Egypt was now imminent – with the Eighth Army in disarray and Rommel's Afrika Corps in full hue. In Alexandria some Egyptians prepared to give a rousing welcome to the Germans and Italians, and Mussolini came to North Africa, complete with white charger, for a triumphal entry into Cairo. However on 25th June the tide began to turn. On that day General Auchlinleck personally took over control of operations from the Eighth Army commander, General Ritchie, and by his calmness, steadiness of judgement and tactical skill retrieved the situation. A strong defensive position was taken up at

British troops attempting to dig trenches in the desert. Rocks just below the surface made this very difficult.

Loading of vital water supplies in the desert. One mug was one man's ration per day.

General Montgomery.

El Alamein, and Rommel found the way to the Nile delta firmly barred. He also found himself in urgent need of reinforcements and supplies, and to provide him with these meant that the projected invasion of Malta had to be called off.

In the lull that followed Churchill decided that the condition of the Eighth Army was unsatisfactory and changes were needed. In the first place its weapons, particularly tanks, were inferior to those of the Germans. In the desert, where there was little cover for infantry and it was very difficult to 'dig in', tanks were of prime importance. By June 1942 the new American tank, the Grant, was beginning to arrive, although these were still few in number and the crews needed time to adapt to them. Even more important than weapons, however, was the matter of the army's morale. This had been badly impaired by the way in which Rommel always seemed able to turn the tables on the Eighth Army. The 'Desert Fox' had become a myth among the British almost as much as among the Germans. Both sides held him in awe and even some affection.[1]

New Commanders

To Mr Churchill it was clear that the Eighth Army was in need of new blood. And so in August General Auchinleck was replaced by General Alexander, and General Mont-gomery took over command of the Eighth Army. The latter lost no time in making his presence felt. He ordered all plans for further withdrawal to be destroyed and declared that he intended to 'hit Rommel for six out of Africa'. He also set about making himself known to his troops, and was to be seen and photographed every-where, usually in unorthodox uni-form, exhorting, instructing and correcting. He was not, himself, personally averse to publicity and he has been accused of liking it too much, but at that time there was good reason for it. The Rom-mel myth had to be replaced by the Montgomery myth. Certainly it had an electric effect on the Eighth Army.

Field-Marshal Rommel. Montgomery had a photograph of him in his caravan.

Bernard Montgomery was not in the ordinary mould of British gen-erals. He had never been a conventional soldier, and in consequence was not greatly popular in the army. He was liable to be quarrelsome and tactless and his cocksureness and egotism often caused resentment. Ever since the death of his wife he had devoted himself single-mindedly

---

[1] One reason for this was that Rommel always 'fought clean'. At one stage when British prisoners complained to him about their water ration, Rommel replied that they were getting the same as himself and the rest of the Afrika Corps.

to the science of war and had a unique mastery of it. His exceptional gifts had been much in evidence when he had been in command of a division during the retreat to Dunkirk, where he had always been composed and even cheerful and at all times in command of the situation. As a general he was completely different from his opposite number, Rommel. Rommel was a brilliant armoured corps commander and liked campaigns where there was plenty of movement. He did not plan his battles with great care but preferred to 'play them by ear'. Always in the forefront, he was quick to seize an opportunity, to spot a mistake on the part of the enemy and then to exploit it to the full. He was also quite ready to take risks and perhaps too ready to take over a junior command where the battle was fiercest. Montgomery, on the other hand, planned all his battles with great thoroughness, took no avoidable risks and kept himself aloof so that he had a clear picture of the battle as a whole. Also he was always looking ahead to the next stage.

Battle of El Alamein

In Egypt Montgomery was soon master of the situation. He realised that Rommel would make an attempt to break through to the Nile delta. He was confident that this could be resisted but he himself would make no immediate counter-attack. The main battle, when it came, would be when he was ready for it and not before.

Rommel's attack did in fact come hardly two weeks after his arrival and was easily contained. Montgomery then spent two months building up the strength of the Eighth Army and was not to be hustled into any early move. By then the strength of the Eighth Army had become formidable: it had superiority in numbers and was equipped with newer and better tanks and guns; it also had complete command in the air; but, above all, its morale was high and everyone was confident of victory. However, the Germans and Italians were in a strongly fortified position, protected by the sea on one flank, impassable desert territory on the other and a large minefield in front. Montgomery was in no doubt that the battle would be a long, hard slogging match; and so it proved. For ten days (23rd October–4th November) the Eighth Army tried to punch a hole through Rommel's defences without success, but on the eleventh day it was at last achieved by the Australian division. Then armoured forces were ready to follow through, and Rommel was forced into a full retreat. If the Eighth Army had been a little quicker in pursuit and there had not been two days of rare desert rain, his army might have been trapped and destroyed completely. As it was 30,000 prisoners were taken and the danger to Egypt was removed for ever.

When the Eighth Army did take up the pursuit there was little to stand in its way. In the next fifteen days it advanced 700 miles. All those places – Bardia, Tobruk, Benghazi – which had changed hands several times in the last years were recaptured. There was some anxiety at El Agheila which twice before had been the limit of the Eighth Army's advance, but this time it swept on irresistibly. By the end of January 1943 the whole of Tripoli had been occupied, and then at the beginning of February it drove on into Tunisia. Tunisia at that time was a colony of France, but much had been happening lately in this part of Africa.

Anglo–American Landings in North Africa

By the end of 1942 it had become urgently necessary for Britain and the United States to undertake some major military operation in order to take the strain off Russia. Stalin had been complaining bitterly that they were leaving all the fighting to the Russians and, heedless of the fact that Britain had been fighting nearly two years longer than Russia, had gone so far as to taunt Churchill with dragging his heels and to question the fighting spirit of the British army. In normal circumstances Churchill would have responded to such remarks with some heat, but because of the tremendous strain on Stalin and the great achievements of the Russian armies, he restrained himself and undertook that something would be done. The great question was what this should be. Stalin was emphatic that a second front should be opened immediately in France, and in this he had agreement from some Americans. The British were convinced, however, that such an operation would be impossible in 1942. There were not enough trained troops, there were not enough arms and equipment, above all the landing craft necessary were not available. The coast of France was heavily fortified and the Germans had over forty divisions in the country; and before the Allies could land anything like comparable forces they would be overwhelmed and swept back into the sea. The operation would be a costly failure and Russia would not have been helped at all.[1]

For a time the argument was carried on vehemently, but in the end the British view prevailed and the invasion of France was postponed. The British proposed that instead there should be an invasion of north-west Africa, but American war chiefs were reluctant to agree to this. The British urged that such an operation would clear the Mediterranean, thus releasing millions of tons of Allied shipping, and would pose a strong threat to Italy. To the Americans, however, the operation was a diversion from the main purpose which was the defeat of Germany; they felt strongly that switching large bodies of troops to the Mediterranean would mean that it would be impossible to open a second front in France in 1943. However, Churchill and Roosevelt were agreed that something must be done at once as the situation on the Russian front was critical, so 'Operation Torch' went ahead.

'Operation Torch' was the first joint Anglo–American operation of the war and, as in most joint ventures, did not proceed without difficulties and disagreements. In the first place the Allies differed as to where the landings should take place; and later there were the usual jealousies and resentments of troops in battle, some feeling that they were bearing the brunt of the fighting, some that they were not getting enough credit, and nearly all finding fault with methods and ideas that were not their own.

The task of welding together the British and American fighting forces was a vital one, and here the Allies were fortunate in finding at an early stage a man well suited for the task. Dwight Eisenhower had no pretensions to being a military genius. Before 1942, when he became Supreme Allied Commander of 'Operation Torch' he had never commanded troops in battle. But he had other gifts of greater import-ance for the job he had to do – tact, charm and persuasiveness. In time he was to prove himself 'one of the great co-ordinators of history'.

Under Eisenhower's guidance a compromise was eventually reached about landing places. One American force, coming direct from the United States, was to land on the Atlantic coast of North Africa near

---

[1] The difficulties of a seaborne attack on the French coast were shown clearly and tragically by a commando raid on Dieppe in August 1942. Of the 5,000 Canadians who took part there were 3,369 casualties.

Casablanca. Another, coming from Britain, was to land at Oran in Algeria, and an Anglo–American force was to land near Algiers. At that time Morocco, Algiers and Tunisia were all French colonies, and it was not certain how the Vichy government would react to these invasions. Even more important would be the reaction of the French commanders on the spot. Would they resist? Or would they decide that the time had come to throw in their lot with the Allies?[1] A number of under-cover negotiations had taken place before the operation was carried out, but on 8th November, when the first landings took place, there was still great uncertainty about French attitudes. In the event strong resistance was encountered in some places and there was much confusion. But it so happened that at the time the French Minister of Marine and right-hand man to Marshal Pétain, Admiral Darlan, was visiting Algiers and, after some prevarication, he was persuaded to order a cease-fire which, despite being countermanded by Vichy, was generally obeyed. The German response to this was prompt: unoccupied France was invaded, troops and aircraft were poured into Tunisia, and an attempt was made to take over the French fleet in Toulon.[2] Drastic though these measures were and great the suffering they caused, they did simplify the situation in North Africa. Frenchmen became much more ready to commit themselves to the Allied cause.

In Morocco and Algiers the fighting soon came to an end. In Tunisia the British First Army made good progress in the early stages and advanced to within fifteen miles of Tunis but then, as the Germans became organised, it was held up and made little progress in the following months. In February 1943, however, the Eighth Army crossed into Tunisia from Libya and at the end of March broke through the strongly fortified Mareth Line which the French had originally built to keep out the Italians. Meanwhile American troops, under heavy pressure from the Germans (now under Rommel) had fought back strongly. At the beginning of May a strong attack was launched on Tunis and Bizerta which was completely successful. After the capture of these cities Axis resistance suddenly came to an end, with the Germans as anxious to surrender as the Italians.

---

[1] As there were at that time some 120,000 French troops in North Africa this was clearly a matter of some importance.

[2] This was unsuccessful. The fleet – some 73 ships – was scuttled.

Eventually then 'Operation Torch' was a great victory. Axis forces were completely removed from North Africa with heavy losses – 250,000 prisoners and huge quantities of equipment. Also squadrons of the Luftwaffe had been diverted from Russia, and Italy lay open to invasion. On the debit side the operation had taken much longer than expected and, as the American chiefs had feared, it would not be possible to open a second front in France until 1944. However, if the Germans gained time in North Africa, the Allies gained invaluable experience without which the invasion of Europe might have failed.

The Bombing of Germany

During the winter of 1940–41, when the 'blitz' of British cities was at its worst, there had been a widespread clamour to 'give it them back'. Churchill had much sympathy with this feeling, and in June 1941 declared: 'We shall bomb Germany by day as well as by night in ever-increasing measure, casting upon them month by month a heavier discharge of bombs, and making the German people taste and gulp each month a sharper dose of the miseries they have showered upon mankind.' This was no idle threat and in time, as Allied air power grew, air raids on major German cities made those on London, Plymouth and Coventry seem minor by comparison.

However, from 1941, when the raids began in earnest, the RAF and later the USAF had to learn the same lessons as had been borne by the Luftwaffe in 1940. They found that precision bombing of strategic targets – factories, oil refineries and radar stations, could only be achieved in daylight; and in daylight losses of bombers became unacceptably high unless they were escorted by fighter planes, and at that time in the war the range of fighters was much smaller than that of bombers. This meant that for the time being vital targets in the centre of Germany were out of reach. It also meant that the Allied Air Forces, like the Luftwaffe in 1940, switched to night attacks where accuracy was impossible, and all that could be done was to drop bombs at random somewhere in the target area. Later it was discovered that the early RAF raids were even wider off the mark than had been thought, and an enquiry in September 1941 came to the conclusion that only one bomber in ten got within five miles of the target. The raids, then, were having only nuisance value and German war production was unaffected by them. Because of this and because of the urgent need for aircraft in other theatres of war, notably in Coastal Command for the battle against the U-boats, it is possible that RAF raids on Germany would have remained on a small scale, anyway until new aids to navigation had been developed.

'Saturation' Attacks

However, at the beginning of 1942 Air Marshal Harris became chief of Bomber Command, and he was convinced that mass attacks on German cities could bring the war to an end. He maintained that if the attack was heavy enough – at least a thousand bombers – and intensive enough so that it was all over in ninety minutes, the air defences would be saturated, the city would be devastated and civilian morale shattered. The threat of this happening to every German city would, surely, cause general panic and compel the German leaders to sue for peace. But, as might have been foreseen from the example of the raids on British cities, this is not what happened. Here it had been found that air raids only dislocated life temporarily, and that far from weakening civilian morale people became angry and obstinate.

At the time, however, Harris's idea had great appeal. If the war could be won without opening a second front in Europe, where losses might be devastating, it seemed worth trying. Also it was becoming urgently necessary to take some action to take the pressure off Russia, and if large-scale land operations were not possible for the time being, heavy bombing attacks were all that could be done. And so Harris had his way and on 30th May 1942, by dint of scraping together every possible aircraft and crew in the country[1] the first thousand-bomber raid was launched on Cologne. However, although great damage was done, it was not enough; life in the city was soon resumed and there were no signs of panic or despair. To some this signified the failure of Harris's plan, but to Harris it simply meant that the attack had not been heavy enough and he must aim to double the bombing force.

And so, later in the war, even heavier raids were carried out on other German cities – notably Hamburg, Berlin and Dresden. These certainly

---

[1] Including flying instructors and their pupils.

caused tremendous damage; they also caused the diversion of valuable resources, notably fighter aircraft, from the Russian front; and they did too have considerable effect on German war production. But in their main aim, to bring the war to an end by sheer terror, they were unsuccessful; and Allied air losses were very heavy.

Technical Advances

Technical advances came rapidly in the later years of the war. Radar devices were developed which were of great help to bombers in reaching their targets.[1] But at the same time other radar devices were fitted to German night fighters which enabled them to hunt down raiding aircraft more easily.

In 1943 the USAF took the leading role in the air war in Europe. At first American air chiefs were determined to strike at strategic targets in daylight and were confident that their heavy bombers, the so-called 'Flying Fortresses', which were heavily armed, would keep at bay the German fighters. However, this hope was not fulfilled, and losses became so heavy that for a time raids had to be discontinued. But this was not to be for long, as soon afterwards long-range fighters, notably the Mustang, came into service and these were able to escort the bombers to targets deep inside Germany. These precision attacks on vital targets, especially oil refineries, had great effect. In conjunction with the night operations of the RAF, they also wore down Germany's air forces so that when eventually Allied forces invaded Europe their supremacy in the air was complete.

War at Sea – Mastery of the U-Boats

Heaviest Losses Yet

In the second half of 1941 there had been a marked drop in British shipping losses, the average monthly losses being down to 170,000 tons from 470,000 in the first half of the year. However, the picture changed

---

[1] At first it was only possible to fit these in a few aircraft whose function it was to seek out the target and light it up for the aircraft which followed. These later became known as 'Pathfinders'. The new devices also made possible highly accurate specialist raids, notably the 'Dambusters' in May 1943.

soon after America came into the war. For the Germans soon discovered that shipping off the American coast was unescorted and unprotected and that a rich and easy harvest was to be gathered in these waters. In the first six months of 1942 over 500 American ships were sunk.

Throughout 1942 the Allies continued to lose the Battle of the Atlantic. In spite of more escort vessels, more long-range aircraft and all the resources of the United States, shipping losses mounted critically – to more than 800,000 tons in some months. The main reason for this was the tremendous pressure on the Allied navies at that time. Not only had the transatlantic lifeline to be kept open, but convoys had to be sent to the Far East, to the Mediterranean and, most hazardous of all, to Russia.

Russian Convoys

Immediately after the German invasion Churchill had pledged all possible aid to Russia, expressing the hope that it would be possible to send a convoy carrying war supplies every ten days. However, these would run into great danger as it would be necessary for them to pass within range of German U-boats, aircraft and surface warships based in northern Norway. At first the Germans were slow to react, and the first convoys managed to get through almost unscathed, but then in the spring of 1942 squadrons of the Luftwaffe were moved to the area as also was the battleship *Tirpitz*, sister ship of the *Bismarck*. In the event this ship was never to fire a shot in anger, but the threat posed by her presence was enough to create terrifying problems. It was because of this threat that the seventeenth and largest Russian convoy was almost annihilated. The Admiralty in London, became convinced, wrongly as it turned out, that the *Tirpitz* was about to attack the convoy and ordered it to disperse so that nearly all the ships fell helpless victims to U-boats and aircraft.

Nowhere did the Royal Navy suffer such hardships and losses as in the Arctic convoys, but they had little thanks for their pains from the Russians who did little to provide for them when they arrived and Stalin complained bitterly about their 'failure' to get through.

Battle of the Atlantic Won

In the first months of 1943 the Battle of the Atlantic reached its climax. By then the Germans had some 240 U-boats in commission and their commander-in-chief, Admiral Doenitz, realised that the time had come for a supreme effort. At first he had great success and in March Allied shipping losses were again fearsomely high. But then, quite suddenly – in about six weeks – the whole pictures changed: losses of U-boats rose sharply and then became so great that Doenitz was forced to withdraw them.

There were several reasons for this abrupt change of fortune. In the first place, following the completion of the landings in North Africa, numerous escort ships were able to return to the Atlantic. Allied resources, both in terms of equipment and expertise, had by then become considerable. It had been known for some time that convoys which had both sea and air protection were almost impregnable, and now for the first time it was possible to provide this. The new escort vessels were of long range and were fitted with radar which enabled them to detect submarines on the surface at night and in dense fog. Even more deadly to U-boats were the new long-range aircraft, also fitted with radar and with a new and more effective type of bomb. In 1942 there had been all too few of these aircraft as Coastal Command had been kept short so as not to interfere with the bombing offensive against German cities. However, in 1943 more were becoming available and further air cover was being given by aircraft from 'escort carriers' — merchant ships with flight decks superimposed on them. These were of decisive importance as they made it possible for convoys to have air protection all the way across the Atlantic.

In April 1943 fifteen U-boats were destroyed; in May the number rose to forty. In June shipping losses were down to about 150,000 tons, and from then until the end of the war on average four ships were being built for every one lost.

And so, after three years, the Battle of the Atlantic was won. Even at the worst time supply lines to Britain had been kept open while those to Germany and Italy had been closed. In 1943 U-boats were temporarily withdrawn from the oceans and were never again a serious menace. In this victory technology and expertise were of great importance, but the main factor, of course, was the courage and endurance of the merchant seamen. In spite of heavy loss of life, heavier than in most branches of the armed services, these men, all civilian volunteers, continued to man their ships even when the chances of survival were small.

Timescale

1941

June 22	Germany invades Russia.
October 2	Germans open final drive on Moscow.
November	British drive Rommel out of Egypt.
December 5	Germans checked in front of Moscow.
8	Japanese attack on Pearl Harbour.

1942

February 15	Surrender of Singapore.
April	Japanese conquest of Burma completed.
	End of resistance to Japanese in Philippines.
May 4–8	Battle of Coral Seas.
27	Rommel drives back Eighth Army.
30	First thousand-bomber raid on Germany.
June 4	Battle of Midway.
July 25	Rommel halted at El Alamein.
October 23	Battle of El Alamein begins.
November 8	Anglo–American landings in North Africa.

1943

March	Eighth Army breaks through Mareth Line into Tunisia.
May 13	Surrender of Axis forces in North Africa.
June	Battle of Atlantic won.

Chapter 14

SECOND WORLD WAR – FINAL VICTORY

Russia – German Armies Retreat

Hitler Aims for the Caucasus

In April 1942 Hitler informed his generals that during the months ahead the principal objective of the German army was to be the oilfields of the Caucasus. He had become convinced, wrongly as it proved, that Germany could not continue the war without further oil supplies.

As in the previous year the German offensive was off to a late start – not until 28th June – due mainly to a large-scale Russian attack to recapture Kharkov. Once again the Germans had great success at first. By 3rd July the Crimea had been cleared and by 23rd Rostov had been captured. The Germans then wheeled south towards the Caucasus and by 9th August had reached Maikop in the foothills and the first oilfields. However, these had been destroyed by the Russians and, partly because of the lack of fuel and partly because of the mountainous nature of the country, the German armoured forces were brought to a halt. If Hitler had persevered with this attack it is possible that his armies would have forced their way through and that the oilfields not only of the Caucasus but also of the Middle East would have fallen into his hands. However, he decided that this was too risky and that, in order to protect his line of supply, he must first drive back all Russian troops across the Volga. In order to do this it was necessary to capture Stalingrad, a long thin strip of a city stretching some ten miles along the west bank of the Volga. Stalingrad then became Hitler's main objective.

The Battle of Stalingrad

This was to be one of the decisive battles of history. Today most people agree that Hitler was wrong in concentrating on Stalingrad; its strategic importance was not great. It seems that he was bemused by the name and the shattering effect he thought the loss of it would have on Russian morale. Certainly Stalin ordered that the city should be defended to the last drop of Russian blood, and in the ensuing weeks the hardest and bitterest fighting of the war took place.

The attack on Stalingrad began on 19th August and on the night of the 23rd the Luftwaffe made one of its heaviest attacks of the war, setting the whole city on fire so that it was possible, so it was said, to read a newspaper from its glow forty miles away. In the fighting that followed the Germans had great advantages – more men and many more tanks and aircraft. However, these advantages were to a large extent offset. For at Stalingrad battle conditions were different from the rest of Russia. On the open steppes the Panzers, supported by the Luftwaffe, were almost unstoppable, but in a confined space among the rubble of a ruined city with Russians ready to fight and die in every nook and cranny, tanks were much more vulnerable. Also with the opposing armies at such close quarters aircraft could give little support. In such conditions everything depended on the infantry, and it soon became clear that in close hand-to-hand fighting – so close at times that one could even hear the breathing of the enemy – the Russians were superior to the Germans.

When their first attacks failed the reaction of the German commanders was obstinate and unimaginative: they would pour in more troops and apply greater force; they would fight a battle of attrition in which both sides would be bled dry until the stronger prevailed. At the beginning of October the fourth

Soviet infantryman in action in Stalingrad. It was he and others like him who caused the greatest German defeat of the war.

German attack was launched and the days that followed were the most crucial of the battle; but, although by now the city had been almost entirely destroyed, the Russians still fought on. And at the same time a plan was taking shape in the minds of the Russian commanders, a plan which was eventually to trap and annihilate the whole German army in Stalingrad. In the weeks that followed, then, the Russians, unlike the Germans, did not pour into the city maximum reinforcements. Instead they fed in the minimum, just enough to keep the battle going. Meanwhile to the north and the south of the city, in strict secrecy, they started to build up large new armies. The plan was that, when the time was ripe, these would converge in a great pincer movement behind the Germans who would then be cut off and caught like a rat in a trap.

The plan was to work with complete success. The northern and southern flanks of the German army in Stalingrad were protected only by Rumanians, Hungarians and Italians who had little stomach for the fight, and when the Russian armies attacked on 19th November they soon broke through. Two days later the two armies joined up and the jaws of the pincers snapped tight behind the German Sixth Army. At first the magnitude of the disaster was not realised by the German high command. A rescue operation was mounted at once, and Goering announced that the Luftwaffe would be able to supply the stranded army with its vital needs. However, neither German land forces nor the Luftwaffe could save the Sixth Army, and on 31st January 1943 the German army commander, von Paulus, along with 90,000 men surrendered. In the course of the battle some 120,000 Germans had been killed.

Resurgence of the Russian Army

Stalingrad was a catastrophe for the Germans. They had suffered enormous losses and the blow to their morale was shattering. For the Russians it had been a miraculous achievement. In spite of their heavy defeats of the previous year and in spite of the fact that so much of their country was in German hands they had managed to put in the field huge new armies, well equipped and well trained. Increasingly the Russian fighting man was showing himself more than a match for the Germans; and in generalship too, especially now that Hitler was in command, the Russians were proving superior. After the disasters of 1941 it was becoming clear that Russian commanders were learning from their mistakes and were beginning to understand the nature of modern warfare. At the same time German leadership was declining. To Hitler the defeat at Stalingrad meant simply that he could not trust his generals and must take more and more on himself. Increasingly he ignored expert military advice and relied more on his own intuition.

After Stalingrad the Russian armies on the southern front surged forwards, but at the end of February they were halted by a well-timed German counter-attack at Kharkov. Then for a time there was a lull in the fighting while the snows thawed. For the summer of 1943 the Germans planned a vast pincer movement from north to south to cut off the large Russian salient at Kursk; but their attack was late in starting and had been anticipated by the Russians who were well pre-pared. Subsequently the largest tank battle of the war was fought, and this showed that in armoured warfare too the Germans were losing their superiority. The new Russian tanks were as good as or better than those of the Germans. Everywhere the German attacks were held off and beaten back. From then on with occasional delays and setbacks the Russian advance westwards swept on inexorably.

The Conquest of Italy

'The Soft Under-Belly of Europe'

After North Africa had been cleared of Axis forces there was again disagreement among Allied leaders as to what should be the next step. Once again the American chiefs of staff urged that the war in the Mediterranean be broken off and the forces there sent either to Britain in readiness for the invasion of France or to the Far East for the war against Japan. To Churchill and his advisers, on the other hand, it was imperative that the victory in North Africa be followed up immediately. Churchill urged how necessary it was to divert as many German forces as possible away from France and Russia by operations in other areas, such as Italy and the Balkan countries, what he called 'the soft under-belly of Europe'. But the Americans disagreed, regarding these as side-lines which achieved little and detracted from the main operation which was to get to the heart of Germany as soon as possible. However, they had to face the realities of the situation which were that it would not be possible to invade France for another year and that in the meantime something must be done to relieve the Russians.

*Invasion of Sicily. British soldiers wade ashore as others
prepare tracks for heavy vehicles.*

Invasion of Sicily

And so, cautiously and with reservations, the Americans agreed to an invasion of Sicily. They were still determined not to become involved in a major operation, and for the time being would agree to no more than this. They would wait and see how things evolved.

The invasion of Sicily was the largest amphibious operation undertaken so far in the war. Altogether some 2,500 ships and landing craft were used and these were escorted by 750 warships and 4,000 aircraft; the total number of troops was 160,000 along with 600 tanks and 14,000 vehicles. At the last moment the operation was nearly wrecked by a freak storm which suddenly blew up, but then equally suddenly subsided. However, partly because of this and partly because of an ingenious intelligence operation,[1] the enemy was taken by surprise and the landings occurred without serious setback. Subsequently the American Seventh

---

[1] The body of a British officer was allowed to be washed up on the coast of Spain with plans showing that the next Allied objective was to be Greece.

Army under General Patton[1] swept round one side of the island while the British Eighth Army under General Montgomery advanced round the other; and in due course they met up at the key port of Messina in the north. The whole operation took 38 days; total enemy losses amounted to 167,000, those of the Allies to 31,000. Meanwhile dramatic events were taking place in Italy. On 25th July Mussolini was deposed by the Italian king and was succeeded by Marshal Badoglio who showed signs of being interested in making peace. Italy, then, seemed ready for a knockout blow, and so an invasion of the mainland was authorised.

Invasion of Italy

On 3rd September 1943 the Eighth Army, meeting only light resistance, crossed the Straits of Messina and, four years to the day after the outbreak of war, British forces returned to the mainland of Europe. On the same day Marshal Badoglio signed a secret armistice. The events leading up to this had been a delicate operation as the marshal was caught between the invading forces of the Allies on the one hand and on the other powerful German forces who were determined to keep Italy in the war. However, in the event the matter was arranged, and Badoglio and the Italian royal family were able to escape from Rome. At first it was not clear what the Germans would do. For a time Hitler considered withdrawing from all southern Italy, but then, partly because of Allied hesitation and partly because of the prompt and effective measures taken by the German commander on the spot, Marshal Kesselring, he came to the decision that the whole of Italy must be defended to the last. At the same time, following a fantastic operation by German paratroopers, Mussolini was rescued from the mountain stronghold where he was imprisoned, and found himself again, temporarily, the ruler of Italy.

The Allied plan of invasion was that the troops crossing from Sicily should tie down as many German troops as possible in the south while another landing was made further north, some thirty miles south-east

---

[1] Regarded by some as America's greatest fighting general of the war, but a somewhat tempestuous character. Wildly indiscreet in some of his public utterances and 'fighting mad' so that he was not always in control of himself, he was often in trouble with his superiors. He was famed at the time for the pair of pearl-handled revolvers he always wore. His troops knew him as 'Old Blood and Guts'.

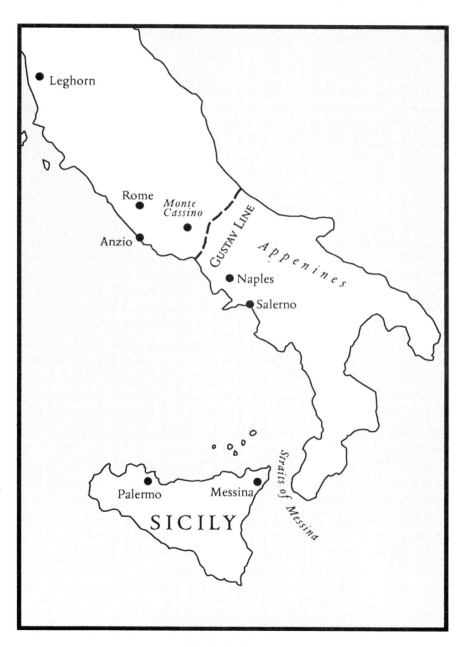

The Italian Front

of Naples in the Bay of Salerno. However, this operation miscarried. The Germans were expecting the landing and were prepared for it. For a week the Allied landing force was in danger of disaster, but then they were reinforced by paratroopers, and naval and air forces supported them with a tremendous bombardment; and the German counter-attack to drive them into the sea was held off. Soon afterwards the Germans withdrew and the Allied forces at Salerno joined up with the Eighth Army which had been advancing persistently, if not very rapidly, from the south. On 1st October the combined forces entered Naples.

The Way to Rome Barred

After the capture of Naples the question arose as to whether or not the Allies should continue their advance northwards. By then they had achieved their principal objectives: Italy had been knocked out of the war, the Mediterranean had been cleared, and airfields had been captured from which vital targets in southern Europe, notably the Rumanian oilfields on which Germany depended heavily, could be bombed. The American war chiefs urged that the Allies should go on the defensive and that only the minimum number of troops be left in the country. However, the British and American commanders in Italy were insistent that the campaign should continue. They thought the captured airfields were not defended in sufficient depth, and they had a great desire to capture Rome. In the end a compromise was agreed whereby some troops and landing craft were to be removed, but the Allied forces were to continue their advance.

The way to Rome, however, was an extremely hard one. The mountains and rivers of the Apennines afforded strong defensive positions of which the Germans made full use. It was the worst possible country in which to attack; anything less like 'a soft under-belly' it would be hard to imagine.[1] At the end of 1943 the Germans fell back to a seemingly impregnable position, running across the narrowest part of Italy, which came to be known as the Gustav Line. So strong was this position that it seemed to Churchill and the new Allied commander-in-

---

[1] Aneurin Bevan, one of Churchill's principal critics in Parliament, declared at the time: 'Is this the soft under-belly of the Axis? We are climbing up his backbone!'

chief, General Alexander,[1] that the obvious move was to make a sea-borne landing behind it. However, this led to dispute as the landing craft needed for such an operation were due to go back to England, and if they were delayed, it would be necessary to postpone again the invasion of France.

In the end, however, Churchill was to have his way, and on 21st January 1944 a large Allied landing was made at Anzio, some seventy miles behind the Gustav Line. This time the Germans were taken completely by surprise and there were hardly any troops in the area, but the commander of the operation, the American General Lucas, was cautious and, instead of striking out at once to cut Highway Seven, one of the main lines of communication to the Gustav Line, he delayed and consolidated his bridgehead. Alexander tried to urge him on but to no avail. Churchill was furious: 'I had hoped,' he said later, 'we would be hurling a wildcat ashore, but all we got was a stranded whale.'

Meanwhile the Germans reacted quickly. Troops were rushed to the area and the bridgehead was sealed off, and there for four appalling months the Allied force remained, hemmed in and frustrated. It was necessary for them to wait until the Gustav Line had been breached – an operation which, it had been hoped, they would make unnecessary.

The Battle of Cassino

The attack on the Gustav Line began in earnest on 15th February 1944 when the ancient Benedictine monastery at the top of Monte Cassino was destroyed by bombing. This later became a matter of great contro-versy. On the one side were those who maintained that the monastery was a unique historical monument,[2] and that it was unnecessary to destroy it as it was not occupied by the Germans until after it had been demolished. Moreover its ruins provided as strong a fortress as when it was intact; and, in any case, it was a mistake to attack at this point which was the strongest part of the Gustav Line. On the other side were those who believed that an attack had to be made at that point and that

---

[1] At the outset General Eisenhower had been commander-in-chief, but he had been transferred to England to command the forthcoming invasion of France. General Montgomery too had gone to prepare for this operation.
[2] This was the birthplace of the Benedictine order of monks. St Benedict had set up a monastery here in the sixth century.

Monte Cassino before the battle . . .

. . . and after.

commanders, when sending their troops into battle, are always under an obligation to remove every possible danger; and even if the monastery was unoccupied, which they could not know, the psychological effect of this large gaunt building overlooking the battlefield would weigh heavily on the attackers.

The Battle of Cassino was to rage for the next three months. During that time the Allies, which included Poles, Gurkhas, New Zealanders and Free French, made many attempts to break through, but it was not until the early part of May that this was finally achieved by the Free French forces from North Africa, all of them hardened mountaineers. This caused Kesselring, the German commander, to pull right back, and the Allies surged forward. On 21st May they joined up with the troops at Anzio, and on 4th June they entered Rome, a glorious occasion and the result of some of the hardest and most skilful fighting of the war. But it did not receive great attention at the time as then all eyes were focused on the Allied landings in France on D-day.

The Invasion of France

'The Atlantic Wall'

The Allies had been planning an invasion of France for a long time. Ever since 1942 the Russians had been demanding it insistently and the American chiefs of staff had been eager to undertake it. However, they had had to face the realities of the situation which were that such an operation would be impossible without complete supremacy in the air and that it would be very dangerous so long as the U-boats were winning the Battle of the Atlantic; also it would have no hope of success unless there were far more landing craft than were then available. Subsequently, as has been seen, further postponements were caused by the invasions of North Africa and Italy. But by the spring of 1944 preparations were complete. By then the Luftwaffe had been driven from the skies, the Battle of the Atlantic had been won, and a vast Allied army of millions had been assembled in England and ready to go. D-day was fixed for 5th June.

The difficulties of the operation were prodigious. Of all military operations an attack from the sea is the hardest. Moreover the Germans were expecting it and had had plenty of time to prepare for it. Along the coast of northern France, Holland and Belgium they had constructed strong defences, including forts, gun emplacements and tank traps, which came to be known as 'The Atlantic Wall'. Millions of mines had been laid and booby traps set, and lately a swarm of underwater obstacles had been set up to sink incoming landing craft.

The breaching of the Atlantic wall was a daunting problem for the Allies, but an even greater one confronted them once they were through. At that time the Germans had sixty divisions in France and, long before the Allies would be able to land forces of anything like comparable size, they could attack with far greater strength and drive them into the sea.

It seemed to some that the Germans were in an impregnable position, and there were those who had visions of another Dunkirk and the Channel seething with dead bodies and the debris of the Allied armada. However, the Allies had one advantage which in the event was to overcome all opposition – overwhelming superiority in the air. As a result of this the Luftwaffe was kept out of the skies completely, the coastal defences were 'softened up' by a tremendous bombardment, and the bombing of roads, railways and bridges prevented the moving into the area of German reserves and supplies.

German Disagreements

At the beginning of 1944 the Germans too had their problems. One of these was that the much vaunted 'Atlantic Wall' was still unfinished, as Rommel discovered when he took command of it at the end of 1943. By his energy and resourcefulness he was able to do much in the next six months to consolidate it, but because of shortages of labour and materials as well as endless Allied air attacks, the Atlantic Wall in June 1944 was still thin in places. The only part where it was complete was in the Pas de Calais area but, as will be seen, this was not where the Allies intended to land.

If Rommel had had his way nearly all German forces in France would have been concentrated on the coast. He was convinced that the only way of defeating the Allies was to prevent them from landing at all or to pin them down on the beaches. To him the first twenty-four hours would be crucial. These were not, however, the views of the German commander-in-chief in the West, Field-Marshal von Rundstedt. He thought it would be impossible to prevent the Allies landing somewhere on the 1,700 miles of Atlantic coast and that the best policy was to build up a large mobile reserve which could be brought into action against any landing forces before they were of sufficient strength to resist. He was unmoved by Rommel's argument that these reserves would be paralysed by Allied air attacks. In the end the dispute was referred to Hitler who decided on a compromise whereby some armoured forces were taken from reserve and committed to the coast. This difference of opinion in the German high command was a serious matter for the Germans but even more serious was Hitler's insistence that all decisions on troop movements and use of reserves were to be referred to him at his headquarters in Eastern Europe. This was to prove fatal.

Plans for D-Day

In making their plans for breaking through 'The Atlantic Wall' the Allied leaders knew that everything would depend on the courage and fighting ability of the first attackers, but there was much that could be done to assist them in their task. In the first place the coastal defences could be heavily bombarded from the sea and the air, but this would not be enough. At the end of it the enemy would emerge from their bomb-proof shelters and would be ready to aim a withering fire on the attackers as they clambered through the minefields, barbed-wire entanglements and other obstacles. The commando raid on Dieppe in 1942 had shown how heavy were the casualties which could be inflicted in these circumstances. In order to counter this danger the British had devised a number of specialised tanks which were to go in with the first attackers. These included tanks fitted with flotation devices so that they could 'swim', bulldozer tanks to clear away rubble and obstacles, tanks carrying bridges to lay over ditches and craters, and tanks fitted with a beating device or 'flail' out in front to explode mines. In the event this assault armour was to prove of great value and did much to keep down casualties.

In preparing for D-Day Allied planners attached great importance to the element of surprise. They could not hide from the Germans that an invasion was coming, but they could deceive them as to time and place. Ever since the decision had been taken to land not in the nearest and most obvious place, the Pas de Calais, but on the beaches of Normandy, great pains had been taken to make the Germans believe otherwise. Large dummy fleets had been assembled in south-east England which German aircraft had been allowed to see while being kept away from the real ones further west; bombing of the Pas de Calais had been as heavy, if not heavier, than that of Normandy; and German agents in different parts of the world had been 'fed' with false information. These methods were to prove highly successful, and right up to D-Day and for some time afterwards most German leaders expected the main invasion in the Pas de Calais and thought the Normandy landings to be only a diversion.

D-Day – The Allies Break In

By the beginning of June the Allied planners had nearly completed their task. To land five divisions on the coast of France simultaneously required massive organisation; but by then timetables, loading schedules, orders of battle had all been drawn up, and a day had been fixed on which moon and tides would be favourable. There was only one factor, of crucial importance, over which the planners had no control, namely the weather. As 5th June approached this caused great anxiety. During May it had been fine, but at the beginning of June there had been an abrupt change and the forecast was so bad that it was necessary to postpone the invasion by one day. The forecast for 6th June was not much better, but rather than call the whole operation off for another two weeks (when moon and tides would again be suitable), Eisenhower gave the order for the invasion to proceed.

The Normandy beaches, stretching for some fifty miles, had been divided into five landing grounds – three for the British and Canadian ('Sword', 'June' and 'Gold') and two for the Americans ('Omaha' and 'Utah'). The first troops to land were the airborne divisions whose task it was to secure the flanks of the beaches and capture other strategic points. The seaborne forces started to arrive at first light after an appalling crossing. Nearly all of them were wet, seasick and exhausted, but in spite of this they forced their way ashore, and on only one beach, 'Omaha', was there serious difficulty. Here the defences were particularly strong and had been little affected by the bombardment, and the amphibious tanks had been unable to land as, owing to the rough weather, they had been put out too far from land. For a time the landing forces here were pinned down on the beach, but in the end they were able to force their way inland, and fortunately there were no German reserves in the area to make a counter-attack. On the British and Canadian beaches the first attackers had little difficulty in getting ashore, but then were unable to capture their main objective, the town of Caen which lay ten miles inland and was guarded by two Panzer divisions.

At the end of the day, the most crucial of the war, the Allies could be well satisfied with their achievement. In spite of exceptionally bad weather all their troops were ashore and more were following. No serious German counter-attacks had taken place, and the number of Allied dead was no more than 2,500.

Battle of the Build-Up

Having succeeded in penetrating the Atlantic Wall the next stage for the Allies was to win the battle of the build-up; this was to ensure that supplies and reinforcements reached the area by sea no less quickly than those of the Germans reached it by land. Extensive preparations had been made for this. It was assumed that no port would be available for some time. The capture of the only one in the area, Cherbourg, was a top priority, but this would take weeks and, because of German demolitions, it would be months after that before it could be brought fully into use. Most of the men and supplies, therefore, would have to come in over the beaches, but as a significant supplement to this the invading armies brought with them their own prefabricated harbours. Two of these Mulberry harbours, as they were called, were towed over and set

American men and equipment pour out of their landing craft on to the Normandy beaches. Barrage balloons were brought as a protection against dive bombers, but were not needed.

North-West Europe.

up soon after D-Day, and although one was lost in a storm a few days later, the other proved of great value. Another effective device for speeding up supplies was an underwater pipeline for fuel, known as PLUTO (pipe line under the ocean). The storm of 19th June which wrecked one of the Mulberry harbours was of exceptional violence and for a time held up the flow of supplies, but this proceeded smoothly again when it had died down. It was not in any way hindered either by the Luftwaffe or by U-boats; the only danger which caused some concern was a new type of pressure mine which could not easily be swept.

As well as building up their own forces the Allies took effective measures to prevent the Germans from building up theirs. Shortly before D-day all Allied air forces had been switched to the bombing of communications in France. Bomber chiefs had been unwilling to break off their strategic bombing of Germany (see p. 206), persisting in their belief that the war could be won in that way and that an invasion of Europe was unnecessary. But they had been overruled and all roads and railways leading to Normandy, all bridges, marshalling yards and engine repair shops had been deluged with bombs. German troops had been able to move by road only at night and then slowly and with difficulty. In keeping German troops away from Normandy the Allies had unwitting help from Hitler who would not allow von Runstedt to bring up his reserves because of his fear of another invasion in the Pas de Calais; fourteen divisions were, therefore, kept out of action, in this area. Even at the end of July only half of these had been transferred to Normandy.

The battle of the build-up was to be another victory for the Allies. At the end of the first month they were well up to schedule with 1,100,000 troops landed along with 200,000 vehicles and 750,000 tons of supplies.

Battle of the Break-Out

Although the Germans had not been able to drive the Allies into the sea, they were able for quite a long time to prevent them from advancing further inland and extending their beachhead. In this they were greatly helped by the Normandy countryside which consisted of small fields surrounded by high, thick hedges. Such country, known as the *bocage*, was ideal for defence and made the use of tanks difficult.

On 26th June American forces captured Cherbourg, but their attempt to break out at St Lo failed, and the British attack towards Caen was repulsed. For a time there was a feeling of frustration in the Allied armies, and much of this was directed at the commander of the ground forces, General Montgomery.[1] It was felt that he was being too slow and cautious and too elaborate in his preparations. However, he himself was entirely satisfied with the way in which the battle was developing and claimed, then and later, that it was just as he had planned it. The essence of his plan was that British and Canadian forces should attack heavily towards Caen, but the main purpose of these attacks was not to break through or capture the city but to hold down in that part of the front as many German forces as possible so that on the part of the front where the Americans were to make the main attack German forces would be at their weakest. Eventually this plan was completely successful but at the time, strangely, it seems that many of the Allied commanders, including Eisenhower, were unaware of it and regarded the British failure to capture Caen as a serious setback.

The Americans were to make their big attack at the end of July. At that time there were fourteen German divisions with 600 tanks in the area of Caen, while on the American part of the front there were only nine divisions with 110 tanks. Within four days the Americans had broken right through the German ring, and their Third Army, which had been held in reserve for that purpose, poured through the gap into Brittany. The commander of this army was George Patton (see p. 216). Since the invasion of Sicily this general had had his ups and downs,[2] but his dynamism and military ability were undeniable, and in France at that time he found himself with a task for which he was supremely well suited – the pursuit and harrying of a defeated enemy.

Closing the Falaise Gap

Patton wasted no time in Brittany; the peninsula was soon sealed off, and he decided that mopping-up operations could be left to others while he directed the advance eastwards towards Paris and the Seine.

---

[1] Montgomery was to hold this position only for the opening stages of the invasion. Later General Eisenhower, who was supreme commander of all Allied forces, took it over from him.

[2] He had been in disgrace for a time after he lost his temper and struck a shell-shocked soldier.

However, a superb opportunity occurred at that moment of striking northwards to meet up with the British and Canadians advancing towards Falaise, and so trapping the whole German army in Normandy which had been ordered by Hitler to resist to the end. In the event the jaws of the trap did not snap tight until many of the Germans had escaped. Even so their losses were enormous and they had to abandon most of their tanks and heavy equipment.

The Battle of Normandy was a disaster for Germany. Total casualties amounted to 500,000 men with the loss of 3,500 guns and 1,500 tanks. At all times the Germans had fought with great courage and determination and their leaders were men of outstanding ability. The man principally responsible for the disaster was Hitler who, remote from the battlefield, insisted on taking all the main decisions. It was his order forbidding any retreat which delayed the German defeat but ensured that, when it came, it would be on a massive scale.

France Liberated

Even before the closing of the Falaise gap Patton's army had reached the Seine where further large numbers of Germans, fleeing from Normandy, were captured. By then France lay open to the Allies. On 24th August Paris was surrendered by the German commandant,[1] and the city occupied by American and Free French forces which had been rushed to the area specially for that purpose. But already by then American forces were pushing on beyond the Seine, and a new American army had landed on the Mediterranean coast of France and, meeting only light resistance, was advancing northwards.

The British and Canadians too were advancing rapidly in the northern part of the front. In the Channel Ports were large numbers of German troops – all those kept there to resist an invasion of the area which never came – with orders from Hitler to fight to the death. The capture of these vital ports was undertaken by the Canadians and was to take time. Meanwhile British forces swept onwards, over the rivers Seine and Somme, over all the French and Belgian territory which had been so bitterly disputed in the First World War, and then,

---

[1] This was against the orders of Hitler who had decreed that Paris should be razed to the ground rather than surrendered.

after a final spurt in which they covered 250 miles in a week, drove into Brussels. The following day the port of Antwerp was captured intact. This might have been of crucial importance, as a port in working order was what the Allies needed urgently; but Antwerp lies at the end of a seventy-mile channel from the sea, and this was dominated by German forces on the island of Walcheren in the Scheldt estuary. It was to be a long time – 85 days – before these were finally cleared out.

'The Underground Armies'

As the Allies advanced into Europe they received valuable help from the 'underground armies' of the occupied countries. These had been active throughout the war with acts of sabotage, intelligence reports and aid to escaping prisoners of war. However, their operations had been curtailed by the ruthless and brutal counter-measures of the Germans. Not only were Resistance fighters, when caught, tortured and put to death, but innocent hostages were shot and sometimes whole villages exterminated.

With the coming of the Allies the Resistance fighters were able to come out into the open and undertook new tasks such as guarding prisoners of war and providing guides. In France the Maquis, as Resistance fighters were called, did much to restore French national pride after the heavy defeats in the early part of the war.

German Recovery

The Allied advance from Normandy had been spectacular, but by the middle of September it had come to a halt. By then the supply situation had come under heavy strain; none of the captured Channel Ports were usable, and everything still had to be transported by road from Normandy. The shortage of petrol in particular had become acute. At the same time German resistance began to stiffen. The remnants from Normandy were being reorganised and re-equipped, new forces were arriving from the Russian front, and the defences of the Siegfried Line, which had grown somewhat rusty in recent years, were being renewed. And the Germans were now fighting with all the doggedness of a people defending their homeland. Back in 1943 the Allied leaders had announced that the only terms of peace they were prepared to accept were unconditional surrender, and the German people were terrified of what might happen to them in this event; they had visions of total chaos and their country being utterly devastated. It was this that made them fight so desperately and remain loyal to Hitler to the end.

In September 1944 with the Allied armies closing in from the east and the west, with the Luftwaffe and U-boats almost inoperative, with oil supplies running out,[1] and industry under continual bombardment from the air, it was clear that Germany was a defeated country. In determining to fight on at all costs Hitler was buoyed up by two main hopes: that the Allies would start quarrelling among themselves, and that his new 'secret weapons' would be destructive enough to bring the Allies to terms.

These 'secret weapons' included a new type of submarine and jet fighters, but the ones of which Hitler had greatest hopes were the self-propelled rockets or 'flying bombs', later known as V-1s and V-2s. These had been in the process of development for some time, but the Allies had got wind of them, and their launching sites in France had been bombed heavily. This meant that it had not been possible to bring them into action until a week after D-Day and then on a comparatively small scale. The V-1s or 'doodlebugs', as they came to be known in England, caused great damage and loss of life in London, but as they did not travel at all fast, it was found possible to destroy them in the air. The V-2s were more formidable. With them no interception was possible. However, they were very expensive and difficult to make in large numbers because of Allied bombing.[2] But they were a serious menace and provided a strong incentive for finishing the war in 1944 if possible.

Disagreements Among the Allies

Hitler's hopes that his enemies would start falling out among themselves were not without foundation. There had already been a number of differences and these became stronger as victory approached. It was becoming increasingly evident that Stalin distrusted and disliked his western allies and was determined to wring from them as many

---

[1] Shortage of petrol was becoming desperate and was crippling all German operations. The Rumanian oilfields were now in Russian hands and synthetic plants were being heavily bombed.

[2] During the winter of 1944–45 most V-2s were directed at the port of Antwerp.

Field-marshal Mongomery jokes with US generals Patton (left) and Bradley (centre). There was not always harmony between them.

concessions as possible about the future of Europe after the war. Between the British and Americans too there had been disagreements, notably the recurring question of whether or not to commit Allied troops in the Mediterranean. Churchill was always strongly in favour of this; he wanted to reinforce the Allied army in Italy so that it could advance into the Balkans and join forces with the guerrilla fighters in Yugoslavia under Marshal Tito. But for this it would be necessary to call off the invasion of southern France, as a large number of troops had been withdrawn from Italy for this purpose. Both Roosevelt and Stalin, for different reasons, were strongly opposed to this idea. Stalin regarded the Balkans as being in the Russian sphere of influence and had no wish to see an Anglo–American army arriving there before his own forces. Roosevelt, who had previously overruled his chiefs of staff on this matter, now supported them and agreed that there should be no more 'diversions', and that all available forces should be poured into France to support the main attack there. He was also desperately anxious to gain the friendship of Stalin; he was going to need his help in the war against Japan,[1] and wanted his co-operation in the re-building of Europe after the war.

There was also a major dispute at the end of 1944 among the Allied commanders in Europe about the strategy to be employed now that the advance from Normandy had been halted. Eisenhower, the supreme commander, thought that all the Allied armies should advance together at the same time along the whole front, exerting as much pressure as possible in as many places as possible. Montgomery, the British commander, strongly disagreed with this. He thought that the Germans were

---

[1] Russia did not declare war on Japan until after the end of the war in Europe.

reeling from their defeat in Normandy and were ready for a knock-out blow. He argued that the supply position made it impossible for all the Allied armies to go on the offensive, and there should, therefore, be one very heavy attack on one part of the front only. He was also clear that that part should be the one which he himself commanded in the north. If he was given the necessary forces and priority in the matter of supplies he was confident that he could carry all before him – past the Siegfried Line, over the Rhine and then, wheeling to the right, cut off the Ruhr, the industrial heartland of Germany. He would then be ready for a final drive on Berlin. This was a bold and attractive plan and, if successful, would have ended the war in 1944. However, it involved great risks and had one great disadvantage, that the remaining Allied armies would have to be kept short of petrol and ammunition, and so would have to go on the defensive; and this would not at all suit 'Roaring George' Patton and other American commanders. Making the main attack a primarily British affair would have serious political repercussions, particularly if it were to miscarry.

And so, after much heated discussion – Montgomery argued his case as forcefully as he knew how – Eisenhower decided that it was not feasible. He would not hold back Patton in the south, but he would give Montgomery's attack in the north some measure of priority.

The Battle of Arnhem

In spite of being overruled Montgomery was determined to allow the Germans no respite and to strike as heavy a blow as possible with the forces he had available. He planned to make a rapid advance into Holland, cross the Lower Rhine at Arnhem, and then strike out further north to the Zuider Zee, thereby cutting off all German forces in the Low Countries. The principal difficulty here was that the country was extremely swampy and the advance to Arnhem would have to be made up one main road only. Moreover it would be necessary to cross a large number of rivers and canals, and if any of the bridges over these were to be demolished, the operation would be held up fatally. Montgomery's solution to this problem was to make use of airborne forces. These were to be dropped in advance to capture the main bridges and then hold on until the arrival of the main British forces pushing up from the south.

This was an exciting plan but a risky one. The air armada, coming

from England, would have to pass through heavy anti-aircraft fire, and
for a time after they had landed the first troops would be very vulnerable.[1] But the main consideration was the weather. In order to transport
all four airborne divisions the aircraft would have to make three drops,
and if the weather became bad and interfered with this, it would be
critical. In the event this was what happened, and as a result the
carefully prepared timetable was disrupted. Other things too went
wrong. Although the Germans were taken by surprise they reacted
quickly and took prompt and effective counter-measures. Also there
was a breakdown of radio communications between the different
groups. But in spite of these setbacks some success was achieved. All
the bridges were captured except one – the all-important one over the
Rhine at Arnhem. Here, after a great fight, the First British Airborne
Division, or what was left of it,[2] had to be withdrawn.

The Germans Attack in the Ardennes

After the setback at Arnhem it became evident that the war would not
come to an end in 1944. For the rest of the winter Eisenhower's plan
was that all Allied armies should advance and clear out all German
forces on the near side of the Rhine. However, he and the other Allied
commanders were in for a shock. For Hitler had decided to mount a
large offensive in the west. Forces were removed from the Russian front
and others were found elsewhere, and by 16th December this formidable new army was ready to strike. The place chosen for the attack was
the Ardennes (see map on p. 226) where German armoured forces had
broken through in 1940; and the German plan was similar to the one
which had been so successful then. The Panzers were to break through
to the Meuse and were then to wheel northwards to Antwerp and so cut
off the Allied armies in Holland. The plan was a desperate one and had
little chance of complete success, but Hitler hoped that it would gain
time for him and might induce the Allies to negotiate.

At first the operation went according to plan. The Allies, thinking
that Germany was on the verge of defeat, did not believe that an

---

[1] This was to be the largest airborne operation ever, involving about 1,000 troop carriers
and 500 gliders.
[2] 2,400 out of 9,000.

offensive on this scale was possible and were completely taken by surprise. The Ardennes was held only lightly by American troops, and these were pushed right back so that there was a large bulge in the Allied line. However, the Americans fought back vigorously and the Germans failed to reach the Meuse, and with some help from the British from the north the situation was restored.

The Ardennes offensive was Hitler's last fling. The troops taken from the Russian front were badly needed there and the Russian advance began to gather momentum.[1] In the west the Allies were checked, but only for a time, and when they started moving again Hitler would have no reserves with which to meet them.

Crossing the Rhine

At the beginning of February 1945 the Allies were able to resume their task of clearing German forces from the west bank of the Rhine. For the British and the Canadians in the north this meant a long, hard slog through the mud and floodwaters of Holland. However, in conjunction with the American Ninth Army, this resulted in a notable victory. A large haul of prisoners was taken and, even more important, nearly all German armoured forces were drawn to that part of the front so that when the American armies of General Bradley attacked in the centre and the south opposition was less strong than it might have been. Certainly Bradley and Patton made brilliant use of their opportunity. On 6th March Cologne was captured, and on the following day, to their surprise and delight, American forces captured intact a bridge over the Rhine at Remagen. Meanwhile in the south Patton had been pushing ahead forcefully and on 22nd March (to his great satisfaction) he forced a crossing of the Rhine just one day before the main crossing by Montgomery's armies in the north. For the latter extensive preparations had been made, as the Rhine in that area was 500 yards wide, double that further upstream. Airborne forces, numerous amphibious vehicles and large quantities of bridging equipment had been amassed for the operation which, in the event, was to proceed without hitch. By the

---

[1] The Russians had advanced into Poland during the summer and had since occupied most of Rumania, Hungary and Yugoslavia. Their last great offensive opened at the beginning of January 1945 and by the end of the month they were in Germany.

second day (24th March) British forces had advanced six miles beyond the river, and two days later twelve bridges were in operation. Just over a week later American forces had surrounded the Ruhr. Here the Germans might have held out for a long time, but on 18th April some 350,000 of them surrendered.

The Last Phase

Already before the mass surrender in the Ruhr the advance troops of the American army had reached the river Elbe, and Eisenhower had then had to make a difficult decision. Should he drive on to Berlin and reach the city before the Russians? Or should he drive into central Germany where there was the possibility of some elements of the German army making a last-ditch stand in the Bavarian Alps? This caused some dissension among the Allies. Relations with the Russians were deteriorating, and Churchill was eager to get to Berlin first, but the Americans thought this would not be worth the heavy losses which might be involved. In the end this view prevailed and, in order to prevent the possibility of any accidental clashes with the Russians, Eisenhower halted the main part of the Allied armies on the Elbe. In the north the British advanced along the Baltic coast, and in the south Patton could not be restrained from entering Czechoslovakia although, following Russian objections, he was not allowed to take Prague.

German resistance was now almost at an end. Russian troops reached Berlin on 21st April, and four days later Russian and American forces joined up near Leipzig. At the same time came news from Italy that the German army there had capitulated. Hitler was now at bay in his underground fortress in Berlin where he had resolved to stay till the end. He was by now a sick man and had become deranged. He was obsessed with the idea that the German people had failed him and were not worthy of him, and that he and they should perish together. He ordered that everywhere a scorched earth policy should be carried out with everything in the path of the invading armies being destroyed. Although this order was not obeyed, it was extraordinary how much his authority lasted to the end. On 30th April, as the Russians closed in, Hitler committed suicide after nominating Admiral Doenitz as his successor. A week later the new government signed terms of unconditional surrender.

During the five and a half years of the war in Europe there had often

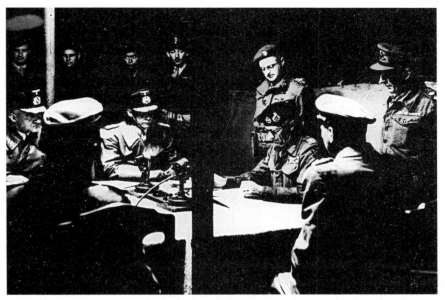

Montgomery in his headquarters on Luneberg Heath dictates terms of surrender to German commanders.

British and Russian troops on the balcony of the German Chancellery from where Hitler had made many of his speeches.

been disagreement among the Allies when the alliance had come under strain, but always hatred of the evils of Nazism and all that Hitler stood for had been enough to keep them together. Just how great these evils were was revealed horrendously as the Allies entered Germany and uncovered the 'death camps'. These were Hitler's extermination centres – complete with gas chambers, incinerators and special railway sidings where Jews, gypsies and so-called 'undesirables' were unloaded from cattle wagons before being put to death. The scenes of misery and degradation in these camps were so appalling that some who witnessed them never recovered from the experience. Perhaps never has man's inhumanity to man been on such a scale. Any doubts about the justness of the Allied cause in the Second World War must have been removed by what the 'horror camps' revealed.

The Defeat of Japan

The Americans Close In

When making their war plans the more far-seeing of Japan's leaders had realised that, although everything might go their way for the first year, after that they would be fighting a losing battle. They knew how much greater were American resources both in manpower and industrial capacity,[1] and that when these were fully mobilised and the war in Europe was over, Japan must be defeated. They realised too how vulnerable Japan was for, like Britain, she depended heavily on overseas trade; much of the country's food, all oil and most raw materials had to come from abroad, and if command of the seas was lost and these supplies cut off, the country's situation would be desperate. The hope of some Japanese was that by forming a strong defensive belt round Japan and by fighting to the bitter end they could make the cost of total victory for the Allies in terms of material and men's lives so great that they would come to terms.

The task ahead of the Americans was, indeed, formidable. They had to gain mastery in the air and on sea, and then make a number of seaborne attacks against heavily defended Pacific islands. Here the

---

[1] It was estimated that Japanese industrial capacity was about one-tenth of that of the United States. Steel production was one-thirteenth.

conditions of fighting would be grim – dense jungle, hot steamy climate and an enemy who would fight fanatically until killed. However, there was no lack of determination among Americans to see the war through to the end. Although it had been laid down officially that the war in Europe was to have priority,[1] many Americans regarded Japan as the main enemy and were eager to avenge Pearl Harbour and the defeat in the Philippines.

In breaking through the Japanese outposts in the Pacific the strategy of General MacArthur, the supreme commander, was to attack only the key islands; those in between, having been rendered unusable, were left to 'wither on the vine'. This process of bypassing certain islands or 'leap-frogging', as it was called, began in August 1942 in the Solomon Islands where the main target was Guadalcanal. Here the fighting was prolonged and intense, and Japanese resistance was not worn down until seven months later. Losses on both sides were heavy, but these could be borne more easily by the United States than by Japan. In particular the Japanese lost 600 irreplaceable aircraft pilots. The Americans were gaining control in the air and this would lead, inevitably, to command of the seas.

At the same time as the battle for Guadalcanal was raging American and Australian forces were having a hard, long fight in New Guinea, and had cleared the Japanese out of Papua which removed the threat to communications with Australia; it also established a base from which the next leap forward could be made. During the remainder of 1943 the Americans occupied the Gilbert and Marshall Islands, and in June 1944 they broke into the Marianas from where the Japanese mainland was within bombing range. Then in September came the operation to which MacArthur had been most looking forward, his return to the Philippines. Here Japanese resistance was fiercer than ever, including 1,900 'suicide bombers' (Kamikaze). The remnants of the Japanese fleet, led by the mighty battleship *Yamamoto*,[2] were also brought into action, but without air support this was in effect another suicide mission and most of the ships, including the *Yamamoto* were sunk by aircraft. After this

---

[1] In spite of this decision for six months after Pearl Harbour the flow of men and resources to the Far East was twice that to Europe.

[2] With her 18-inch guns the most powerful ship afloat at that time.

command of the seas passed almost completely to the United States. The ring round Japan would move in ever closer.

The Reconquest of Burma

While the Americans were closing in on the Japanese in the Pacific, British and Indian forces had won a notable victory in Burma. Since arriving on the borders of India in the spring of 1942 the Japanese had for a time made no attempt to advance any further. They had achieved their main objective which was to close the Burma Road so that Allied supplies to China were cut off.[1] Also they had routed the British forces in such a way that there was little chance of their being able to fight back effectively for the time being. Moreover there were political troubles in India at that time. Talks about independence had broken down, and Britain had found it necessary to arrest a number of Indian political leaders who had advocated helping the Japanese. This had caused widespread unrest and, although it died down in time, it had meant that forces from Burma had had to be brought back to maintain order in India.

The difficulties facing the British in mounting an offensive in Burma were formidable. There were few good roads or railways from India to the Burmese frontier which meant that there was always a problem about supply. Also the morale of the British Fourteenth Army was low. This was partly due to the extremely rigorous conditions of jungle warfare and the fact that during the long retreat the Japanese had shown themselves better able to survive these. There was too a feeling among the troops in Burma that they were being neglected by the government and people back at home. It seemed to them that all eyes were focused on the war in Europe and there was little recognition of what they were enduring and achieving. It was with some bitterness that they referred to themselves as 'The Forgotten Army'.

However, when British fortunes were at their lowest, the tide began to turn. It was realised that reconstituting and revitalising the Fourteenth Army would be an immense task, but it would be possible provided that

---

[1] At the time China was rent by civil war between the Nationalist forces of Chiang Kai-shek and the Communists led by Mao Tse-tung, but the Chinese were still containing the majority of the Japanese army (see p. 193).

Chindits make their way with mule through the Burmese jungle.

time was allowed. The first task was to win command in the air, and with the construction of new airfields and the arrival on the scene of modern aircraft this was achieved in 1943. At the same time the morale of British troops was boosted by the activities of special forces behind the Japanese lines. These forces, which came to be known as 'Chindits', were led by a brilliant and unorthodox soldier, Orde Wingate, who had had experience of guerrilla fighting in Abyssinia. The first Chindit operation suffered considerable losses and achieved little in material terms apart from the blowing up of bridges and railway lines and generally harassing the Japanese. However, it did show that British troops, when properly trained and well led, were more than a match for the Japanese in jungle fighting. Also an important lesson had been learned which was that, if full use was made of air power and radio communications, quite large forces could be kept supplied by drops from the air. Later this was to prove vital.

During 1943 and the first part of 1944 the re-equipping and retraining of the Fourteenth Army made great progress. This was in large measure due to its commander, William Slim, a man of outstanding ability. Modest, unassuming and shunning the limelight, Slim had great drive and determination and an exceptional gift for getting the best out of the men under him. Under his command 'The Forgotten Army' regained its self-respect and, when the time came, surged ahead from one victory to another.

The first major test came in the spring of 1944 when the Japanese launched an offensive towards the two key towns of Imphal and Kohima. But Slim took prompt action. He airlifted troops into the area from another part of the front and then kept them supplied during a long and gruelling siege. And in the ensuing battle of endurance it was the British and Indian troops who prevailed. The Japanese commander was incompetent and his troops so badly supplied that even they could not keep going. In June they made a complete withdrawal. Then, in spite of the fact that it was the monsoon season, Slim gave the order to advance. The conditions were appalling – deep mud, thick tangled undergrowth, leeches, pythons and sheeting rain so that the men were always soaked to the skin – but the men of 'The Forgotten Army' pressed on. They had been well prepared and this time malaria took only a small toll. At every stage supplies were brought to them by air, as Churchill described it, 'like manna from above'. By December they had crossed the Irrawaddy river. By April 1945 they had captured Mandalay and a month later were in Rangoon. In the north of the country meanwhile the Chinese and American forces under General Stilwell had advanced and re-established a supply route into China.

The victory in Burma was then complete. The Japanese had been outfought and out-generaled. The basis of the victory had been the overcoming of the problems of supply and disease. Here the Japanese had failed and their starving and disease-ridden soldiers had been left to fend for themselves. In this, it should be said, some of them performed unbelievable feats of heroism and endurance.

The Final Surrender

After the invasion of the Philippines the Americans planned to take two more islands before the final assault on the Japanese mainland. The capture of Iwo Jima and Okinawa took up the first half of 1945. Once again the Japanese resisted fanatically. American losses were high and, on the basis of these, terrifying estimates were made of what the death-

Japanese officer surrenders his sword as token of submission.

roll might be in the final invasion. For this a British fleet was now on the scene and it was planned to bring out a large army. However, in the event both the Allies and Japan were spared this bloodbath. For some time British and American scientists had been working on the manufacture of an atomic bomb, and on 17th July one was successfully exploded in the Mexican desert.

The question of whether or not to use the bomb against the Japanese was an intensely difficult one. It rested with President Truman who had succeeded Roosevelt on the latter's death in April 1945. A hitherto unknown politician of no great standing, it was for him an awesome responsibility. But he faced up to it manfully and came to a clear decision, supported by Churchill, that the bomb should be used. It would cause fearful destruction and loss of life and some of its after-effects, notably from radioactive dust, were incalculable. However, it was estimated that perhaps as many as a million Allied casualties would be saved, and that loss of life among the Japanese too would be far less than if an invasion were to be carried out.[1] On 26th July Allied leaders called on Japan to surrender or face complete destruction. Then, when there was no response, an atomic bomb was dropped on Hiroshima on 6th August and another on Nagasaki three days later (see p. 320). Then at last on 10th August Japan surrendered. 'The atomic bomb had,' as Churchill later wrote, 'brought a speedy end to the Second World War and perhaps to much else besides.'

---

[1] Dead and injured among the Japanese from the two atomic bombs dropped amounted to about 280,000.

Timescale

1942

August	9	Germans reach Caucasus.
	19	Battle of Stalingrad begins.

1943

January	31	Surrender of German Sixth Army at Stalingrad.
July	4	Battle of Kursk begins.
	9	Allies land in Sicily.
	25	Mussolini deposed.
September	3	Allies land on mainland of Italy.
	7	Italians sign armistice.
	9	Allied landing at Salerno.

1944

January	21	Allied landing at Anzio.
February	15	Battle of Cassino begins.
June	6	D-Day. Allies land in Normandy.
July	27–31	Americans break through into Brittany.
August	15	American landings in south of France.
	25	Allies enter Paris.
September	3	British enter Brussels.
	17	Battle of Arnhem begins.
December	16	German offensive in Ardennes begins.

1945

March	22–23	Allies cross the Rhine.
April	30	Hitler commits suicide.
May	4	Germans sign armistice.
	7	Germans agree to unconditional surrender.
	3	British Fourteenth Army captures Rangoon.
June		Capture of Marianas brings Japan into range of American bombers.
August	6	Atom bomb dropped on Hiroshima.
	9	Atom bomb dropped on Nagasaki.
	10	Surrender of Japan.

Chapter 15

EUROPE IN CHAOS

The Aftermath of War

With the coming of peace fearful responsibilities were lifted from the shoulders of Allied leaders; they no longer had to send men into battle nor order the destruction of whole cities; but the war left a daunting legacy of chaos and misery. Some European cities were no more than piles of rubble, many millions were homeless and many more stateless refugees. Everywhere there was a desperate shortage of food, fuel and the necessities of life; the main transport systems had been shattered; and in some places money had become virtually worthless – cigarettes or tins of food being a more effective form of currency.

The number of people killed had been less than in the First World War; but damage to property and disruption of civilian life had been much greater. In 1914–18 most of the actual fighting had been confined to the battlefields of France and Belgium, but in the Second World War, owing to air raids and the movements of great armies over great distances, there had been widespread destruction of houses, factories, railways, bridges and roads. Many civilians had been killed and many more bombed out of their homes; many too had been expelled from their homes or taken off to work in foreign countries.

The worst devastation had occurred in Russia, Germany and Poland; it was there that starving people were eking out some form of existence in holes and hovels of ruined cities. It was here too that millions of people, who had fled from invading armies or been evicted from their homes, were roaming the country, to be accommodated eventually in camps for 'displaced persons'. In other countries damage and disruption, though on a smaller scale, had still been formidable, notably in Italy where there had been a long hard-fought campaign over the whole length of the country. In France there had been great destruction in Normandy where the fighting after D-Day had taken place; and the country's roads and railways had suffered heavily from Allied air raids;

but Paris and other large cities had escaped comparatively lightly. In Britain London and other cities had taken a heavy battering from air raids and people were war-weary and on short rations, but because there had been no foreign invasion there had been less interference with everyday life than in other countries. The war had brought changes but not upheavals.

Very different was the situation in America at the end of the war. Here there had been no destruction and, despite enormous war expenditure, the economy was booming, shortages were almost unknown, and the country was by far the richest and most powerful in the world. Europe was to have great need of America in the years ahead.

The Break-up of the Grand Alliance

Although the coming of peace was greeted with great rejoicing and thankfulness, there were many at the time who had deep fears for the future. Winston Churchill recorded that on VE Day, the moment of his greatest triumph, there were few whose hearts were more heavily burdened with anxiety than his own. For Churchill had already realised

Belsen concentration camp after the arrival of allied forces.

what others were only beginning to suspect that the Grand Alliance of Britain, Russia and the United States was at an end, and that Britain's principal war aims, notably the independence of Poland and the right of people everywhere to choose their own type of government, were not going to be achieved. He realised too that Europe was facing a new sinister threat from Soviet Russia. At the same time Britain's days as a world power were ending.

Ever since the German invasion of Russia Churchill had tried hard to establish trust and friendship with the Russian leaders, but he had usually been met with cold response. Before the war relations between the two countries had been, almost always, suspicious and hostile. Churchill himself had been one of the most vehement and outspoken opponents of Communism. After the First World War he had spoken of 'the baboonery of Bolshevism' and it was he, more than anyone, who had been responsible for sending British troops to assist the White Russians in their fight against the Communists (see p. 105). Later Stalin and other Russian leaders became convinced that the capitalist countries were planning to surround Russia so that Communism was hemmed in and would ultimately be destroyed. This feeling came to a climax at the time of the Munich settlement (see p. 143) when it seemed to Stalin that the Western powers had made a deal with Hitler in order to divert him away from themselves and towards Russia. From then on it became Stalin's main object to break up this alliance, and he regarded it as a great triumph when in 1939 he signed a treaty of friendship with Hitler which led to the invasion of Poland and Britain and France declaring war on Germany.

For the first twenty months of the war Stalin was openly friendly with Hitler, hoping that by appeasing him he would avoid a German invasion. In June 1941 it was shown how dreadfully mistaken this policy had been and in the following years Russia was to pay a terrible price for it. But even in the darkest moments of the war, when Russia was almost at her last gasp, Stalin was reluctant to stretch out the hand of friendship to the Western powers; he could not rid himself of his old suspicions. He was convinced (perhaps because it was what he himself would have done in their position) that the Allies were deliberately delaying the opening of a second front in Europe so that Germany and Russia would destroy each other. He was deeply suspicious too of Churchill's ideas of invading the Balkans, and in the closing stages of

The 'Big Three' (Chruchill, Roosevelt and Stalin) meet in the Crimea, February 1945.

New 'Big Three' (Atlee, Truman and Stalin) meet at Potsdam, July 1945. Also present Ernest Bevin (second from left), new British foreign secretary and Russian foreign secretary Molotov (right).

the war he was obsessed by the thought that the Allies would make a separate peace with Germany, leaving Russia to her fate. Later again, perhaps with more reason, he was resentful that he had not been told about the development of the atom bomb until the last moment, and then that the Allies were not prepared to share its secrets with him.

For a long time, despite insults and complaints, Churchill had persevered resolutely in his attempts to come to an understanding with Stalin, hoping that 'with the deepening experience of comradeship in arms against Hitler the countries would be drawn together.' Certainly he was prepared to forgive much in consideration of the heroic Russian resistance to Hitler's armies. However, as the fortunes of war turned in favour of the Allies and the danger from Germany diminished, Stalin became more and more insistent in his demands: he required that the Western powers should recognise his claims for territory in Poland, Rumania, Finland, Turkey, Persia and even North Africa. Bearing in mind Russia's immense war losses and appreciating her need for maximum security from invasion in the future, Britain and America were not unsympathetic to some of the Russian claims; but some were in flagrant breach of the Allied war aims as set out in the Atlantic Charter[1] (see p. 8). This stated positively that there would be no territorial changes without the consent of the people concerned and that all people everywhere had the right to choose the form of government under which they would live.

At first Britain and America made a number of concessions to Russia, but when it became evident that this had the effect not of lessening Russia's demands but of increasing them, it was necessary to stand firm.

Poland

Hitler was always convinced that the Grand Alliance of Communist Russia, capitalist America and imperialist Britain could not last and that before the end of the war the differences between them would have become so great that they would fall out among themselves. In this he was not altogether mistaken; it was only dread of him and all his works

---

[1] A statement of principles for post-war world issued after the first meeting between Churchill and Roosevelt in August 1941.

that kept them together; once he was removed from the scene wide disagreements did, indeed, arise. There were a number of points at issue, but the most important was that of Poland, on which both Britain and Russia had strong feelings.

It was to save Poland that Britain had declared war in 1939 and there would be no true victory if at the end of the war Poland was not free and independent. To the Russian leaders, however, Poland held the key to her security; for it was through Poland that any invading forces from the West would have to pass. A friendly government in Poland was, therefore, essential to them and this could only be a Communist government.

Since the Russian invasion of Poland in 1939 (see p. 147) relations between the Russians and the Polish government in exile in London had been very strained, and in 1943 diplomatic relations were broken off when the Poles asked the International Red Cross to investigate the mass grave, discovered by the Germans at Katyn which contained the bodies of hundreds of Polish officers said to have been killed by the Russians.[1] In August 1944, when the Russians were driving the Germans back into Poland, the Polish underground army in Warsaw, on orders from the government in exile, rose in revolt against the Germans, but they received no help from the Russians; the Russian army halted its advance outside Warsaw, and it seemed that they were deliberately standing by and allowing the Poles to be slaughtered. Whether or not this was the case, they certainly made it difficult for anyone else to bring help to the beleaguered Poles.

At the Yalta Conference at the end of the war Stalin promised that there would be free elections in Poland, but later, when he realised that these would result in a government not altogether friendly to Russia, he went back on his word. At the beginning of 1944 the Russians set up a 'Government of National Unity' which included other parties besides Communists, but with the Russian army behind them it was not long before the Communists gained the upper hand.

The question of Poland's frontiers was also discussed at Yalta where it was agreed that Russia should keep the part of Poland which she had taken in 1939[2] and that Poland should be compensated with part of East

---

[1] After the war established as a fact.
[2] This had been part of Russia before 1918.

Germany, the actual frontiers to be fixed at the peace conference. In this matter too Stalin did not keep his word; the Poles, with Russian support, were allowed to take over a much larger part of Germany so that more than seven million Germans were driven from their homes. At the time Churchill urged strongly that the Allies should stand firm on this issue and, if necessary, have an open confrontation, but the Americans disagreed and Churchill was soon to be out of office.

Germany

The question which caused the greatest disagreement between Russia and the West and which nearly brought war between them was that of Germany. For a brief time after the war there was a measure of unity. The zones of each of the occupying powers were agreed, and a Control Commission was set up for the whole country. There was no thought then of dividing the country in two, and the Russians were making no great efforts to impose Communism in their zone. They were more interested in keeping Germany weak so that she would never again be a threat to Russia. At first the Western powers were in agreement about this: Germany was to be completely disarmed and demilitarised and her industrial capacity reduced. Also the country was to be purged of Nazism and the principal Nazi leaders were to be brought to trial.

These trials took place in Nuremberg where the charges against the Nazis fell into two main groups: the waging of aggressive war and crimes against humanity including the death camps, the shooting of prisoners of war and the imposition of forced labour. On the first of these the Court ran into difficulties as the defendants were able to produce numerous cases from history of aggressive war being waged by such kings and emperors as Louis XIV and Napoleon. They also pointed out that Russia had been branded an aggressor by the League of Nations for her attack in Finland in 1939 (see p. 151), and if Germany had invaded Poland, so too had she. On the second group of charges the Nazis were on much weaker ground, although they tried to put all the blame on to Hitler and the dead Gestapo chief, Himmler, pleading that they knew nothing about the atrocities or were only obeying orders. In the end some of them were sentenced to death and others to terms of imprisonment. At the time some people were uneasy about executing in cold blood the leaders of a defeated country, a proceeding without precedent in history. Others felt that the crimes of the Nazis were so great that they called for unique retribution.

Allied unity on Germany did not last long. It came to an abrupt end in the spring of 1946. The main reason for this was the matter of reparations which the Russians were determined should be as large as possible. These mainly took the form of industrial plant and machinery, large quantities of which had been despatched from the industrial areas in the Western zones to Russia. But the British and Americans expected that in return the Russians would send to them food from the agricultural lands in their zone; but this the Russians did not do. The consequence of this was that in order to prevent the Germans in their zones from starving the Western powers had to buy food from abroad – something which the British, with a tottering economy, could ill afford to do. Obviously this situation could not last: as fast as the Russians were taking resources out of the country, the British and Americans were bringing them back, thus in effect paying for Germany's reparations. And so on 3rd May 1946 the Americans announced that no more reparations would be sent from the Western zones for the time being. This was a turning point in post-war Germany. From now on the idea of a weak and united Germany began to fade, and more and more the country came to be divided into two parts, East and West. In the East the Russians began to impose Communism and in the West the British and Americans began to rebuild German industry on capitalist lines.

It soon became evident to the Western powers that the policy of deliberately keeping Germany weak was not feasible. The economies of the Western European countries were too dependent on each other, so that if Germany was weak, so too would be other countries. Also if Germany was going to pay for the food she needed for her large population,[1] she could only do so by the export of manufactured goods. For a time Germany's economy was caught in a vicious circle: food could only be paid for by exports which needed raw materials from abroad which could also only be paid for by exports. This cycle was eventually broken by massive aid from the United States which enabled

---

[1] Although some four and a half million Germans had been killed in the war, her population in 1945 was seven million higher than in 1937. This was due to between ten and twelve million refugees from East Europe.

the German 'economic miracle' to take place and Western Germany to emerge as the strongest capitalist country in Europe. This was, of course, exactly what the Russians wanted to avoid and so they did all they could to strengthen and consolidate the countries of Eastern Europe, including East Germany, under their control.

And so Germany reaped a rich harvest from the divisions and quarrels of her conquerors. She soon came to be regarded no longer as a defeated enemy to be subdued and kept down but as a future ally who was to be strengthened and whose goodwill was to be won.

Communism in Eastern Europe

During the last part of the war Winston Churchill had been very uneasy at the thought of Russian troops occupying the countries of Eastern Europe. He thought that once they were there they would remain and would impose Communist types of government. Accordingly he urged strongly that the Allied army in Italy should be reinforced and allowed to invade the Balkans. Later in the war too, during the invasion of Germany, he had urged General Eisenhower to allow his forces to advance so that they could occupy Vienna and Prague. But the Americans, still hopeful of coming to terms with the Russians, held back and let them get there first. Three years later it was evident how well-founded had been Churchill's fears: by then seven countries of Eastern Europe were under Communist domination.

Stalin did not impose Communism on Eastern Europe at once; the process was gradual and cautious. In two countries no imposition was necessary: in Yugoslavia the Communist resistance fighters of Josip Tito took over the government immediately after the war, and in Albania those of Enver Hoxha did the same. In other countries, however, Communism came only with pressure from the Russians or, as Tito later put it, 'on the bayonets of the Red Army'.

The pattern of Communist takeovers was always the same. First there would be a coalition government in which Communists shared power with other parties, but made sure that they held the key posts, particularly those controlling the police and armed forces. Then, in time, the Communist leaders, most of whom were Moscow-trained, would seek to discredit and destroy their opponents. Sometimes these fought back, but always there was the menacing spectre of the Russian army in the background. Thus in Bulgaria in September 1946 the monarchy was abolished and a People's Republic set up, and a year later the Communists were in complete control. In Rumania it took them longer to build up their power and it was not until the end of 1947 that King Michael was forced to abdicate. At the time the Communists were a small minority in parliament but by skilful manoeuvring and intimidation of their opponents they managed to gain the upper hand; but it was not until ten years later that it was considered safe for the Russian army to be withdrawn from the country. In Hungary the anti-Communist Smallholders' Party won a clear majority in the election of 1945 but were not allowed by the Russians to form a government on their own. In the years following there was strong opposition to the Communists, particularly from the Roman Catholic Church, but in the end this was unavailing and by 1948 the Communists were in control. In Poland, in spite of Stalin's promise at Yalta, elections were not held until 1947 and then they were certainly not free, having been rigged in order to exclude the Peasant Party which derived from the anti-Communist wartime government in exile in London. From then on the Communists here too became all-powerful.

The country to hold out longest against Communism was Czechoslovakia. In the elections of 1946 the Communist Party won only 114 seats out of 300. A coalition ensued and in the next years, as was their usual custom, the Communists managed to pack the police with their supporters and to gain control of the radio services and printing unions. The showdown came at the beginning of 1948 when, with the country on the brink of civil war and a Russian army poised to intervene, President Benes, a highly respected figure, felt obliged to accept a Communist-dominated government. Two weeks later the country's principal anti-Communist, Jan Masaryk, the son of Czechoslovakia's first president, died in mysterious circumstances.[1] Soon afterwards a Communist-style general election was held – one in which no opposition parties were allowed to stand. This was followed by the retirement and death of Benes and thereafter the Communist takeover was complete.

---

[1] He fell from a window of the Foreign Ministry. It has not been conclusively established whether this was suicide or murder.

Russian Intentions

After the war, under the plea that they must have maximum security from another German invasion, the Russians had taken possession of territories in Poland, Rumania and Eastern Germany; they also took over the Baltic States of Estonia, Latvia and Lithuania and regained territory from Japan in the Far East. Altogether some twenty-four million people had been added to the Soviet Union. And further claims were made to parts of Iran, Turkey and Finland.

At first the Western powers, bearing in mind how often Russia had been invaded in the past and eager to gain her friendship, had some sympathy for her demands; but it was not long before they became seriously alarmed and wondered what were the true motives of the mysterious men in the Kremlin.[1] Did they really want nothing more than security for their country with a protective belt of friendly Communist countries? Or was this demand for security merely a cloak to conceal other designs? Was their main aim to extend Communism into Western Europe and the rest of the world? And did they have genuine fears about a Western threat to Russia? Or was it necessary for them to fabricate this in order to create a sense of danger at home to justify their tyrannical government and to require even greater efforts and sacrifices from the long-suffering Russian people? Whatever may have been their true motives, most European and American leaders soon became convinced that Russian policy was to bring down the capitalist countries by undermining their economies and by causing trouble for them at home and abroad. It also became evident to them that Winston Churchill was right when he said that the Russians respect strength and despise weakness and that concessions made to them as goodwill gestures are looked on by them as signs of weakness. From this it followed logically that the Western countries should lose no time in rebuilding their armed forces.

---

[1] Winston Churchill once described Russian actions as 'a riddle wrapped in a mystery inside an enigma'.

The United Nations Organisation

In the last years of the war President Roosevelt had stressed the importance of a new international organisation which would take the place of the League of Nations and be responsible for keeping the peace of the world.

The United Nations Organisation (UNO) came into being in 1945 when fifty nations at San Francisco signed its charter. The new organisation was to have a General Assembly where all countries had equal voting rights, but the task of keeping the peace fell mainly on the Security Council where there were five permanent members (United States, Russia, Britain, France and China). On Russian insistence no decision could be taken unless all of these agreed; this meant that each of the permanent members had the right to block or 'veto' a decision, and this was much resented by smaller countries. In the post-war years the Russians used their veto frequently which did much to hamstring the workings of UNO and to make it ineffective. Consequently some countries lost faith in it and felt that they could not rely on it for protection and must, therefore, take independent action. However, UNO has always carried more weight than the League of Nations ever did.

Chapter 16

POST-WAR BRITAIN

A Massive Labour Victory

At the end of the war in Europe Churchill and some of the leaders of
the Labour Party wanted to continue the National Government until the
end of the war against Japan. But the majority of the Labour Party
thought otherwise and so the coalition was ended at once and a general
election held as soon as possible. At the time most people thought the
Conservatives would win; it was considered unlikely that the country
would turn against Churchill in his moment of triumph and remove him
from office before victory was complete. But when the result became
known it showed a massive Labour victory with a majority over all
other parties of more than 150. The people of Britain had decided that
it was time for a change. They remembered the distress of the years
between the wars – the unemployment, the poverty and squalor – and
held the Conservatives mainly responsible for these. And so, much as
they admired Churchill as a war leader, they felt he was not the man
to establish a new order in Britain.

The Labour Government

The Labour government which took office in 1945 was a strong team.
Most of the leading members had had experience of office in the wartime coalition and were men of ability and stature. The prime minister,
Clement Attlee, had been leader of the Labour Party since 1935 and
deputy prime minister since 1940. In nearly every way he was a complete contrast to Churchill – a man of few words, no orator, unimpressive looking and completely lacking in showmanship. Churchill
is said to have once described him as 'a sheep in sheep's clothing', but
this was a misjudgment. In the years ahead Attlee was to show himself
a firm and capable leader and in some ways a more effective and

businesslike prime minister than Churchill. If Attlee was low key and unassuming the same cannot be said of his two principal colleagues – Herbert Morrison and Ernest Bevin. Morrison, the son of a policeman and a one-time errand boy, had been Home Secretary during the war and the man mainly responsible for Labour's 1945 election victory. Bevin too had come from a working-class home and had been a van driver for a mineral water firm before becoming a full-time official of the Dockers' Union. He had also played the main part in building up the country's largest trade union – the Transport and General Workers' Union. During the war he had had one of the hardest jobs in the government, that of Minister of Labour where he had been in charge of mobilising and directing all resources of manpower. This involved taking some very unpopular measures, but working people had been ready to accept them from him. Bluff, rugged, genial and in every sense a heavyweight, Bevin had unique influence with the rank and file of the trade unions. As a trade union negotiator he had been tough but flexible, qualities he was also going to need when, as foreign secretary, he was to carry on hard and frustrating negotiations with the Russians.

Labour Objectives

The Labour Government had set itself a heavy programme for its period of office. It intended to nationalise a number of industries including the coalmines, the railways, road transport and gas and electricity undertakings. It was also committed to introducing a national insurance scheme and a national health service. Such a programme would have been formidable at the best of times, but in the post-war years, with the national economy never far from collapse, it was exceptionally difficult. It was a considerable achievement that it managed to carry it out.

Britain's economic plight in 1945 did, indeed, seem desperate. Early in the war all the country's foreign investments[1] had been sold and huge debts had been incurred. Since 1941 the British economy had been entirely dependent on Lend-Lease (see p. 188), but at the end of the war this had ceased abruptly, and Britain was left to fend for herself in very disadvantageous circumstances. In order to pay the interest on her

---

[1] These were mainly shares in foreign companies which brought in large amounts of foreign currency.

Ernest Bevin, a massive figure and minister of labour during the war,
joins factory workers in the canteen queue.

debts and to buy raw materials for industry and enough food not only
for her own people but also for the Germans in the British zone (see
p. 251), it was reckoned that Britain would have to export nearly twice
as much as before the war; and in 1945 this was impossible. In the first
place, due to the war, Britain had lost many of her old export markets,
and not all of these could be regained. Also Britain did not have at that
time the necessary industrial capacity; most of her industry had been
turned over to war production, much of it had suffered from bomb
damage and much of what remained was worn out or obsolete. A
complete reorganisation and re-equipment was needed; but in order to
keep going in the meanwhile help from abroad was essential, and this
could only come from the United States. It will be seen later (p. 268)
that America was to respond magnificently to this need but at first,
partly perhaps because of her dislike of the socialist measures of the
Labour Government, there was some reserve. A large loan was made
available, but on hard terms which were to cause great difficulty in the
future.

In the years after the war the relentless problem of every British
government was to be to strike some sort of balance between the
country's exports and imports without causing widespread unemployment.
Methods of achieving this varied; those of the post-war Labour Government were to restrict spending at home by rationing and heavy taxation

and to build up exports by every possible means. This policy was mainly associated with Labour's second Chancellor of the Exchequer, Sir Stafford Cripps. Before the war Cripps had been a highly successful lawyer with extreme political views which had caused him to be expelled from the Labour Party. However, he was later readmitted, and during the war was a member, albeit an uneasy one, of Churchill's government. When Cripps became Chancellor at the end of 1947 the country's economic crisis had become acute. A devout Christian and a man of austere habits (he was a vegetarian and a teetotaller), Cripps was clear what had to be done: the British people must tighten their belts, cut down their spending and eliminate luxuries. This was certainly not a popular policy but it says much for Cripps's force of character that for a time he induced the British people to accept it. In the struggle he never spared himself. Ill health forced him to retire in 1950 and he died soon afterwards.

Nationalisation

During the successive post-war economic crises the Conservatives strongly urged the government to put off their nationalisation plans and to concentrate on more urgent matters; but the government was not to be deflected and went ahead with its programme. To some of its measures there was only small opposition. Most people felt it was inevitable that the coalmines should be taken into public ownership; many of the pits were run down, productivity was low and labour relations were bad. It was hoped that nationalisation would bring not only new capital but a new spirit into the industry. There was too a strong case for nationalising the railways. These had been used heavily during the war when little had been done to maintain or improve them. Now huge sums were needed to restore them, and these would be beyond the means of the railway companies. And so in 1948 all the railway companies – the London Midland Scottish, the Great Western, the Southern and the London North Eastern – were taken over and merged to form British Railways. To the nationalisation of road transport and, later, steel there was stronger opposition, as the reasons in these cases were theoretical rather than practical. There was nothing wrong with the industries – indeed they were flourishing – but Socialism required that all basic industries should be in public ownership.

The Welfare State

The Beveridge Report

During the Second World War, as in the First, there was great hope among the forces taking part that they were fighting for a better world. Many remembered how, after the First World War, these hopes had been dashed and 'the land fit for heroes' had become a mockery. Now they were desperately anxious that the same thing should not happen again and that this time they really would go back to a different world where there was no unemployment, no festering slums, no dole queues and no half-starved children. It was because of this strong feeling that a government report on social security, which appeared half way through the war, caused particular interest. It had been prepared by a civil servant, Sir William Beveridge, and contained a carefully worked out plan for abolishing the worst poverty. Until that time there had been a number of separate schemes for insurance – covering illness, unemployment, pensions – but these were all unconnected and there were many gaps. With Beveridge, for the first time, there was a complete system covering everything – 'interruption of earnings' (such as unemployment or illness), family allowances for each child and old age pensions. The idea of the plan was that every citizen would pay a contribution each week in the form of a stamp on his insurance card, and for this he could expect a basic minimum for life or, as it was put at the time, 'from the cradle to the grave'.

It was laid down that everyone, rich and poor alike, would pay the same contribution and receive the same benefits. There was some disagreement about this, but Beveridge maintained that only in this way would people come to realise that benefits under the scheme were a right and not a charity. Also it would do away with the means test which had been so bitterly unpopular before the war.[1]

The Beveridge Report gave great hope to the British people in their long wartime ordeal. The forces felt that now they had something to fight for as well as against, and there soon arose an irresistible demand

---

[1] This had required a man to supply details of the earnings of all his family before he became eligible for unemployment pay.

for the Beveridge Plan to be put into operation. At the general election of 1945 both the main parties were firmly committed to introducing a scheme based on Beveridge; and the Labour Government, when it came to office, lost no time in honouring its pledge. The plan, which it introduced in 1946, differed from Beveridge in only one important way. Beveridge had recommended that pensions and other benefits should be adjusted automatically to meet rises in the cost of living. But this was not provided for; instead there was to be a review every five years. In the event this proved inadequate; it meant that benefits, particularly old age pensions, did not keep pace with the cost of living. Partly because of this and partly because there were, inevitably, some people for whom social security benefits were not enough, National Assistance was also established. This was to provide for those in need in special circumstances, but here it was necessary to have a means test, although this was different from and less offensive than the one before the war.

National Health

In his report Beveridge named five giants to be overcome after the war: Want, Disease, Squalor, Ignorance and Idleness. Of these he himself aimed only to overcome the first. But urgent action was also needed against the second.

It has often happened in history that a war has roused people from inertia and opened their eyes to the wrongs and sufferings of their fellow countrymen. This occurred early in the Second World War at the time of evacuation (see p. 148) when it became apparent how appalling was the health of large numbers of city dwellers. Country people were horrified to find children ill-fed, unhealthy, undersized and, in some cases, vermin-ridden. From that time British people became much more health conscious. A number of welfare foods such as milk, cod liver oil and orange juice were provided free or heavily subsidised to young children and expectant mothers. Even Winston Churchill, whose interest in social welfare was not great, declared that there was no finer investment for any community than putting milk into babies.

Partly because of this growing concern with health and partly because it was convinced that a National Health Service was an essential part of a welfare state, the Labour Party was fully committed to setting one up which would provide all medical attention free to everyone who needed it. The establishment of such a service would not be easy; it would be complicated and expensive and liable to stir up strong opposition from parts of the medical profession. To some doctors the idea of 'socialised medicine' was abhorrent; they had no wish to give up their private practices and become salaried employees of the state. They felt strongly that National Health would lead to a lowering of medical standards and to the disappearance of the special relationship between doctor and patient. But the need for a health service was evident. Under the system of private practices there were numerous doctors in well-to-do districts but all too few in poorer areas; and many in need of medical attention were not getting it.

The member of the government who was given the task of setting up the National Health Service was Aneurin Bevan, the son of a Welsh coalminer who had himself worked in the mines in his youth. Gifted with compelling eloquence and a brilliant mind combined with outspokenness and frequent indiscretion, he was the most exciting and controversial of Labour leaders. With his mercurial temperament – all charm and warmth at one moment, all rage and contempt the next, he was someone about whom it was impossible to feel neutral; one either loved him or loathed him. Among the rank and file of the Labour Party he had fervent support but, being a difficult and sometimes overbearing colleague, he had enemies among other Labour leaders. Among Conservatives he was cordially disliked, although some had a grudging respect for him. The setting up of the National Health Service was Bevan's great triumph. In cajoling money out of a nearly empty exchequer, coping with formidable administrative problems and winning over reluctant doctors, he showed not only persuasiveness, but also unexpected qualities of patience and tact. The Service began operating in July 1948. By then most doctors had agreed to participate, and nearly all hospitals had been nationalised. Since then the Health Service has been under great strain due to inadequate hospitals, too few doctors and everlasting shortage of money. The costs have, indeed, been immense, and this has meant less money for other urgent needs such as education, housing and pensions. But few people today would deny that the National Health Service has been a great boon to the country.

Housing

The third of Beveridge's giants, Squalor, referred to housing conditions. After the war this was Britain's most crucial problem. The situation was desperate. There had been no building of new houses for six years; one house in three had been destroyed or damaged during the blitz; and many of those remaining were slums which ought to have been demolished long ago. There was an immediate need for 5,000,000 new houses, but the Labour Government reckoned that no more than 200,000 could be built in one year. Labour's achievement in housebuilding was not outstanding – later the Conservatives were able to increase the number to 300,000. One of the reasons for this was that both housebuilding and the Health Service came under the direction of Aneurin Bevan, and such a task was too much for one man; he could not give it enough personal attention. It is likely that more houses would have been built if he had allowed private builders to build more private houses for sale and had not relied, almost entirely, on local councils building council houses to rent.

Housing remains one of the great unsolved problems in the United Kingdom. Waiting lists for houses are still long, and thousands of families are still homeless or living in overcrowded or wretchedly inadequate conditions. Not all the methods used to overcome the housing shortage have been successful. Prefabricated houses and caravans have served some useful purpose, if only temporarily, but high-rise flats, which are quick to build and need little building land, have been found to have great disadvantages and have not always been agreeable places in which to live. Not everyone too has been happy in the carefully planned new towns built to take the overspill from large, overcrowded cities. In spite of being neat and convenient these have sometimes proved to be strangely 'unlivable in'.

Education

The main measure for dealing with Beveridge's fourth giant, Ignorance, had been taken during the war. The Education Act of 1944 aimed to give secondary education to all. It required local councils to educate children according to 'age, aptitude and ability', and laid down that the school leaving age would be raised from fifteen in 1947 and to sixteen in due course. For this new programme of secondary education the Act provided three types of school – Grammar, Technical and Modern. It was hoped that all three would be of equal status, but this was not what happened. The Grammar Schools with their traditions of scholarship were much sought after; it was from these that a pupil would be most likely to gain a place at a university with the prospects of a better job afterwards. There was, therefore, keen competition to pass the exam into a grammar school taken at the age of eleven; and this had unfortunate consequences. It meant that a child's future might depend on the result of one exam taken at an early age and, there being an element of chance in all exams, this might entirely fail to do the child justice. Also the exam put young children under great strain and restricted unduly the curriculum of primary schools which felt obliged to 'cram' for the exam to the exclusion of other subjects. For these reasons and because Grammar Schools were said to be creating a new class system, there developed a body of opinion opposed to any kind of selection and in favour of large comprehensive schools which would cater for children of all abilities.

Chapter 17

AMERICAN INVOLVEMENT IN EUROPE – THE COLD WAR

End of Isolation

At the end of the war there was a great longing in America to get back to normal as soon as possible. Everyone hoped that the armed forces would be demobilised quickly, that industry would at once be switched to peacetime needs, and that all, or nearly all, American troops would be brought home. It had been the great hope of President Roosevelt, and later President Truman, that an understanding could be reached with Russia and that the two countries, with Britain, would be the mainstay of a new international organisation to keep the peace of the world. In the last years of the war Roosevelt, ignoring the objections of Churchill, had made great concessions to Stalin in the hope of winning his trust. But, as has been seen, these were merely regarded as signs of weakness and only encouraged Stalin to ask for more.

At one time it seemed as if Roosevelt was more suspicious of Britain than of Russia, referring scathingly to 'archaic medieval Empire ideas', and making it plain that America was not fighting the war to prop up the British Empire. Truman too, at first, had great hopes of Russia and was inclined to keep Britain at arm's length so as not to give the impression of 'ganging up', as he put it. However, with the British Labour government losing no time in giving independence to India (see p. 291) and Russia losing no opportunity of expanding her frontiers, it was not long before his eyes were opened to the real situation and he was declaring roundly that 'unless Russia is faced with an iron fist and strong language another war was in the making'.

In May 1946 Winston Churchill, who was then Leader of the Opposition, made an historic speech at Fulton, Missouri. In this he referred to an iron curtain which had descended across Europe and appealed for a special Anglo–American relationship as a prevention of war. This speech had a great effect on President Truman and other Americans who were coming to realise that isolation was no longer possible for their country and that if the spread of Communism in Europe was to be halted, massive American aid would be necessary.

The Truman Doctrine

The first substantial American commitment to aid Europe came early in 1947. In February of that year the British government announced that it could no longer continue to supply military aid to Greece and Turkey. British troops had been in Greece since 1944 when they had prevented a Communist takeover of the country. Since then, however, Greek Communists had received considerable help, particularly from neighbouring Yugoslavia, and it had been necessary for British troops to remain and give further support to the Greek government. But at the beginning of 1947, with the British economy near to collapse and in the middle of the coldest winter for a hundred years, which had brought a food and fuel crisis worse than at any time during the war, the British government decided that it could no longer afford to give this aid. It seems that this announcement was not unexpected by American leaders and that they were ready to fill the gap caused by Britain's departure. Certainly Truman acted quickly and in the following month asked Congress for a large sum of money to aid Greece and Turkey. At the same time he declared that it must be the policy of the United States to 'support free people everywhere who are resisting attempted subjugation by armed minorities or by outside pressures'. Thus America came forward as champion of the free world. A clear warning was given that in future help would be made available to any country resisting a Communist takeover. The Cold War had been declared.

Marshall Aid

The Cold War has been described as 'all hostilities short of general war'. It was to be fought with varying degrees of intensity in different parts of the world. At times it came near to erupting into full-scale open war, but always the fear of nuclear weapons caused the great powers to draw back.

In the waging of the Cold War strong military forces have been a major consideration, but of great importance too have been economic forces – the ability to maintain full employment, reasonable prices and a fair standard of living for all. It is when these break down in capitalist countries that Communism has its opportunity. This was fully realised by American leaders in 1947. At that time most of the countries of Eastern Europe were fast succumbing to Communism and those in Western Europe were in desperate financial difficulties. In France and Italy especially the Communists were making headway, and it seemed that they were just waiting for final economic collapse before taking over. To most Americans, therefore, it was manifest that large-scale economic aid must be provided in order to prevent this. Such aid would enable existing European industries to be re-equipped and new ones to be started up. It would give the economies of these countries an opportunity to recover so that they would be able to provide for themselves.

And so in June 1947 the American Secretary of State, George Marshall, propounded the plan which later came to be known as Marshall Aid. He made it clear that this aid was unconditional and that the United States was not seeking to interfere in the government of European countries. It was from them that a plan for European recovery must come. He also emphasised that this aid was not directed against 'any country or doctrine, but against hunger, poverty, desperation and chaos'. It was, therefore, available to Russia and East European countries if they chose to cooperate. At the time several of these, notably Czechoslovakia, were eager to respond, but Stalin forbade it. To him Marshall Aid was just 'capitalist propaganda' and 'a plan for the interference in the domestic affairs of other countries'. It would certainly have been greatly to Russia's advantage to avail herself of America's offer, but cooperation with America was something Stalin could not undertake. In order to maintain his despotic powers at home he needed an enemy abroad with which to frighten the Russian people. And so it was necessary to build up the idea of a threat to the world from American 'imperialism'.

In spite of the Russian attitude Marshall Aid was to have outstanding success in reviving European economies and in stemming the tide of Communism. But it did also have the effect of deepening the division of Europe into East and West. More and more the Russians tightened their hold on Eastern Europe and took an increasingly belligerent attitude to the West. At the same time the Western countries began to draw together, pool their resources and build up their armed forces in order to meet any Russian aggression.

And so in the last part of 1947 and the beginning of 1948 the 'communization' of Eastern Europe was completed and the Cominform was established to coordinate the activities of the Communist countries and to ensure Russian control of their foreign affairs and armed forces. And in the West in March 1948 the Treaty of Brussels was signed whereby Britain, France and the Benelux countries[1] agreed to come to each other's aid in the event of being attacked. At the same time disagreements between Russia and the West began to intensify, notably on the introduction of a new currency in Germany, and this resulted in Russia quitting the Allied Control Council for all Germany, and then embarking on a foolhardy venture, which nearly brought open war, of trying to force the Western powers out of Berlin.

The Blockade of Berlin

Berlin was the obvious place for Russia to apply pressure. The Western sectors of the city (British, French and American) constituted a tiny island over a hundred miles inside the main Russian zone, dependent on the Russians both for electricity supply and for road and rail links with Western Germany. It seemed that it lay at Russia's mercy. Even so the Russians proceeded with caution. It was at the end of March 1948 that they first started to interfere with land traffic to West Berlin and to close down roads and railways, making the excuse that repairs were necessary; but it was not until the end of June that all land communications were cut off completely. It seems likely that the Russians were not carrying out a well-prepared plan, but were 'playing it by ear', experimenting cautiously to see what they could get away with.

To the Western powers it seemed at first as if there were two possible courses of action: either they could submit to being squeezed out of Berlin or they could blast their way through. The first would mean an impossible humiliation, the second would mean open war. But then a third possibility became apparent – to keep West Berlin supplied with all needs by air. This was a daunting prospect: it would involve flying in every day thousands of tons not only of food but also of fuel. On

---

[1] Belgium, Netherlands and Luxembourg.

examination, however, the scheme seemed feasible and on 25th June the Berlin airlift began.

The Berlin airlift was an amazing achievement and a notable Western victory in the Cold War. After six months an average of 552 flights a day were being achieved,[1] and by then 700,000 tons of food, fuel and other supplies had been brought in. A few months later on 16th April 1949 a record 1,400 flights were made, carrying some 13,000 tons, so that more goods were then coming into the city than before the blockade. This tremendous display of strength had great effect both on the Russians and on the inhabitants of West Berlin. Throughout the bitterly cold winter the West Berliners were ready to accept any hardship rather than be absorbed into the Russian sector. For their part the Russians realised that they had failed; they were not going to be able to force the Western powers out of Berlin; it had been clearly demonstrated that they were not there on sufferance. On 12th May 1949 the blockade was lifted, although the airlift continued for another four months in order to build up ample reserves.[2]

The Berlin blockade was one of the most acute crises of the Cold War. It was the nearest the two sides had come until then to open war. Neither side wanted this; the Russians were deterred by American superiority in atomic weapons; while the Americans were deterred by the huge Russian preponderance in conventional forces.[3]

North Atlantic Treaty Organisation

The Berlin blockade had the effect of drawing the countries of Western Europe closer together. Already alarmed by Communist takeovers in Eastern Europe and the enormous size of the Russian army (far larger than was needed just to defend Russia), they realised that they must take urgent measures for their common defence. In April 1949 the North Atlantic Pact was signed by Britain, France, Benelux, Italy, Portugal, Iceland, Denmark, Norway, the United States and Canada. This set up a North Atlantic Treaty Organisation (NATO) which was to

---

[1] The proportion was about two thirds American and one third British.
[2] By then 2,300,000 tons of goods had been airlifted.
[3] At one time Russian forces outnumbered the West by 125 divisions to 14.

provide for collective defence, it being stated that an attack against one of these countries was to be considered as an attack against them all.

At the same time (May 1949) the American, British and French zones of Germany were united to form the German Federal Republic with the capital at Bonn. Thanks to Marshall Aid, the new currency and the efforts of the German people, the economy of the country soon began to burgeon and in time to become the strongest in Europe. It was not long too before America was urging that Germany should be rearmed and her forces integrated into those of NATO. This, inevitably, caused great consternation to the Russians who affirmed that NATO and the rearming of Germany were all part of an aggressive plot directed against their country.

In the years that followed the NATO countries took steps to reduce the gap in the size of their armed forces and those of the Russians, but they were always much smaller. At the end of 1949, however, two things happened which strengthened the Russians' hand. In the first place, much sooner than expected, they developed an atomic bomb, and secondly the Chinese Communists completed the conquest of China (see Chapter 18) which meant that the Cold War would be extended to the Far East.

Unrest in Eastern Europe

During the Berlin blockade and the years following, Stalin had been feeling increasing anxiety about the loyalty of the countries of Eastern Europe. In particular he was agitated by the activities and attitudes of Marshal Tito of Yugoslavia. During the war no-one in occupied Europe had fought so fiercely and so effectively against the Germans as the Yugoslav partisans. In their mountain fastnesses they had proved to be invincible and in the last months of the war had emerged to liberate Belgrade before the arrival of the advancing Russians. Their leader was Josip Broz, the son of a blacksmith and a dedicated Communist, who had assumed the name of Tito. On the withdrawal of the Germans he lost no time in taking over the government of the country and in disposing of his rivals. And so in Yugoslavia Communism had been brought in with no pressure or assistance from the Russians.

Soon after establishing himself Tito began taking a strongly Communist line in European affairs, giving much help to the Communist rebels in Greece, demanding Trieste from Italy and championing anti-

Western policies generally. But this was not at all to the liking of Stalin to whom there was room for only one star in the Communist firmament and who strongly disapproved of independent action from other Communist leaders. It was not long before relations between them became strained. And then on 28th June 1948 Yugoslavia was formally expelled from the Cominform. Stalin had decided to crush the country and eliminate its presumptuous ruler. He had little doubt that this would be achieved quickly. 'I will shake my little finger and there will be no more Tito,' he exclaimed. But he was wrong. He had underestimated Yugoslav obstinacy and pride; for despite threats and intimidation and an economic blockade Yugoslavia and its leader held firm; and Stalin stopped short of an open invasion of the country. At the moment of crisis help was forthcoming to Yugoslavia from the Western powers. Since the war relations with Britain and America had been hostile, but Tito had never entirely let go the links which had been established when he was a guerrilla chief in the mountains fighting the Germans, and the Allies had sent help including men who had fought by his side. Now these links were revived and trade and economic aid were made available which enabled Tito to prevail.

With the survival of Tito and the failure of the Berlin blockade Stalin felt it necessary to strengthen his position in the other Eastern European countries. His method was to strike terror into the hearts of their rulers. Accordingly a series of purges, similar to those in Russia before the war (see p. 125), were instigated, and at the end of 1948 and the beginning of 1949 Communist leaders in Poland, Hungary, Bulgaria and Albania were executed or imprisoned on trumped up charges. During this time there was great unrest in these countries and great resentment at Russian domination and exploitation. Collectivisation of agriculture (see p. 124) was forced on them as also were five-year economic plans which took more consideration of Russian needs than their own. In addition vast quantities of food and other goods were demanded as reparations from those countries which had fought against Russia during the war (Rumania, Hungary and East Germany).

This discontent could not be kept down indefinitely. In 1953 there were riots in East Germany and Czechoslovakia, but it was not until 1956 that serious outbreaks occurred (see Chapter 20).

Timescale

1946

May   Churchill's 'Iron Curtain' speech.

1947

March   US agrees to supply aid to Greece and Turkey.

June   American Secretary of State, George Marshall, offers economic aid to European countries (Marshall Aid).
Cominform established.

1948

March   Treaty of Brussels.

June   Land traffic to Berlin cut off by Russians.
Berlin airlift begins.
Yugoslavia expelled from Cominform.

1949

April   North Atlantic Treaty signed.

May   Berlin blockade lifted.
American, British and French zones of Germany united to form German Federal Republic.

September   Russians explode atomic bomb.

Chapter 18

COMMUNISM IN THE FAR EAST

The Rise of Communism in China

If it is the case that Communism flourishes where there is hunger, corruption and chaos, then it was always likely it would come to China. Since the middle of the nineteenth century China, once the proudest and most civilised country in the world, had been subjected to one humiliation after another. Foreign forces had invaded the country and imposed ignominious terms which gave them special rights and privileges and, when it suited them, taken over Chinese territory. For a long time there had been no effective central government and the country had been dominated by local warlords and powerful foreign merchants. In the 1920s one party had emerged as more powerful than any other, the Kuonmintang or Nationalist Party led by Chiang Kai-shek, a one-time invoice clerk. But this did not control the whole country. At first the Nationalist Party contained a large Communist element, and received some support from Moscow, but in 1927 Chiang turned against the Communists and put a number of them to death. Later he tried to eliminate them altogether, but in 1934 some of them escaped and, after a famous Long March of 6,000 miles, reached a part of the country where Chiang could not get at them. The leader of this group was Mao Tse-tung, an ex-assistant librarian of peasant stock who in his youth had aspired to being a poet. Mao was a leader of genius. He was destined to rule a quarter of the human race for a quarter of a century.

The civil war in China did not come to an end when the Japanese invaded the country in 1931 (see p. 111). In the years that followed the Communists extended their power as Chiang had to deploy many (although not most) of his forces against the Japanese. The end of the Second World War, coming as it did suddenly with the dropping of the atomic bombs, took both Nationalists and Communists by surprise, and there followed a scramble by both to gain possession of strategic points and arms dumps left by the Japanese. For a time after

1945 there was a truce between them while the Americans tried to bring them together, but fighting broke out again in 1946 when these efforts came to nothing.

The civil war was to continue for three years longer. At first it seemed that the Communists had little chance of success. They were outnumbered by more than two to one, they had no air or naval forces, and the Nationalists were receiving extensive help from the Americans. However, they also had great advantages, for they were winning the battle for the hearts and minds of the Chinese people. Their forces were well led and well disciplined, and their treatment of the civil population was less brutal and unjust than the Nationalists'. Also their morale was high; they believed passionately in their cause and were determined to win at all costs. By contrast the fighting spirit of the Nationalists was poor; they were disorganised, underfed and unpaid so that there was much looting; and their leaders were inefficient and corrupt and associated in the minds of the people with warlords and rich landowners. It was not long before large numbers of Nationalist troops began to desert to the Communists, taking with them their American arms and equipment. By 1948 everything was going the Communists' way, and final victory came at the end of 1949 when Chiang resigned the presidency and withdrew with the forces still loyal to him to the island of Formosa (later Taiwan). At the same time Mao proclaimed the establishment of the Chinese People's Republic.

The Communist takeover in China was different from those in other countries after the war in that it owed nothing to outside pressure or assistance. In particular it received no help from Russia. It seems that from an early stage Stalin decided that the cause of the Chinese Communists was hopeless and urged them to come to terms with the Nationalists. Also he regarded Mao with some suspicion and thought him a bogus or, as he put it, 'a margarine Communist'. Stalin never had any love for rivals and, perhaps, he preferred the idea of a weak, divided China under the Nationalists on Russia's eastern border rather than a strong one under Mao.

China under Mao Tse-tung

After twenty-five years of civil war and fourteen years resisting the Japanese the condition of China in 1949 was woeful. Roads and railways were in ruins, food was in desperately short supply, manufacturing output was half what it had been before the war, and inflation was rampant so that money was often valueless. Faced with these conditions Mao set about the creation of a new China, and in this he was prepared to be totally ruthless. The lives of millions of people would be disrupted, millions more would be 're-educated' or, as he put it, 're-moulded', and, if necessary, millions more would be put to death. The new China would be based on Communism, but Mao was determined to incorporate many of his own ideas and was quite prepared to rewrite the Communism of Marx and Lenin when it suited him. In the coming years Mao's rule, as also his lifestyle, were to bear more resemblance to ancient Chinese emperors than to revolutionary Communist leaders.

Mao was determined to make China a major industrial country as soon as possible. This was a massive task and would require all Chinese people to work their hardest with minimum in return. To this end Mao sought to fill everyone with revolutionary zeal, and mighty propaganda campaigns were launched exhorting everyone to spare no pains. In 1952 a Five Year Plan was introduced to boost production, and this had some success notably in coal, electricity and steel production. After seven

Mao Tse-tung inspecting troops of the Chinese army.

years Mao had achieved much. China was once again an independent, united country, free from foreign interference; the dignity and pride of the Chinese people had been restored and most of them were ready to make any sacrifice on behalf of Chairman Mao and his version of Communism. But there had too been fatal failures. Of these the most notable was in agriculture. One of Mao's first acts had been to break up the estates of the large landowners[1] and distribute their land among the peasants; but he was to find, as Russian Communists had found before him, that small plots farmed by peasant proprietors were inefficient and resulted in low production. The smallholders could not afford modern machinery and most of them were not interested in new, scientific methods. And so, as in Russia, twenty-five years before, it was decided to 'collectivise' farm holdings – that is to form them into communes where everything was owned in common and all workers were paid employees. But, as in Russia again, farming communes were not popular. Farmers wanted their own land and property and to farm in their own way; they were not prepared to work as hard for a commune nor to take the same amount of care with livestock and machinery that did not belong to them.

By 1956 Mao was feeling that his position was insecure. It seemed to him that the Revolution, *his* Revolution, was being taken over by others – intellectuals, scientists, technocrats – who were becoming much too independent. And so, with great guile, he proclaimed a campaign known, poetically, as 'Let a Hundred Flowers Bloom' which invited criticism of his regime. But this was in reality a trap for his enemies; for those who made criticisms, and there were many of them, were soon exterminated – perhaps as many as half a million.

In 1957 Mao announced another Five Year Plan called 'The Great Leap Forward', but this was dogged by disaster. Partly because of opposition to collectivisation and partly because of exceptional floods and drought agricultural production slumped, and there were three years of famine in which it is believed over forty million people starved to death. And then in 1960 came another major setback when relations with Russia reached breaking point, and Khruschev suddenly ordered the withdrawal of all Russian aid to China; all Russian engineers and other technical experts were recalled, taking their plans and blueprints

---

[1] He also put them to death – perhaps as many as one and a half million of them.

with them, leaving vast projects, such as bridges and factories, half finished and machinery idle and useless because there were no spare parts for them.

Rift Between Russia and China

An open breach between Russia and China had been boiling up for some time. It has been seen that in his revolution Mao received little help from Stalin, but he always had a great admiration for him, and after he came to power he signed a treaty of friendship with Russia, and it was generally assumed that this would be firm and lasting and that the two countries would work together to further the advance of Communism. During the Korean War (see p. 279) this impression was strengthened, and it was not until several years later that it became evident how great were the stresses of the alliance and how much hatred and suspicion existed between the two countries.

This antagonism lies deep in history. Among Russians there remains an instinctive dread of invaders from the East, dating from the fourteenth century when Genghis Khan and his Mongols swept through Russia, leaving behind them, as they went, grisly memorials of towering piles of human skulls. Ever since that time Russians have had an innate fear of 'the yellow hordes of Asia'; and in modern times this fear has increased with the prospect of a strong, united China with a hungry, exploding population. In China too there has been great fear – fear of Russian strength and intentions. There has been too considerable resentment that Russia still holds lands that were once Chinese. In the nineteenth century, when China was weak and divided and lay at the mercy of foreigners, large areas of borderland were taken over by the Russians. At the time of the Russian Revolution a promise had been given that these would be returned, but this had not happened, and after the Second World War the Russians were not prepared even to discuss the matter.

The first sign of a major rift appeared in 1956 when Khruschev made his famous denunciation of Stalin and his brutal methods (see p. 310). Mao was outraged by this; it seemed to him a great betrayal; he may also have had a great dread that someone one day would treat him in the same way. At the same time Khruschev sought better relations with the West, and this too appalled Mao; it was not for true Communists to compromise with capitalists; rather they should be confronting them and seeking to bring them down.[1] From that time Mao was always urging the Russians to make greater use of their rapidly growing nuclear capacity and, if necessary, to have a show-down with the Americans. He himself seemed ready to contemplate the prospect of a nuclear attack on China. 'We may lose more than 300,000,000 people,' he once declared. 'So what? War is war. The years will pass and we'll get to work producing more babies than ever before.' The Russians, however, since coming into possession of atomic weapons and witnessing their devastating effect, had a more responsible attitude. In waging the cold war they were prepared to go to the brink but no further.

The War in Korea – Aggression Checked

Korea ('The Land of the Morning Calm') had been part of the Japanese Empire since 1910. At the end of the Second World War it was occupied by both American and Russian forces, and for the sake of convenience was divided into two parts along the 38th line of latitude, the North under the Russians and the South under the Americans. This division was not meant to be permanent and it was expected that in time the country would be re-united under a government of its own choice. However, this was prevented by the Russians who, despite a United Nations resolution, refused to allow free elections in the North. And so the two parts remained separate as the South Korean Republic and the People's Democratic Republic. Relations between the two became increasingly hostile, but most people were taken by surprise when on 25th June 1950 the North invaded the South. The reaction of the United States government was prompt: it immediately summoned a meeting of the Security Council of the United Nations which passed a resolution calling for a cease-fire and the withdrawal of the North Koreans. Soon afterwards another resolution was passed promising all necessary assistance to the South Koreans.[2] It was considered by most countries that

---

[1] To show his contempt of Khruschev Mao received him, when he came on a visit to China, in his swimming bath, dressed only in swimming trunks.

[2] These resolutions would certainly have been vetoed by the Russians if they had been there; but at the time they were boycotting the United Nations because of its refusal to admit Communist China into the Organisation.

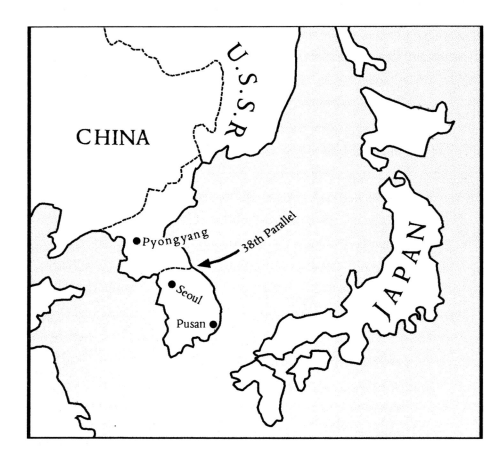

Korea.

the action of the North Koreans was open aggression which should not be overlooked and that the United Nations should not make the same mistake as the League of Nations and fail to check it. Altogether fifty countries pledged support, although only fourteen eventually sent forces to fight in Korea. Of these the great majority were American; the British force was the second largest.

Although US forces were sent at once they were nearly too late to save South Korea. At first the armies from the North carried all before them and overran the whole country apart from a defensive perimeter round the port of Pusan in the extreme south of the peninsula. But then the tide turned and the UN supreme commander, General Mac-Arthur, carried out a bold operation, landing large forces nearly two hundred miles behind the enemy lines, thus threatening to cut them off. This resulted in the complete defeat of the North Korean army which by the end of September had been driven back across the 38th parallel.

Chinese Intervention

At this point a crucial decision had to be taken. Should the United Nations consider their task to be completed? Or were they to invade North Korea and bring about the reunion of the two parts of the country? To do so would involve risk of war with Russia or China or both. President Truman was cautious, as were other United Nations leaders, but General MacArthur urged it strongly and managed to get his way, and so on 1st October UN forces crossed into North Korea. At first everything went well and MacArthur expected the war to be over by Christmas, but then resistance stiffened and it became evident that large numbers of Chinese 'volunteers' were fighting alongside the North Koreans. More and more of these appeared on the scene so that by the end of the year the UN force found itself in an entirely different situation – confronted with a new, powerful army being supplied from bases in Manchuria which could not be bombed. In the following months the Chinese, attacking recklessly with little regard to loss of human life, pushed the UN forces back into South Korea. But then the position stabilised. The Americans and their allies, with their great superiority of fire power, were able once again to force the Chinese back across the 38th parallel (3rd April 1951).

It was at this time that there was a serious disagreement between President Truman and General MacArthur: the latter wanted to extend the war to China, bring in the forces of Chiang Kai-shek from Formosa and, if necessary, to use atomic weapons. Truman, strongly supported by the British, was opposed to this. He maintained that open war should be avoided, that it was necessary only to 'contain' Communist aggression and that the idea of reuniting the two parts of Korea should be abandoned. In the end this difference of opinion became so acute that Truman felt himself obliged to dismiss MacArthur, an act requiring considerable courage as MacArthur was a great American hero. By July it was evident that a deadlock had been reached and the first armistice talks took place, but these came to nothing as the Chinese insisted on the forcible repatriation of all Chinese prisoners of war who, facing almost certain death or disgrace, were desperate not to go. The war was to drag on for another two years until July 1953 by which time General Eisenhower had become American president, and he let it be known that if a treaty was not signed, he was prepared to use nuclear weapons. Also in Russia Stalin had just died and the new Russian leaders, for the time being, were anxious not to provoke a crisis.

The Korean War took a heavy toll of human life: 142,000 Americans, 300,000 South Koreans and perhaps as many as 2,000,000 Chinese and North Koreans. Altogether, including civilians the total death roll was of the order of 4,000,000. The results of the war were far-reaching and disastrous. It is true that the authority of the United Nations was upheld; aggression was checked and South Korea saved from Communism. But on the other hand great damage was done to relations between the United States and the new China. But for the Korean War America might not have withheld recognition from Communist China and given strong support to Chiang Kai-shek. For the time being the most populous country in the world was to be excluded, on American insistence, from the community of nations.

End of European Empires in Asia

Before the war nearly all the countries of South East Asia had been colonies of European powers. When these were overrun by the Japanese it was unlikely that this situation would be restored, and at the end of the war there were many nationalist movements ready to demand independence and take over the government of their countries.

In some countries independence came comparatively peacefully, but in others there were long and hard-fought wars. In the Dutch East Indies, which comprised some 2,000 islands, the leader of the Nationalist movement, Achmet Sukarno, who had collaborated with the Japanese during the war, lost no time in proclaiming the independent Republic of Indonesia. This the Dutch refused to recognise and three years of war ensued at the end of which, partly owing to pressure from America and the United Nations, the Dutch were compelled to give way. In French Indo-China, comprising Vietnam, Cambodia and Laos, there was a far longer and more bitter struggle. The French, determined to regain France's status as a world power, would not come to terms with the Viet Minh, the nationalist movement led by the Communist Ho Chi Minh. For eight years a grim war was waged. The French fought with great valour, but they failed to win over to their side the people of Vietnam and were unable to track down the Communist forces under a guerrilla leader of genius, Vo Nguyen Giap. From 1949 these forces received great help from China and in 1954 they succeeded in trapping a large French force in the village of Dien Bien Phu and completely destroying it. This made French withdrawal inevitable, although at the end America was giving considerable aid, and at one stage was even planning to use nuclear weapons to rescue the beleaguered French forces. At a peace conference in Geneva a treaty was signed whereby Vietnam was divided in two – the North under the Communists and the South under a non-Communist regime. Peace, however, had not come to Vietnam for long.

After the Communist victory in China it was likely that there would be Communist uprisings in other parts of Asia, and in 1948 these broke out in Burma, Indonesia, the Philippines and Malaya. All of these were subdued quite quickly except in Malaya where war was waged for twelve years before the final victory of the British and Malayan forces (see p. 293).

In 1954 the United States, Britain, France, Australia, New Zealand, Pakistan, Thailand and the Philippines formed a defensive alliance to contain Communism in the Pacific. This was known as South-East Asia Collective Defence Treaty or SEATO for short, and for a time it had some success, but, being Western-dominated, it was always suspect to the people of Asia.

War in Vietnam

In 1960 John F. Kennedy was elected 35th President of the United States, at forty-three the youngest man to hold that office. In his Inaugural Address he declared the time to be an hour of maximum danger for freedom and that his generation had been given the role of defending it. He went on to say that Americans would 'pay any price, bear any burden, meet any hardship, support any friend, oppose any foe to ensure the survival and success of liberty.'

On taking office Kennedy was to find that a friend in great need of support in the fight for liberty was South Vietnam. Since the 1954 treaty (see p. 283) there had been great rivalry and hostility between North Vietnam under the Communist leader Ho Chi Minh, and South Vietnam under a pro-West dictator, Ngo Dinh Diem. It was the aim of each to reunite the whole of Vietnam under his leadership, and in this confrontation it soon became clear that the North was gaining the upper hand; it had stronger and more determined leadership and an army of experienced and highly skilled guerrillas. There was too a Communist guerrilla force inside South Vietnam, known as the Vietcong, which was bent on bringing down the government of Diem. Before Kennedy came to office the United States had been sending aid to the South including a number of military 'advisers'. It did not take Kennedy long to decide that this aid should be extended, and by 1962 the number of American troops in Vietnam had risen to 15,000. From then on America became more and more involved in Vietnamese affairs; or, as it has been put, 'drawn into the Vietnamese quagmire.'

The task in Vietnam proved extremely difficult. The Vietcong, fighting by night and hiding by day, could not be pinned down; and they were receiving increasing assistance from North Vietnam who, in turn, was receiving modern weapons and other war supplies from Russia. In consequence American commanders in South Vietnam were demanding more and more troops: by 1965 there were 125,000, by 1966 400,000 and by 1968 550,000. And still the Vietcong was undefeated. In 1965 President Johnson, who had succeeded Kennedy after his assassination, ordered the bombing of North Vietnam, and some very heavy raids were carried out; but these too failed to shake the determination of Ho Chi Minh to win the war at all costs.

It seemed that a deadlock had been reached and that it was a war which neither side could win. But the situation in the South was deteriorating. President Diem had been assassinated in 1963[1] and his successors were weak and irresolute. In spite of immense American fire power the Vietcong and North Vietnamese continued to prevail. At the same time there was a wave of opposition to the war in the United States. The press mounted a massive campaign against it and pictures of the horrors of the war were shown on television throughout the country. Protestors were probably a minority, but they were extremely active and vocal,[2] and opposition to the war spread to other countries where the spectacle (often exaggerated and fallacious) of American warplanes bombing Vietnamese peasants and setting fire to their villages with napalm caused outrage.

In view of these outcries L. B. Johnson decided not to stand for re-election as President and was succeeded in 1967 by Richard Nixon who decided to pull American troops out of Vietnam and seek an honourable end to the war. But this could not be achieved. Ho Chi Minh was as uncompromising as ever and negotiations dragged on interminably. In 1973 some sort of cease-fire was signed in Paris; Vietnam was to remain divided for the time being, and American troops were to be withdrawn. But Ho Chi Minh was still determined to bring both Vietnams together under his rule, and fighting between North and South continued. In 1975 the North Vietnamese, still receiving massive help from Russia, mounted a strong offensive which the South, without American help, was unable to resist; and on 21st April the war ended with a complete American evacuation and Ho Chi Minh taking over the whole country.

This was America's most humiliating defeat; nearly 46,000 Americans had been killed and none of the American objectives had been achieved. The American climb-down was to have momentous consequences. In neighbouring Laos the Communist Pathet Lao took over and in Cambodia a particularly brutal and ruthless Communist clique, known as Khmer Rouge, gained power and proceeded to carry out perhaps the greatest crimes against humanity ever. Millions of inhabitants of the capital, Phnom Penh, and other cities were driven out into

---

[1] The US government had connived at this as Diem was regarded as a ruthless and unpopular dictator.

[2] Their slogans included: 'Ho Ho Ho Chi Minh, the Vietcong are going to win!' and 'Hey, Hey, L.B.J. How many kids have you killed today?'

the country where they were put to death or left to die; it is estimated that 1,200,000, one fifth of the population, perished. Later Cambodia and Vietnam were to become pawns in the power struggle between Russia and China; Vietnam which was in the Russian camp invaded Cambodia which was on China's side, and set up a new government in place of the Khmer Rouge. This resulted in China temporarily invading Vietnam to 'punish' the Vietnamese.

Another consequence of the Vietnamese debacle was the effect it had on American public opinion. The idea of America coming to the aid of all countries fighting for freedom became less popular. From that time Americans were to become chary of getting too deeply involved in other countries' affairs.

The 'Cultural Revolution' and the Death of Mao Tse-tung

Since the rift between Russia and China in 1960 relations between the two countries had gone from bad to worse, and at times it had seemed as if open war might break out between them. One of the consequences of these strained relations was that the Chinese started to have much greater trade with the West, particularly Japan; and partly because of this Chinese industry began to go ahead again. This was shown significantly in 1964 when the first Chinese atom bomb was exploded.

In spite of these great improvements, however, Mao was not content, for they had been obtained at the expense of those things he hated most – large industrial cities and a rapidly growing middle class of managers and technical experts which inevitably come with industrialisation. More and more Mao was feeling edged out, and not only by industrialists but also by rival politicians and intellectuals who were deviating from the 'thoughts' which he had enunciated in his 'Little Red Book'. He was also concerned that at seventy-two he was considered by some to be too old for his job and that people were laying plans for a new regime after his death, perhaps even before it. And so he decided that ruthless and dramatic action must be taken. First, to show how fit he still was, he went on a nine-mile swim in the river Yangtse. Then he launched on China the 'Cultural Revolution', proclaiming that if the purity of Communism was to be maintained and China was not to go down the same road as Russia, the country must be in a state of

Two Red Guards with armbands.

'continuous revolution'. But the real purpose of the Cultural Revolution was to rid China of all those whom Mao looked on as his enemies. It was the last desperate bid of an old man to regain lost prestige and power.

The 'Cultural Revolution', then, was not cultural at all. It was, in fact, anti-cultural as some of the main victims were artists, writers and university teachers; and those who carried out the revolution – the so-called Red Guard – consisted of ignorant unlettered peasants, some as young as thirteen or fourteen, who could do little more than destroy and shout slogans they did not understand. In 1967 these vandals, egged on by Mao and his minions, were let loose to rampage through the streets of Peking and other cities with orders to remove or destroy anything showing signs of Western 'decadence'. Temples of religion were smashed, books burned, shops closed down and plays and other forms of entertainment banned. Eminent artists, writers and university teachers were denounced as 'monsters' and forced to kneel down and confess their 'faults' on pain of having their hair torn out, and then paraded through the streets wearing dunces' caps and surrounded by screaming youths waving the 'little red book'.[1] More humble citizens too were not safe: girls with long 'Western-style' hair were shorn and boys wearing tight trousers had them removed. For three years the people of China was ravaged by these mobs.

The consequences to China of the 'Cultural Revolution' were disastrous. Schools and universities had to close down, factories and businesses came to a halt as key workers were taken away to listen to political harangues or to take part in demonstrations. It was not long before the antics of the Red Guard stirred up strong opposition and there were many clashes with heavy loss of life. Altogether some half million people were believed to have been killed. Eventually more moderate Communists came

---

[1] The title was *Quotations from Chairman Mao*. Some three thousand million of these had been distributed free.

to the fore including, notably, Ten Hsaio-ping (Deng Hsaioping), a long standing colleague of Mao, dating from the Long March, but with more realism and less fanaticism who called for an end to 'shouting and yelling' and for everyone to get back to work. And even Mao came to see that things had got out of hand, and in time the Red Guards were disbanded and despatched to farms in remote country areas.

In the years that followed China remained a totalitarian state, in theory dedicated to Communism. But it became evident that increasingly economic considerations were being given priority over Communist theory. Increasingly too China became involved in the community of nations. In 1971 she at last joined the United Nations, and in the following year there was a notable development when President Nixon visited China and came to an understanding with Chinese leaders. For many years American relations with China had been bitter and hostile. The Korean War, the war in Vietnam and American support for Taiwan had all contributed to this. But it seemed to Nixon that the time had come for reconciliation; China comprised one quarter of the world's population; she was not yet a major power but one day would surely become one. And so Nixon extended the hand of friendship and the Chinese leadership responded. As a result the American ban on trade with China was lifted with great benefit to the Chinese economy.

Mao died in 1976 and this was followed by a power struggle in which his widow, Chiang Ching, a scheming and ambitious woman, attempted to take over the government.[1] However, she was thwarted and later sent to prison where later she committed suicide. In the post-Mao era Deng Hsaio-ping, after a period in the shadows, again emerged as the leading member of the government. He seemed to be bent on modernising China, if necessary at the expense of Communist dogma. But that he presided over a harsh and repressive regime was shown blatantly in 1989 when riots in Tibet were put down brutally,[2] and then in Peking when students, demonstrating in Tiananmen Square for more democracy, were ruthlessly cleared out by the army using tanks, with 2,600 killed and more than 10,000 injured.

---

[1] She was Mao's fourth wife. She had previously been an actress of dubious repute.
[2] Tibet had been annexed by China in 1950.

Suppression of student riots in Tiananmen Square.

Timescale

1927	Beginning of civil war in China
1931	Japan invades China.
1934	Long March led by Mao Tse-tung.
1949	Chiang Kai-shek resigns presidency and withdraws to Formosa (Taiwan). Mao proclaims Chinese People's Republic.
1950	
June	North Korea invades South Korea.
September	North Korean forces driven back across 38th parallel.
October	UN forces invade North Korea. Intervention of Chinese 'volunteers'.
1951	
April	MacArthur dismissed by Truman.
1953	
July	Korean War ends.

1954	French withdraw from Indo–China after surrender of large French force at Dien Bien Phu. Vietnam divided in two.
1957	Mao announces 'Great Leap Forward'.
1960	Open rift between Russia and China. All Russian aid withdrawn.
1962	President Kennedy increases US forces in South Vietnam.
1965	President Johnson authorises US bombing of North Vietnam.
1967	President Nixon announces US withdrawal from South Vietnam. 'Cultural Revolution' in China.
1971	China joins United Nations.
1972	President Nixon visits China.
1973	Ceasefire in South Vietnam.
1975	Complete US withdrawal from Vietnam.
1976	Death of Mao Tse-tung.
1989	Suppression of student riots in Tiananmen Square.

THE DISSOLUTION
OF THE BRITISH EMPIRE

Although it had always been expected that in time Britain's colonies would achieve independence and full nationhood, few people realised how soon this would happen. During the war and afterwards there was a strong body of opinion, particularly in America and the United Nations, that the days of colonies and overseas empires were over, and in colonial territories there was a rapid growth of nationalism and the demand for self-government.

The Partition of India

During the war a number of Indian leaders had shown open hostility to Britain and had advocated coming to terms with Japan so that it had been necessary for the British government to imprison them. At the end of the war, however, the newly elected Labour government professed itself ready to grant independence to India at as early a date as possible; but it soon became clear how great were the difficulties in achieving this. In the country there were divisions which could not be bridged, notably between Hindus (two thirds of the population) and Moslems (one quarter). It had always been the hope of British statesmen that, when the time came for British rule to end, India would be preserved as one country. The unification of the sub-continent had been Britain's great achievement. However, this was to prove a vain hope. The Moslem minority was too afraid of domination by the Hindus, and so it became necessary to hive off the Moslem areas in the Punjab and Bengal to form a separate state of Pakistan. It had also been the hope of the British that the transfer of power to the Indians would be peaceful and orderly. But this too proved impossible. In order to achieve it a large and dependable army would have been necessary and, with Britain exhausted at the end of the Second World War and her economy in ruins, this could not be provided.

At the time there were many who believed that Britain was still unwilling to leave India and would always be finding reasons for remaining there, but this was not the case. The Labour Government, beset with many other relentless problems, could not have been in more of a hurry to get out. For a time efforts were made to find a settlement acceptable to all Indian groups, but then, when these were unavailing, the British prime minister, Clement Attlee, announced in February 1947 that, whatever the circumstances, British rule in India would end by June 1948. The wisdom of this decision has been questioned. There are those who maintain that it was the only way

Pandit Nehru and his daughter, Indira Gandhi. Between them they were prime ministers of India for 33 years.

to compel Indian leaders to reach some sort of agreement. Others, however, insist that this sudden move, far from stimulating Indian unity, diminished it; that the sense of urgency which it created intensified Moslem fears and made them more intractable; and the hurried, last-minute division of the country, with the mass migrations and massacres which this involved, was the cause of much future strife. But in the circumstances it is doubtful if any other course was possible.

Following the prime minster's announcement strenuous efforts were made by the new viceroy, Lord Mountbatten, to persuade Indian leaders to agree on a scheme of partition, and these had some success. Lord Mountbatten also tried hard to prevent riots and communal strife, but this proved impossible and it can never be known for certain how great the death roll was.[1] But in view of the anger and hysteria in India at that time and the upheavals that were occurring, it was a considerable achievement that bloodshed was not on a much greater scale.

Eventually Indian independence was fixed for 15th August 1947. Communal strife continued for some time afterwards, and on 30th January 1948 Mahatma Gandhi (see p. 95) was assassinated by Hindu

---

[1] 250,000 is one estimate. Others are much larger.

extremists who blamed him for agreeing to the establishment of Pakistan. In 1950 India proclaimed herself a republic but asked to remain in the Commonwealth, and this was agreed. This marked the final development of what had been the British Empire. The British monarch was acknowledged as head of the new Commonwealth but all member countries were entirely equal and independent. All they had in common was that once they had been British colonies.

Postscript

For seventeen years after independence the prime minister of India was Jawaharial Nehru, a well-to-do lawyer, educated at Harrow and Cambridge, who had later become an ardent disciple of Mahatma Gandhi and had spent some nine years in gaol for his political activities. After him his daughter Indira Gandhi (no connection with the Mahatma) was prime minister (on and off) for sixteen years, and then for four years his grandson, Rajiv Gandhi held the office. During these years, with overwhelming problems at home (due primarily to an exploding population and chronic food shortages) and disputes with neighbouring states which led to wars with China (1961) and Pakistan (1965 and 1971) democracy in India might have given way to dictatorship. It is the great achievement of the Nehru family that it did not. And only a few years after independence the Republic of India, as the world's largest democracy, had gained a prominent position on the world stage as a dominant force in the 'Non-Aligned Countries' which sought to arbitrate in the Cold War between East and West.

Civil War in Malaya –
Communist Threat Overcome

In several British colonies after the war there were threats of Communist infiltration, but in most cases these were soon contained. Only in Malaya did the danger become formidable.

In Malaya there were special circumstances favouring the Communists. It was here during the war that the British had suffered their most humiliating defeat, and this had been a heavy blow to their prestige. After the British surrender the Malayan Communists had carried on an underground war against the Japanese for which they had been supplied with arms by the Allies, and when peace came these were not handed in; they were carefully hidden away for a future struggle with the imperialists. At the beginning of 1948 it seemed that the time for their use had arrived. There was much disorder in the country at that time, and with the victory of Mao Tse-tung in China it seemed that Communism was on the march. At the same time it appeared that the British, who had recently withdrawn from both India and Palestine, were in retreat. And so in June 1948 a twelve-year-long war began.

At first the Communists had considerable success. Strikes were called, trains derailed and officials murdered; also attacks were made on rubber plantations, the trees being slashed and workers killed or terrorised. The British response to these tactics was not as prompt as it might have been, and it was not until 1950 that effective counter-measures began to be taken. By then rubber estates, tin mines and all isolated communities had been turned into armed camps, and strict control had been imposed on all food and essential supplies to prevent them falling into the hands of the terrorists. But it was realised that the main battle would be for 'the hearts and minds of the people', and it was here that the Communists were soon shown to be at a disadvantage. For in waging war against rubber estates, tin mines and all 'forces of imperialism' they had murdered and mutilated many workers and inflicted great hardship on many more. Very few had joined the Communists willingly, certainly not the Mohammedan Indians and Malays and not many of the Chinese. The main object of British policy, then, was to isolate the Communists and cut them off from all sources of aid. And so in 1950 they began the process of resettling all inhabitants of outlying regions into the New Villages. This proved a great blow to the Communists as these were the people from whom they hoped to extract most help, and they were now being withdrawn from their grasp.

In 1952 the war against the Communists took a new turn with the arrival in Malaya of a new commander-in-chief, Sir Gerald Templer. Templer came armed with supreme powers over both the civil and military authorities, but he also brought with him an undertaking from the British government that Malaya would now proceed towards self-government. This had great effect on public opinion and did much to take the wind out of the Communists' sails. From then on all anti-Communist forces could feel that they were fighting for a free and independent Malaya, not just for the continuation of British rule.

During the next two years under Templer's dynamic leadership the hunting down of the Communists was greatly intensified. Systematically they were isolated and starved out, and at the same time specially trained 'hunter-killer' platoons were sent into the jungle to destroy them. By 1954 the Communists had been overcome but, although hungry, demoralised and heavily outnumbered, they continued to fight on, and the war did not finally come to an end until 1960.

Complete peace, however, had not yet come to Malaya, for in 1963 there began the so-called 'confrontation' with Indonesia. This arose from the foundation in that year of the Federation of Malaysia consisting of Malaya, Singapore and the British colonies of Sarawak and Sabah in North Borneo. This was strongly opposed by President Sukarno of Indonesia (see p. 283) who loudly declared his intention of crushing it. In the following years, however, he did little to achieve this aim; it seemed that 'confrontation' meant little more than numerous threats, a few small-scale raids and some interference with trade. During this time Malaysia depended to a large extent on British forces for protection, and although these were only involved in minor operations, their presence in the area was one of the main reasons for the failure of 'confrontation'. In 1965 Sukarno was overthrown by army leaders and 'confrontation' came to an end.

The Middle East – Decline of British Influence

In the granting of self-government to the British colonies the area where there was greatest difficulty, and on one occasion disaster, was the Middle East. Officially the only British colonies in the Middle East were Cyprus and Aden, but Britain's power and influence extended to most other countries as well. It was Britain who, during the First World War, had freed the Arabs from the Turks (see p. 42). And after the war Britain was granted a Mandate by the League of Nations to govern Palestine and was responsible for the setting up of a Jewish national home there (see p. 99). Also for more than sixty years Britain had been the effective ruler of Egypt and the Sudan.

At the end of the Second World War Britain was still the dominant power in the Middle East. The Anglo–Egyptian Treaty of 1936 (see p. 99), which gave her the right to station troops in the Canal Zone, made her the guardian of the Suez Canal; she had special treaty rights in Libya, Iraq and Jordan (then known as Transjordan); and she was still the official ruler of the Sudan.

In the post-war years most British statesmen felt it necessary to try to maintain Britain's position in the Middle East. More and more the country was coming to depend on Middle Eastern oil and on the Suez Canal through which, in those days before the arrival of supertankers, all the oil had to be transported. And so, despite a desperate economic situation, British troops continued to be stationed all over the area and Britain continued to make her influence felt. It soon became clear, however, that the problems of the Middle East were too much for Britain to handle alone. A series of crises erupted which Russia was always ready to exploit and which in some cases led to strong disagreement with the United States.

British Withdrawal from Palestine

The first crisis was in Palestine. Here after the war the Jews were clamouring loudly for the immediate admission of large numbers of Jewish refugees from Europe. This was strongly opposed by the Arabs in Palestine who demanded immediate independence for the country while they were still in a majority. For a time the British attempted to hold the balance between the two sides and to work out a settlement which both could accept. But the problem was insoluble, and the British received little thanks for their efforts, many brutal attacks being made against them by terrorist gangs.

Finally in 1947 the British government announced that it was going to give up its Mandate and hand it over to the United Nations. After that events moved swiftly. In November the United Nations voted for the partition of Palestine so that one part would be predominantly Jewish. The state of Israel was proclaimed on the day the British mandate came to an end (14th May 1948) and was at once recognised by the United States and Russia. But already before then fighting had broken out between Jews and Arabs and this now erupted into open war with the Jews struggling desperately and effectively to withstand their five Arab neighbour states. In 1949 United Nations mediators managed to bring about a truce, but a state of war continued with no permanent settlement in sight. By then nearly all the Arab population had left

'The blame is on your head if you fire on this unarmed ship.'
Illegal Jewish immigrants arriving in Palestine, defying all opposition.

Israel, and the greatest of all Middle Eastern problems, that of the Arab refugees, had begun.

Withdrawals from Persia and Egypt

British prestige in the Middle East had certainly been damaged by events in Palestine, and it took a further knock when the Persian government suddenly announced the nationalisation of the Anglo–Iranian Oil Company. This was a serious blow to Britain and the situation was made more difficult by the hysterical rantings of the Persian prime minister, Dr Mossadeq and by apparent American support for the Persian case. Eventually a settlement was patched up, but it had been demonstrated for all to see that in the modern world Britain could be abused and defied with impunity.

Soon after the takeover of British oil interests in Persia there began to take place in Egypt a series of events which were to lead to a far more serious crisis and humiliation. In 1952 King Farouk was expelled and the country taken over by army officers of whom Gamal Nasser in time emerged as the dominant power. The result of this was that activities against Israel were stepped up,[1] and a campaign was mounted to rid Egypt and all the Middle East of the remains of British power. The first step was to get the British troops out of the Canal Zone and this was soon achieved. The British government, still in desperate economic straits, had for some time been concerned about the cost of maintaining this garrison and with an increasingly hostile Egyptian population the position became almost untenable.

In spite of concessions by Britain relations with Egypt did not improve. Cairo radio continued to pour out a stream of anti-British propaganda and then in 1955 Nasser concluded an arms deal with Russia. This caused serious alarm. It meant that the delicate balance the Western powers had been trying to maintain in the supply of arms to Jews and Arabs would be upset. It also looked as if Russia was about to extend the Cold War into the Middle East and to stir up trouble there. For the time being, however, Britain continued to try to establish good relations with Egypt and in 1956 the last British troops were withdrawn. Also Britain and the United States agreed to provide finance for the construction of the Aswan dam on the river Nile. Russia too had offered to provide money for this project, and for a time Nasser attempted to play off one major power against the other. The consequence of this was that the United States abruptly, without any word to Britain, withdrew their offer. Whereupon Nasser announced that in order to provide the finance required he would nationalise the Suez Canal (July 1956).

For the British government and for the prime minister, Sir Anthony Eden,[2] in particular this was a turning point. Up to then he had been trying to come to terms with Nasser and to remove his grievances. But the nationalisation of the Suez Canal (owned principally by Britain and France) was a breach of an international treaty and, so Eden maintained, an illegal act, and to allow Nasser to get away with it amounted to appeasement. Appeasement was a sensitive subject with Eden. Before

---

[1] Israeli shipping was kept out of the Suez Canal and the Gulf of Akaba. Also special commando units, known as Fedayeen, were sent on raids into Israel.
[2] He had succeeded Churchill in 1954.

the war he had resigned from the British government of the time because of its policy of appeasing the European dictators, and he had later seen how this policy had led to the Second World War. In 1956 he was determined that the same mistake should not be made again. Nasser's actions since becoming President, in particular the way that one concession to him only led to further demands, convinced Eden that here was another dictator out to get what he could. It seemed to him that Nasser's aim was the leadership of the whole Arab world along with the extinction of the state of Israel. He also thought it intolerable that one of the world's main waterways, of vital importance to Britain and all Western European countries, should be solely under Egyptian control. 'Nasser must not be allowed,' he declared, 'to have his thumb on our windpipe.' For these reasons Eden and some, but not all, of his colleagues decided that this was an occasion where force might have to be used.

The 'Suez Affair'

It was tragic that Eden, who was essentially a man of peace and whose record of peaceful achievement since the war as Foreign Secretary had been outstanding, should have felt himself obliged suddenly to resort to force. Perhaps it was because he was acting out of character that everything was to go wrong for him. The basic trouble was that there was no agreement about Middle Eastern affairs between Britain and the United States. The policy of President Eisenhower and his Secretary of State, John Foster Dulles, was inconsistent and sometimes baffling. At times it seemed that they were firmly behind Britain and talked of forcing Nasser to 'disgorge', but at other times it seemed that this support had been abruptly withdrawn. In their relations with Middle Eastern countries since the war American statesmen had been anxious not to appear to be always on the side of the old colonial powers. In their struggle with the Communists for the 'hearts and minds' of the underdeveloped countries they had always to be showing themselves firmly opposed to old-fashioned imperialism. Also at that time they did not depend to the same extent as Britain on Middle East oil – obtaining only 4% of their supplies from there.

During the months following President Nasser's announcement efforts were made to come to an agreement about the future control of

Scuttled ships block the Suez Canal at the time of the Anglo-French invasion.

the Suez Canal, but Eden was convinced that no agreement with Nasser had any value as he could not be trusted to keep his word and that force would have to be used. In this he had strong support from the French government which had been enraged by the assistance given by Nasser to the rebels in Algeria. And so it came about that the governments of Britain, France and Israel came to an agreement and devised a plan by which Israel would attack Egypt with whom she was still officially at war and that Britain and France should then intervene to 'separate' the antagonists and at the same time gain control of the Suez Canal. The plan was put into effect in October 1956, and although the military operations were successful, everything else went disastrously wrong. In order to obtain secrecy none of Britain's allies, not even members of the Commonwealth, had been informed of the plan and were stunned by what was happening. At home too people were greatly confused and could not make out what the government was up to. At first the natural patriotism of the British people came to the fore and they thought the government must have good reasons for what they were doing. Later, however, opposition became angry and outspoken, and the country was bitterly divided on the issue. Opponents pointed out that the use of force was unwarranted and out of date and that Britain's action was a breach of the United Nations Charter. Abroad opposition was almost universal and Britain and France found themselves completely isolated. For a time they persevered with the operation, even though it meant using the veto in the Security Council to block a cease-fire. However, the forces against them were too strong; they had completely underestimated the reaction of the United States. It was expected that the American government would protest but no more; but in the event it reacted angrily and ruthlessly. For once it joined forces with Russia to condemn the operation at the United Nations and, more seriously, made use of its all-powerful economic force to bring pressure on Britain and France to end the operation.[1] And so, faced with hostile world opinion, strong opposition at home and the imminent collapse of the pound, the British and French had to give way and make a humiliating withdrawal with none of their aims achieved.

The 'Suez Affair' was a sobering lesson to Britain. It failed on every count. Nasser was not brought down; his power increased and he became, for a time, the hero of the Arab world; also he retained possession of the Suez Canal. At the same time it led to a growth of Russian influence in the Middle East and caused a rift among Western powers at a time when unity was particularly needed to confront the Russians over their invasion of Hungary (see p. 311). For Britain the essential truth that had to be grasped was how much in the modern world the country depended on the United States and that independent action was difficult if not impossible.

A Long-Drawn-Out Struggle in Cyprus

Perhaps in no other British colony did the achievement of independence cause so much difficulty and bloodshed as in Cyprus. Although Cyprus has always been predominantly Greek in character and more than three-quarters of the population are Greek, it lies just off the coast of Turkey

---

[1] This severe treatment of two of America's main allies was later to be described by President Eisenhower as his major foreign policy error.

and had been under Turkish rule for many years. Britain's first connection with Cyprus (apart from Richard Coeur de Lion at the time of the Crusades) occurred in 1878 when the Sultan of Turkey, anxious for British support in that area against Russia, placed the island under British rule, but the island did not formally become a British colony until 1925. At first, owing to the absence of deepwater harbours, Cyprus was of little use to Britain as a base; but later, with the advent of air power and following British withdrawal from other countries in the Middle East, it became of considerable importance.

However, as the importance of Cyprus grew, so too did the national feelings of the Greek population and their desire for Cyprus to be united with Greece. The movement for this, known as Enosis, erupted into violence in 1955 when there arrived from Greece a Colonel Grivas who began to organise an underground guerrilla movement known as EOKA. The leader of the Greek population was Archbishop Makarios, an adroit and devious politician, who was usually, but not always opposed to the use of force. But during the next four years there was great violence and bloodshed in the country while the British government tried vainly to find a settlement acceptable to the Greeks and the Turks and to itself.

Makarios III – archbishop, rebel leader and president of Cyprus.

At first the Greek demand for independence had been met with a flat refusal from Britain. Cyprus was considered a vital British base and it was thought that independence would lead to union with Greece which would stir up strong opposition not only from the Turks of Cyprus but also from those on the mainland – no more than 14 miles away. Efforts to reach an agreement dragged on over the next four years. The Greeks were determined to have Enosis while the Turks insisted that the island should be divided into Greek and Turkish sectors. In 1960 Cyprus became an independent country within the Commonwealth under joint Greek and Turkish rule, but this arrangement did not last and in 1964 a United Nations peace keeping force had to be sent to the island to prevent fighting between the two races. In 1974, when conditions had again become chaotic a Turkish invasion force landed and established a 'Turkish Federated State' in the northern part of the island, and the country has remained divided since then.

Africa – 'The Wind of Change'

After the war the general belief in Britain was that the African colonies would not be 'ready' for self-government for many years and that, in any case, they did not greatly want it. It soon became clear, however, that in Africa, as in Asia, national feeling was growing and that more and more Africans were eager to be rid of white rule and to be their own masters. In 1958 on a visit to South Africa the British prime minister, Harold Macmillan,[1] declared: 'The wind of change is blowing through this continent, and, whether we like it or not, this growth of national consciousness is a political fact.'

When it had become accepted that self-government had to come sooner rather than later, the process of decolonisation in Africa proceeded without undue difficulty. Problems and crises did arise, but there were no long drawn-out bloody wars as in Indo–China and Algeria where the French attempted to maintain their rule, and no chaotic situation as in the Congo (Zaire) where the Belgians pulled out suddenly, leaving no form of government behind them. It was the great hope of the British that when they left they would leave in each colony a democratic system of government similar to their own which would be workable and which would last. But this was expecting too much. It had taken Britain many centuries to establish democracy at home; it was unlikely that it would be achieved at once in Africa. In the years following British withdrawal it usually happened that the power of parliaments declined, opposition parties were subdued and despotic powers taken by the countries' rulers.

---

[1] He succeeded Sir Anthony Eden in 1956, soon after the 'Suez Affair'.

Apartheid in South Africa

Although Britain had responded promptly to the 'wind of change' in Africa, there was one country on which it made little impression. In South Africa there was a larger white population than in any other African territory, many of whom, the Afrikaners or Boers,[1] had been there for 300 years and more and were utterly determined to maintain white supremacy. Their relationship with the later British settlers had never been an easy one, and since the Boer War (1899–1902) it was the latter who had had the upper hand. After the Second World War, however, this position began to change and in 1948 the Boer Nationalist Party won the general election and set about imposing on the country a system known as *apartheid* which involved the complete separation of black and white races. This was enforced ruthlessly: blacks were compelled to live in separate townships (being evicted from their existing homes where necessary), went to separate and inferior schools, travelled in separate parts of public transport, and used separate public buildings and beaches; in addition blacks had no political rights and their freedom of movement was restricted by 'pass laws' which required them to carry at all times a kind of identity card saying to which racial group they belonged and which barred them from going into certain areas. At the same time the government took dictatorial powers to suppress riots, to put away political opponents and to censor the press. In theory apartheid meant 'separate development' and did not involve racial superiority and white domination, but it had that effect. Black people became second-class citizens while the white population depended on them completely for labour, and the economy of the country would have collapsed without them.

Inevitably such a policy caused outrage in the outside world and nowhere more so than in the new style Commonwealth; this was growing rapidly as new countries joined after attaining independence.[2] As the essence of the Commonwealth was that all members were equal regardless of race, it was clearly not the place for a country with racist

---

[1] These were mainly of Dutch, German and French origin.
[2] Between 1945 and 1968 the Commonwealth had grown from 5 members to 28.

policies. It was only a matter of time before South Africa left the Commonwealth which she did of her own accord in 1961.

Postscript

In the following years South Africa became more and more cut off from the rest of the world, but isolation was something to which Boers were accustomed and hostility made them all the more obstinate. In 1962 the United Nations imposed sanctions on the country, cutting off all foreign trade, but ways were found round these and for the time being they did not make a great impact on the South African economy. More irksome to many South Africans was their exclusion from world sporting events, notably cricket and rugby.

By the end of the 1970s it was becoming evident to most South Africans, notably the business community, that South Africa could not exist indefinitely in isolation from the rest of the world. In 1978 there was some relaxation of apartheid: black trade unions were allowed as also were mixed marriages. But these concessions, far from damping down black militancy, only increased it. In the following years further concessions were made, and the major break through came in 1989 when F. W. De Klerk became President. He was on the liberal wing of the Nationalist Party and was determined that apartheid had to go. He announced the ending of it in the following year and at the same time ended the ban on the African National Congress (ANC) and released from prison, where he had been for twenty-six years, Nelson Mandela, the most famous and most charismatic of its leaders. These measures immediately led to white 'backlash' from the far right Afrikaner Resistance Movement, determined at all costs to prevent black rule in South Africa. There was also much ferocious fighting with great loss of life between ANC supporters and the Zulu 'Inkatha Freedom Party' led by Chief Buthelezi. But nothing could now stop the movement for reform. In 1992 a referendum was held among the white citizens of South Africa which showed that 70% were in favour of ending apartheid and the introduction of parliamentary government with one man one vote. But the problem of finding a settlement acceptable to all groups – Boer extremists, other whites, the ANC, the Zulus and other African tribes – seemed almost insuperable.

Rhodesia Declares Independence

The only British colony in Africa where there were serious and lasting difficulties was the one where there was a comparatively large white population.[1] The white people in Rhodesia, as in South Africa, were strongly aware of being a small minority in the middle of a much greater number of blacks. They maintained that they and their fore-fathers had worked hard and lived dangerously to build up the prosperity of the country which, they thought, would disappear with black rule. But, as has been seen, this attitude was becoming increasingly outdated. To most people in Britain, as in the rest of the world, it was essential that there should be majority rule.

Rhodesia (previously known as Southern Rhodesia to distinguish it from Northern Rhodesia, later Zambia) had originally been founded by the English multi-millionaire, Cecil Rhodes and for a number of years was the property of the British South Africa Company. In 1923, after a referendum which decided that the country would not join up with South Africa, it became a self-governing British colony which meant in effect that it had independence in all matters except foreign affairs and laws relating to the rights of Africans.

After the war a scheme was devised by which Northern and Southern Rhodesia along with Nyasaland (later Malawi) would be united to form a federation. The economic advantages of this plan were considerable. Northern and Southern Rhodesia would provide their mineral and agricultural products, notably tobacco, and Nyasaland, a poor country with few natural resources, would be provided with employment opportunities for her population. However, this arrangement took little account of the 'wind of change', and from the first it was strongly opposed by the Africans, especially in Northern Rhodesia, who saw in it a device for depriving them of complete independence and for main-taining white supremacy. The British government hoped that these objections would be overcome when it was seen how great were the economic advantages, and in 1953 it went ahead and formed the Central African Federation of the three colonies. But opposition to it did not die down and grew more intense over the years. It was to last until 1964

---

[1] There were about 241,000 Europeans and 4,400,000 Africans.

when it was clear to most people that it could not survive, and Northern Rhodesia and Nyasaland were granted independence.

The leaders of Southern Rhodesia confidently expected that it would be granted to them too, but the British government would not agree to this unless there were binding provisions for more political rights for the Africans. It was not expected that there would be 'one man one vote' immediately but a reasonably rapid advance to this goal should be made. However, on this point no agreement could be reached with the Southern Rhodesian leaders. In 1965 there was a general election which was won by the Rhodesian Front party led by Ian Smith, an ex-fighter pilot, who immediately declared Rhodesia's independence from Britain. This was an illegal act, constituting rebellion, and there were some in Britain who urged that force should be used to restore the situation. The Labour government, however, decided against this and instead imposed sanctions which aimed at establishing a blockade, cutting off Rhodesia's trade with the rest of the world. However, to be effective the blockade had to be complete and this could not be achieved; goods continued to come in and out of the country mainly through South Africa and Mozambique, at that time still a Portuguese colony.

For a time the Rhodesian Republic (as it became in 1970) existed without undue difficulty, but the forces opposed to it could not be withstood indefinitely. In 1974 Mozambique became an independent country with black rule which resulted in guerrilla fighters based in the country operating against Rhodesia, and then in the Mozambique border being closed. This put Rhodesia in a desperately difficult situation as its only access to the outside world was now through South Africa, and at the same time guerrilla fighting increased and pressure from abroad, particularly from Britain and the United States, to allow political rights to the blacks was intensified. In 1976 Ian Smith was compelled to climb down and accepted the principle of black rule. He managed to hold on to power for a few years longer, but in 1979 a conference was held in London which worked out a new constitution for the country, now renamed Zimbabwe. In the following year a general election was held in which a large majority was gained by the party of Robert Mugabe who has remained in power ever since (1994).

Timescale

1947

February   British prime minister announces end of British rule in India.

August   Indian independence.

1948

January   Assassination of Gandhi.

May   British Mandate in Palestine ends. State of Israel proclaimed.

June   Beginning of civil war in Malaysia.

1950   India proclaimed a republic within the Commonwealth.

1953   Formation of Central African Federation.

1955   EOKA subversion in Cyprus begins.

1956

July   Nasser announces nationalisation of Suez Canal.

October   'Suez Affair'. British and French armed intervention in Egypt.

1960   End of civil war in Malaysia.
           Cyprus becomes independent country within the Commonwealth.

1961   South Africa leaves Commonwealth.

1963   Confrontation with Indonesia in Borneo begins.

1964   End of Central African Federation.

1965   Rhodesia declares independence from Britain.

1979   End of white rule in Rhodesia. Country renamed Zimbabwe.

1990   de Klerk announces end of *apartheid* in South Africa.

Chapter 20

EUROPE AFTER STALIN

The Death of Stalin

Stalin died on 5th March 1953. As with most events in his life it was encompassed by an element of mystery. A few months before there had been rumours of a 'doctors' plot', and as there were indications that he was about to embark on another of his great purges, the suspicion arose that his death had been hastened by some of his intended victims.

Few dictators have had such great power as Stalin. At the time of his death his authority stretched from North Korea to Central Europe. In Russia his power was absolute, far greater than any of the tsars, and extended over all aspects of Russian life. Russian thinkers and writers were compelled to keep rigidly to the party line; history was rewritten to fit in with Stalin's image; even art and music were dominated by his tastes, and all Western or 'bourgeois' influences were banned.[1] Stalin's death was followed by a power struggle among his subordinates, but by 1955 Nikita Khruschev had emerged as the main power in the land. Like Stalin Khruschev was a ruthless and devious politician, but both in personality and style of leadership he was different. He was more open and forthcoming; he was capable of great furies but could also be genial and humorous. Also he did not remain all the time cooped up in the Kremlin, brooding suspiciously, but travelled extensively both in Russia and abroad. Above all he did not make the same use of terror and mass purges; his political opponents were not exterminated.[2]

---

[1] This had disastrous results: it meant that new work was old-fashioned and uninspired. Russian artists were obliged to paint such things as machinery and large peasant women doing heavy manual labour.

[2] The one exception was Lavrenti Beria, head of the secret police, who was shot.

The 'Thaw' – A New Attitude in Russia

With the coming of Khruschev there was some relaxation in Russian attitudes both at home and abroad. In Russia the activities of the secret police were curtailed, a number of political prisoners were set free and, for a time, more freedom was given to the Russian people to write and say what they believed.

In 1956 in the Twentieth Congress of the Communist Party Khruschev made a long and forthright denunciation of Stalin and all his ways.[1] He accused him of flagrant abuse of power, brutality and wilfulness. He described how, on Stalin's orders, old Bolsheviks had been disgraced and put to death, and how innocent people had been tortured into confessing crimes which they had not committed; he also blamed Stalin bitterly for Russia's unpreparedness for war at the time of the German invasion. As can be imagined, this speech caused a tremendous sensation; the sudden debunking of the man whom all Russians had been brought up to regard as godlike brought great confusion and doubts and led to further divisions in the Communist ranks, particularly in China where Mao Tse-tung was horrified and where relations with Russia were soon to reach breaking point (see p. 278).

In relaxing Stalin's iron rule Khruschev soon realised that he was releasing forces which he might not be able to control. For once having been given a taste of freedom, the Russian people were going to want more and, if this were given, it would endanger the dictatorship of the Communist Party. Khruschev, therefore, felt it necessary, as later did his successors, to put on the brakes and to show clearly and forcefully that there were limits to the freedom that could be allowed.[2]

---

[1] Although this was not published in the Soviet Union news of it leaked out and it was soon spread all over the world.

[2] Two of the most famous 'dissidents' who suffered from allowing themselves too much freedom were the writer, Alexander Solzhenitsyn, who was exiled from Russia, and Andrei Sakharov, Russia's leading scientist who was put under house arrest in a remote part of Russia.

Revolt in Eastern Europe

Nowhere were there stronger repercussions to Khruschev's denunciation of Stalin than in the Communist countries of Eastern Europe. Here the long-suffering people thought they saw the chance of ridding themselves of their harsh, repressive, Russian-dominated governments and replacing them with more liberal and more independent regimes.

In Poland riots broke out in June 1956 and soon afterwards Wladyslaw Gomulka, a Communist leader who had been purged by Stalin in 1948 and imprisoned ever since, was elected First Secretary of the Party. At this the Russian leaders took fright, fearing he might prove to be another Tito. They arrived suddenly in the country and ordered Russian tanks to move in; but Gomulka was able to persuade them that he had no intention of taking Poland out of the Eastern bloc, and the Russian forces withdrew without bloodshed.

In Hungary, however, there was considerable bloodshed. Here feelings were running high. Not being a Slav people, the Hungarians particularly resented Russian domination and were seething with indignation at the brutal and tyrannical methods of their Stalinist leaders. In October 1956 riots broke out and the moderate Communist, Imre Nagy, previously dismissed for offending the Russians, became prime minister. At the same time there was a loud and insistent clamour that Hungary should leave the Warsaw Pact and adopt a neutral position in Europe similar to Yugoslavia. For several days the crowds ran riot in Budapest. The hated secret police were lynched, home-made bombs were flung at Russian tanks and, to general delight and hilarity, an immense bronze statue of Stalin was toppled from its pedestal and smashed. Then for a time there was a lull when the Russian tanks, sent in at the request of Hungary's Stalinist rulers, withdrew from the city, and Russian leaders debated what they should do next. For a time they hesitated, but then the decision was taken that Hungary could not be allowed to go her own way. And so the tanks, heavily reinforced, were sent back into Budapest where hard and bitter fighting took place. However, the Russians were ruthless and in ten days all resistance had been ground down. As a result of the rebellion 25,000 Hungarians were killed, 50,000 wounded and about 140,000 became refugees.

Before the fighting came to an end the Hungarians sent out an appeal for help to the United Nations and to all free people everywhere, but there was no effective response to this. It was tragic that at the time the attention of the world was distracted by the ill-fated Suez venture of Britain and France (see p. 299). But the only way in which the West could have intervened to save Hungary was by nuclear war, and this was too heavy a price to pay.

The solemn lesson to be learned from the Hungarian revolution was that the Russians were not prepared to let any of the satellite countries out of their control – rather than that they were ready to invade and use force. At the same time it became evident that the United States was not prepared to prevent this happening by force. The bitter truth for the people of Eastern Europe was that in seeking freedom they could expect only moral support from the West and, for the time being, should expect only gradual change in their situation.

The lessons learned in Hungary were underlined by events in Czechoslovakia in 1968. In that year a liberal Communist, Alexander Dubcek, was brought to power by popular acclaim and proposed certain reforms; but these were too sweeping for the Russians and, once again, the tanks were sent in. This time there was no popular resistance and the Czechs sadly resigned themselves to their fate. The time for liberation was not yet.

Street fighting in Budapest with the burning of Communist literature.

Peaceful Co-existence

After Stalin's death the 'thaw' in Russian attitudes was also felt in Western countries. Khrushchev conceded that, contrary to orthodox Communist doctrine, war between Communist and capitalist powers was not inevitable and the two could co-exist peacefully (although he

Czech civilians confront Russian tanks in Prague.

continued to believe that capitalism would eventually collapse of its own accord). This new attitude was manifested in deeds as well as words. Thus a peace treaty with Austria, which Russia had been obstructing, was signed; the Korean War at last was brought to an end; and Khruschev visited Yugoslavia and apologised for Russian 'mistakes'.

Russia's new outlook, however, did not prevent the further division of Europe into two camps. The Russians recently had made rapid advances in the development of nuclear weapons,[1] and American superiority in this field was no longer as great as it had been. Partly for this reason and partly because the effect of using nuclear weapons was now so horrendous, the Americans maintained that it was urgently necessary to build up the conventional forces of NATO, and that this could only be done by rearming the Germans. There was some opposition to this in France and Britain and even in Germany itself, but the Americans insisted and in October 1954 West

---

[1] The first Russian hydrogen bomb was exploded in 1953, only one year after the Americans.

Germany became a member of NATO (see p. 270). Inevitably the Russians reacted strongly to this: the remilitarisation of Germany leading to another invasion of their country was a nightmare that haunted them perpetually. And so in May 1955 all the Communist countries of Eastern Europe were drawn together into a military alliance, similar to NATO, known as the Warsaw Pact.

It has been seen that the doctrine of peaceful co-existence was not accepted by all Communists. As well as the Chinese there were some Russians who opposed it strongly, and their case was strengthened by the rebellions in Eastern Europe and by the building up of NATO. If Khruschev was to maintain his position he must have some success to show for it. It was perhaps for this reason that he become involved in some foreign adventures which nearly brought about a world war – what came to be known as 'brinkmanship'. The first of these was another attempt to force the Western powers out of Berlin.

Crisis in Berlin – The Wall

Khruschev once described Berlin as 'a fishbone in the gullet'. It had always been very objectionable to the Russians to have this Western capitalist enclave in the middle of Communist Eastern Germany. This was especially the case as West Berlin had become noticeably more prosperous than East Berlin. A stream of refugees from the East was pouring across the border all the time which was not only a bad advertisement for Communism but also a serious loss to the East German economy as many of these were skilled workers.[1]

The Potsdam Agreement at the end of the war gave the Western powers a legal right to be in Berlin and this had been substantiated at the time of the Berlin airlift (see p. 269). However, in a speech in 1958 Khruschev declared bluntly that it was time this situation came to an end and that all occupying powers should leave Berlin and the city become part of East Germany. He added that if this had not taken place in six months Russia would sign a separate treaty with East Germany, handing over East Berlin and control of all access routes to the city. He indicated as well that in any dispute about these with the West, East

---

[1] Since 1945 the number of refugees amounted to about 2,000,000.

Germany, as a member of the Warsaw Pact, would be entitled to help from all the other members.

This announcement caused great consternation. If Khruschev were to carry out his threat it would mean that Western Berlin would become completely isolated and could no longer exist, and this would be a momentous blow to the prestige of America and her allies. There followed a war of nerves in which Khruschev blew hot and cold. At times he was calm and reasonable and had friendly meetings both with President Eisenhower and with the British prime minister, Harold Macmillan. But he was under pressure from hardliners in Russia and could not afford to be too accommodating. Great hopes were placed in a summit conference to be held in May 1960, but this had to be abandoned as a few days before an American U-2 spy plane had been shot down over Russia. At the conference Khruschev angrily demanded an apology for this incident and when this was refused by Eisenhower, he walked out of it.

The following year Khruschev met the new American president, John F. Kennedy, but no agreement was reached. Perhaps because he wanted to test Kennedy's nerve Khruschev was tough and uncompromising, talking freely and fiercely of nuclear war. However, Kennedy was not to be intimidated and support for Berlin was maintained and even increased. As the crisis intensified the number of refugees from the East grew ever larger; in July of 1961 there were as many as 30,000. This the East German government could not allow to continue and in August, with Russian consent, it sealed off all entrances into West Berlin except for a few official checkpoints. Then a few days later the East Germans began to build a six-foot-high wall surrounded with barbed wire. Escape to the West then became almost impossible and anyone attempting it was shot mercilessly.

The Berlin Wall was a breach of the Potsdam Agreement and was bitterly resented by the West Germans, but it did take much of the heat out of the crisis. The flow of refugees was halted; the Russians did not sign a treaty with East Germany; and in time the cold War veered away from Berlin to other parts of the world.

The Cuban Missile Crisis – The Edge of the Abyss

Cuba had been a thorn in the flesh of America since 1956. In that year Fidel Castro landed in the country with 82 supporters and started

The Berlin wall under construction by East German security forces.

guerrilla warfare against the corrupt and despotic government of Fulgencio Batista. It seemed a desperate venture but in the course of the next two years he won over thousands of Cubans to his side and in 1959 he led his forces into the capital, Havana.

At first Castro was at pains to deny that he was a Communist, but when he nationalised land and some American property and then set up Communist-style farm cooperatives, the American government took fright and banned the purchase of Cuban sugar, the staple crop of the country on which its economy depended. The result of this was that Castro was driven further into the Communist camp. Khruschev, sensing the possibility of a Russian satellite just off the coast of America, undertook to buy Cuba's sugar crop and to prop up her economy with substantial financial aid. This caused great alarm in America and a number of plots were hatched to bring about Castro's downfall. These came to a climax in 1961 when a band of discontented Cuban exiles with American backing set out to invade the country, landing in the Bay of Pigs. The expedition proved a disastrous failure and was a great embarrassment to the newly elected President Kennedy. It also resulted in Castro seeking military protection from the Russians who sent a considerable quantity of modern weapons, and then, in September 1962, began the construction of missile bases. It was not long before these were discovered by American spy planes, and this brought about the greatest crisis of the Cold War. For if these bases, only 90 miles from the American mainland were allowed to be completed, every city in the Western hemisphere would be exposed to nuclear attack.

President Kennedy at once decided that missile bases in Cuba could not be tolerated. But how were these to be prevented without

Khruschev and Castro show unity at the United Nations Assembly.

precipitating a nuclear war? For one week the situation was extremely tense. On 22nd October Kennedy announced that American forces would invade Cuba on the 30th if the bases had not been removed. He also announced that Cuba would be 'put into quarantine' and no ships carrying war supplies would be allowed to land. These were strong measures but Kennedy was at pains not to drive the Russians into a corner; he wanted to leave them room to back down without too much loss of face; and in the end this is what they did. At first they tried to extract an undertaking that, in return, the United States would withdraw their bases from Turkey, but this was ignored by Kennedy, and then on 28th October, two days within the limit, Khruschev climbed down and announced that the missile bases would be withdrawn provided only the Americans promised never to invade Cuba again. Although this was a notable victory for Kennedy, there was no exultation over it. The crisis had had a very sobering effect, and both the great powers had been deeply shocked by how near they had come to a holocaust. Soon afterwards they signed the Partial Test Ban Treaty, banning the testing of nuclear weapons in the atmosphere. They also established a direct line between the White House and the Kremlin, known as the hot line, so that in future crises would not occur because of lack of communication.

Another result of the Cuban missile crisis was the dismissal from office two years later of Nikita Khruschev. An indictment against him was drawn up which included 'grave errors of policy, by introducing missiles into Cuba in the autumn of 1962'.

Timescale

1953	
March 5	Death of Stalin.
1954	West Germany becomes a member of NATO.
1955	Nikita Khruschev establishes himself as chief power in Russia.
	Establishment of Warsaw Pact.
1956	Khruschev denounces Stalin.
	Riots in Poland. Russia intervenes and then withdraws.
	Hungarian uprising. Suppressed by Russians.
1959	Fidel Castro gains power in Cuba.
1961	Building of Berlin Wall.
	Unsuccessful US invasion of Cuba at Bay of Pigs.
1962	
September	Russia starts to build missile launching pads in Cuba.
October 22	Kennedy threatens invasion of Cuba.
28:	Khruschev climbs down and agrees to withdrawal of missile bases in Cuba.
1964	Dismissal of Khruschev.
1968	Rebellion in Czechoslovakia. Alexander Dubcek becomes president. Russian troops sent into the country and he is deposed.

Chapter 21

THE ATOMIC AGE

Splitting the Atom

For centuries it was accepted by scientists that every substance was made up of atoms and that atoms were the smallest particles in existence and could not be split. The first upset of this theory came in 1896 when the French physicist, Henri Becquerel, discovered that the atoms of uranium gave off particles or rays. This discovery of 'radiation' or 'radioactivity' was developed further by another French scientist, Pierre Curie and his Polish wife Marie, who discovered a new element which became known as radium. Soon afterwards Albert Einstein put forward the theory that vast amounts of energy were contained in a small amount of matter and that if more were known about the structure of atoms it might be possible to release this energy. In the following years research into atomic science was carried out in several European countries – by Enrico Fermi in Italy, by Niels Bohr in Denmark, by Otto Hahn in Germany and by Ernest Rutherford and a team of Cambridge scientists in England. There was considerable cooperation between these scientists, and their work came to a head in 1938 when in Germany the atom was split for the first time.

The Development of the Atom Bomb

The outbreak of war in the following year meant that in England and Germany atomic science turned mainly to the quest for an atomic bomb. In this field Germany at first took the lead, but soon after the attack on Pearl Harbour British and American scientists joined forces and immense resources were devoted towards 'Manhattan Project' as it was called.[1]

---

[1] Altogether three new towns were built in the United States specially for the purpose.

Within a year the main breakthrough had been made when in a disused Chicago squash court Enrico Fermi, who had emigrated from Mussolini's Italy, achieved the first chain reaction; this was the beginning of nuclear energy on a large scale. There were still numerous problems to be overcome, but two and a half years later an atomic bomb had been constructed and was exploded in the New Mexico desert on 16th July 1945. Onlookers were overawed by the colossal explosion. As the great column of purple fire shot into the air and a cloud of smoke billowed out into the shape of a gigantic mushroom, there were those who feared that the chain reaction had got out of hand. Afterwards it could be seen how immense was its destructive force:

> ... all life, vegetable as well as animal, was destroyed within a radius of about a mile. There was not a rattlesnake left in the region, nor a blade of grass. The land within a radius of 400 yards was transformed into a glasslike substance the colour of green jade ... The tower at Zero was completely vaporised. A herd of antelope that had been grazing several miles away had vanished completely. It is believed that they started on a mad dash that ended in the wilds of Mexico.[1]

Hiroshima and Nagasaki

Three weeks after the successful test in New Mexico an atomic bomb was dropped on the Japanese city of Hiroshima which, in a fraction of a second, was reduced to a mass of radioactive ruins. The attacking aircraft (known as Enola Gay) was badly shaken by the explosion and the crew stunned:

> Those inside Enola Gay first saw a little pinpoint of light, purplish red. In an instant the pinpoint grew into a giant ball of purple fire, half a mile in diameter. The great fireball suddenly exploded into a huge mass of swirling flames and purple clouds. Out of it came gigantic, concentric white rings of fog, as though the earth itself was blowing mighty smoke rings.
> The mass seemed to hesitate for a brief second. Suddenly out of

---

[1] *Dawn Over Zero* by William L. Laurence.

the swirling purple clouds came a huge white column of smoke. Up it went, higher, ever higher, until it reached 10,000 feet.

Then came another phase. The 10,000-foot column suddenly grew into a giant mushroom, with tremendous clouds of dust swirling about its base for a distance of three miles. The mushroom kept rising, growing to tremendous heights ... It kept climbing upward until it reached a height of 45,000 to 50,000 feet, breaking into several layers of a creamy white mass with a purplish tinge.[1]

Down below in Hiroshima everyone within half a mile of the explosion was killed and many more besides – about 90,000 altogether. This was the experience of Mrs Nakamura who was about three-quarters of a mile away and survived:

As Mrs Nakamura stood watching her neighbour, everything flashed whiter than any white she had ever seen. She did not notice what happened to the man next door; the reflex of a mother set her in motion towards her children. She had taken a single step when something picked her up and she seemed to fly into the next room over the raised sleeping platform, pursued by parts of her house.[2]

Two days later another atomic bomb was dropped on the city of Nagasaki and within a week Japan had surrendered. But the ordeal of these cities was not over; for many were to die slow and agonising deaths from radiation and many more became diseased or deformed.

The Control of Nuclear Weapons

The atom bomb brought with it a host of problems. People everywhere were aghast at the thought of what might happen when even bigger bombs were invented and fell into the hands of unfriendly nations. There was a general feeling that the world was a less safe place and would never be the same again.

One of the first problems was whether the United States should share the atomic secrets with her allies or keep them to herself. It was argued by some that failure to share them would lead to great

[1] *Ibid.*
[2] *Hiroshima* by John Hersey.

mistrust between America and Russia and that an atomic war would be less likely if both the great world powers had the bomb. However, by the end of the war tension between East and West was mounting, and in the event the United States government decided not to pass on details of the bomb.

The problem of controlling atomic weapons, so vital to mankind, was to remain unsolved. It was not long before Russia had made her own bomb.[1] This was exploded in 1949, and from then on there developed something of a race to build up the largest armoury of atomic weapons. In 1952 the Americans exploded the first hydrogen bomb, which had a hundred times the power of the bomb dropped on Nagasaki; but in the following year the Russians did the same. At first the Americans were well in the lead, but the Russians caught up much sooner than expected, and in one field they took the lead: in 1957 they launched Sputnik 1 into space and it became evident that in rocketry the Russians were ahead and had superior methods of delivering the bomb to its target.

Nuclear Disarmament

As the nuclear 'race' intensified there were many who felt that the situation had become intolerable. In time both the great powers had enough nuclear weapons to destroy totally whole cities, and although some of them might be stored away, others were at the ready in aircraft, submarines and launching sites, and could be discharged at the press of a button. It seemed that it needed only a misunderstanding or a mis-judgment or a moment of panic for one to be let off, and so bring about a nuclear holocaust.

Because of these fears there grew up in many countries strong, vociferous movements for nuclear disarmament. It was maintained by their supporters that the stockpiling of nuclear weapons must lead inevitably to their use, and that the only way to prevent this was by unilateral disarmament, that is not to wait until agreement has been reached with the other side, but to go ahead and get rid of all your own nuclear weapons at once and forswear their use for ever. Such a policy

---

[1] This was largely due to German experts who had been taken to work in Russia, also to the betrayal of atomic secrets by Western scientists and diplomats sympathetic to Communism.

would mean being at the mercy of your enemy, but better this than a nuclear war. In the event, however, none of the atomic powers was willing to take this step, preferring to wait until some agreement was reached on international inspection and control.

Peaceful Uses of Atomic Energy

In the early days of atomic power governments were much more interested in its military applications than in its peaceful uses. But these were not entirely neglected, and after the war it was in Britain that a lead in this field was taken. Several nuclear power stations were built which contributed significantly to the nation's electricity supply. These have a number of advantages: they are cleaner than coal or oil, can be sited anywhere and do not depend on vast masses of fuel – one lump of uranium producing the same power as many hundreds of tons of coal. However, there are also great disadvantages. In spite of every precaution accidents do sometimes occur, and just how devastating these can be was shown horrifyingly at Chernobyl in the Ukraine.[1] In Britain the accident rate has been very good – better than in most other industries – but the effects of nuclear power stations on the surrounding country and its inhabitants are still uncertain. There is also the problem of radioactive waste; there are large quantities of this and it can neither be rendered harmless nor disposed of completely safely.

If these problems can be overcome and atomic power can be produced which is clean, cheap and safe, the possibilities for its use are immense. Vast schemes of irrigation could be undertaken to bring desert land under cultivation, new harbours could be created and desalination plants set up to provide fresh water where it is needed. No other power in the hands of man has such potential for good or evil.

---

[1] A major accident occurred in a nuclear power station here in 1986. It devastated the country nearby, causing many deaths and great sickness. The effects of it were felt thousands of miles away.

Into Space

'All Moonshine'

As late as the 1950s there were some eminent scientists who were still maintaining that all ideas of space travel were 'moonshine'. But then on 4th October 1957, for all to see and hear, the Russians put into orbit the first space vehicle known as Sputnik 1. From then on developments came rapidly: within four years the first man had made a space flight and eight years later (1969) the first men landed on the moon.

The difficulties of these achievements had been immense. It was necessary to fire a rocket, weighing several tons, over a hundred miles into the sky at a speed of seven miles per second (125,000 m.p.m.). The rocket had to be capable of withstanding the tremendous heat – enough to melt any known metal – and to carry with it not only enough fuel but also enough oxygen so that the fuel could be burned. To put a man into space there were further problems. How could he be provided with air to breathe? How could he be protected from the extremes of temperature? How would he be affected by weightlessness? What were the dangers from meteorites (shooting stars) and solar rays? Above all how was he to be brought safely back to Earth? In the event these difficulties and dangers proved less great than expected, but the overcoming of them was a miracle of technology. Accidents did occur but loss of life was small compared with other great ventures.

The Early Pioneers

Work had been taking place on rocket research, particularly in Germany and America, before the Second World War. After the outbreak of war all efforts in Germany were directed into the development of a military missile capable of being used against the Allies, and this came to completion in 1944 when the V-2s were launched against London (see p. 231). At the time these had little effect on the outcome of the war and the defeat of Germany occurred soon afterwards. However, the V-2 was well in advance of any other rocket at that time, and it was of great importance to American research when, after the war, its chief designer, Werner von Braun, emigrated to the United States and carried on his work there.

Russian Advances

In the post-war years the arms race between the United States and Russia meant that both countries spent enormous sums of money on rocket research. Here at first the Russians were ahead, and it was they who first developed new propellants (fuels) which made it possible for larger and more powerful rockets to be used. Sputnik 1 was followed a month later by Sputnik 2 which contained a live dog, Laika. Laika stood no chance of survival, but has won a place in history as the first living creature to go into outer space. In 1959 the Russians started aiming spacecraft at the moon and one of these, Lunik III, succeeded in photographing the further hidden side.

Meanwhile American space projects were lagging behind, and there was a disaster when, in the full glare of publicity, their first space vehicle, the Vanguard, blew up on its launching platform (December 1957). Two months later, however, a tiny satellite, known as Explorer 1, was put into orbit, and a month later a second and successful attempt was made to launch Vanguard. But the Russians were to maintain their lead for some time, and in April 1961 they achieved the historic feat of sending the first man into space.

Yuri Gagarin had been born on a collective farm and his family had suffered intense hardship during the German invasion of Russia. In spite of a badly interrupted education he later became a test pilot and then, after a long period of training, was selected to make the first space flight. On 12th April 1961 he was strapped into the tiny cabin of Vostok 1. As the rocket accelerated to a speed of 17,500 miles an hour the pressure in the space vehicle mounted and the feeling of being weighed down became overwhelming. But then quite suddenly it vanished and Gagarin was experiencing the sensation of weightlessness. One circuit only of the Earth was made and then came the most dangerous part of the operation, the re-entry into the atmosphere; but this too was achieved successfully, and after a flight of no more than one hour forty-eight minutes Vostok arrived back safely in Russia.

The Americans Aim for the Moon

The flight of Vostok 1 was a historic occasion; it showed conclusively that space flights were possible. It was also a notable triumph for the

Russians, and this had the effect of spurring the Americans into greater activity. In the following month President Kennedy made a rousing speech in which he called for the landing of a man on the moon within the next ten years. Soon afterwards (February 1962) John Glenn made the first orbital flight from the United States.[1]

By the end of the 1960s American space technology was advancing rapidly, and it seemed likely that President Kennedy's target would be reached with time to spare. By 1969 all was ready for the great event, and on 16th July Apollo 11 was blasted off with Neil Armstrong, Edwin Aldrin and Michael Collins on board. Four days later the lunar module, known as Eagle, touched down on the moon's surface in the Sea of Tranquillity. Soon afterwards, with a television camera carrying all his movements to millions of people on Earth, Armstrong emerged from the module and started to climb down the ladder on to the moon. As he reached the last rung he paused and said so that everyone could hear him: 'I'm going to step off the lunar module now. That's one small step for a man, one great leap for mankind.' Then for two hours and forty-seven minutes he and Aldrin, who followed him, moved about the bleak, desolate surface of the moon, performing their allotted tasks. They collected rock samples and set up scientific instruments. They also planted the American flag and a commemorative plaque and chatted with President Nixon. The withdrawal from the moon, like the approach, proceeded faultlessly, and soon afterwards Armstrong and Aldrin were reunited with Collins in the Command Module. Three days later they splashed down in the Pacific – thirty seconds behind schedule.

The moon landing had been a marvellous achievement, but the cost of it had been colossal, and there were many who wondered if it had been worth it. Some gains to scientific knowledge were made, but these had not been of great importance, and to many the whole project had seemed no more than a prestige exercise. As against this there were many who maintained that it was one of the most exciting ventures in the history of mankind and that it had to be done. In reply to the question: 'What is the use of space travel?' they replied: 'What is the

---

[1] The first American astronaut into space was actually Alan Shepard, but his craft only went straight up and straight down without going into orbit.

Buzz Aldrin on the moon (July 1969).

use of any great scientific discovery in its first stages? Electricity for example. Come to that what is the use of a new born baby?'

While the argument was being carried on more space probes were made, going further and further afield. Spacecraft visited Mars and Venus and flights to Mercury and Jupiter are being planned.

Timescale

1938	First splitting of the atom.
1945	
July 16	First explosion of atomic bomb in New Mexico.
August 6	Atom bomb dropped on Hiroshima.
9	Atom bomb dropped on Nagasaki.
1949	First explosion of atomic bomb in Russia.

1952	Americans explode first hydrogen bomb.
1957	Sputnik 1 launched into space.
1959	Lunik III photographs far side of moon.
1961	
April 12	First manned space flight of Vostok 1 (Yuri Gagarin).
1962	First US orbital space flight.
1963	Test Ban Treaty between Russia, United States and Britain.
1969	First moon landing.

Chapter 22

THE UNITING OF EUROPE

'A Supreme Opportunity'

During the Second World War there were few who dared to use the words 'A war to end wars'. These were too much associated with the First World War which had failed so sadly in this respect. In 1945, when the fighting at last came to an end, there were many who wondered whether it was only a matter of time before war broke out again. It seemed that Europe, for so long the centre of civilisation, was fated to have everlasting wars, and that treaty after treaty had done no more than patch up a temporary peace. No-one pondered this question more deeply than Winston Churchill. In a speech in 1947 he described Europe's plight in ringing words:

> Here is the fairest, most temperate, most fertile area of the globe. The influence and the power of Europe and of Christendom have for centuries shaped and dominated the course of history. The sons and daughters of Europe have gone forth and carried their message to every part of the world. Religion, law, learning, art, science, industry, throughout the world all bear, in so many lands, under every sky and in every clime, the stamp of European origin, or the trace of European influence.
>
> But what is Europe now? It is a rubble-heap, a charnel-house, a breeding ground of pestilence and hate ... Is there then to be no respite? Has Europe's mission come to an end? Has she nothing to give the world but the contagion of the Black Death? Are her peoples to go on harrying and tormenting one another by war and vengeance until all that invests human life with dignity and comfort has been obliterated? Are we all, through our poverty and our quarrels, for ever to be a burden and a danger to the rest of the world?

Churchill was convinced that the agony need not be repeated. There was a way out. Europe must unite. Old rivalries and barriers must be eliminated. The people of Europe must be persuaded to join forces:

> If they come together and work together for mutual advantage, to exchange blessings instead of curses, they still have it in their power to sweep away the horrors and miseries which surround them, and to allow the streams of freedom, happiness and abundance to begin again their healing flow.

Churchill did not expect the union of Europe to happen all at once; it would be a step by step process. But it was essential to start immediately when the continent was in ruins. This was 'a supreme opportunity'.

At that time no-one in the world carried more weight than Winston Churchill, and his words had profound effect. The difficulties were formidable, as he himself realised, but to more and more people the need for European union was becoming apparent. The people of France had in the last seventy-five years seen their country invaded by Germany three times. After the First World War they had attempted a policy of keeping Germany weak, but this had proved impossible. Now they were realising that a more constructive and more realistic policy was for the two countries to join together and so become dependent on each other. Then war between them would be impossible. To the Germans too there were strong reasons for union. They needed to be taken back into the family of Europe and needed support against the Russians. Many of them too, as much as the French, dreaded a revival of German militarism, and saw that this could be prevented if Germany were to be absorbed into a European body. Konrad Adenauer, the future chancellor of West Germany, once said that he preferred the unity of Europe to that of Germany.

In Britain, however, the Labour government showed only moderate enthusiasm for European union. It was ready to work closely with other countries in such matters as finance and defence, but it was not prepared to give up any of Britain's sovereign power to a supra-national body, that is a body in which Britain is only one of several and which has the power to overrule governments on matters concerning their own affairs. The surrender of national sovereignty was the crux of European unity; without it no union would have any true meaning.

First Steps

The first significant step taken to achieve European unity was the setting up in 1949 of a body known as the Council of Europe. This was open to all non-Communist European countries and consisted of two parts – the Council of Ministers and the Consultative Assembly. The former was usually attended by the foreign ministers of the member countries but had little real power, as all decisions had to be unanimous which meant in effect that any one country had the power of veto. The Assembly too had little power but was useful as a debating chamber for members of parliament of all parties from all countries where they could get to know each other and discuss their ideas on future plans for union.

The Council of Europe, then, did no more than prepare the way for European union. However, by 1951 the need for this in some form was becoming urgent. By then the Korean War had broken out (see p. 279); the Russian threat was looming larger; and there was strong American pressure for the re-armament of Germany. This caused some alarm in France, but to many Frenchmen it was evident that, provided German and French industry were linked in some way so that each had some control over the other, there was little to fear. Accordingly a plan was drawn up for merging their two basic industries, those of coal and steel. This plan, which was mainly the work of the French foreign minister, Robert Schuman, provided that the coal and steel industries of France, Germany and any other European countries wanting to join should be placed under a High Authority. Here decisions would be taken by majority vote which meant that it was possible for one country to be overruled by a combination of the others. This was enough to frighten off the British government which had visions of British coal-mines and steel mills being closed down by order of foreigners. In the event these fears were shown to have been exaggerated, as most of the decisions of the High Authority were unanimous and few were of a drastic nature. While Britain held back four other countries – Italy, Belgium, Holland and Luxembourg – took the decision to join, and so was formed the famous 'Six' which was soon to form an even closer union.

Soon after the setting up of the European Coal and Steel Community (ECSC) an attempt was made to establish a European army known as the European Defence Community (EDC). The idea of the French, and many Germans too, was that if Germany had to be rearmed, her troops, staff and high command should be incorporated into a European army so that independent action by the Germans was impossible. However, EDC never came into existence. Once again Britain held back and then the French withdrew. Instead Western European Union was formed to which all countries contributed forces, but at the same time kept control of them themselves.

The Common Market

The success of the European Coal and Steel Community soon led the leaders of the Six to consider further schemes of union. In 1955 their foreign minsters declared that the time had come for a new stage in the building of Europe. They had in mind more common institutions as, for example, for the development of atomic energy and the bringing into line of social policies on such matters as health, pensions and social security. They also planned that over a period of years the economies of the member countries would be merged and a Common Market formed. In this new organisation, to be known as the European Economic Community (EEC) all customs duties (tariffs) and restrictions of trade between member countries would be abolished and they would all adopt the same tariffs for the rest of the world. In time too they would adopt the same policy towards agriculture, and there would be freedom for workers of one country to work in another.

There was some long, hard bargaining before EEC was brought into being, but it was finally achieved by the Treaty of Rome which was signed on 25th March 1957. At the time the man in charge of the negotiations, Paul Henri Spaak of Belgium, declared that it was a triumph of cooperation over national selfishness.

Britain Stands Aloof

In later years it came to be regarded by many as a fundamental mistake that Britain took no part in the negotiations at Rome and was not one of the founder members of EEC. It is certain that at the time the country could have obtained much better terms, both for herself and for the Commonwealth, than she did later. But for some years under governments of both parties Britain had been dragging her heels in the matter of European unity. European leaders had hoped that when Churchill became prime minister again in 1951 Britain's involvement in Europe would be much greater, but they were disappointed. Churchill soon made it clear that, while he was still as much in favour of European union as ever, Britain was not to be included. As he put it: 'Britain is with but not of Europe.' And so the chance of leading a united Europe was lost and the other countries, regretfully, went ahead on their own.

There were, of course, serious difficulties for Britain in joining the Common Market. There were the ties with the Commonwealth, notably the special trading arrangements[1] which, to a large extent, would have to be abandoned. There was also Britain's so-called 'special relationship' with the United States which would diminish. And there were great fears about British agriculture. Above all there still remained in Britain a strong feeling of isolation and prejudice against foreigners. The idea of Britain losing her independence and being subject to the decisions of foreign officials alarmed both Conservatives and Socialists.

A Change of Heart

Another consideration which held Britain back from taking part in the negotiations at Rome was the belief that these would almost certainly fail. In the event, however, the Six reached agreement without undue difficulty, and in the following years the newly established Community had great success. Trade between member countries increased, their industries expanded and the standard of living of their peoples became higher. This rapid development of one of the world's largest trading groups so close at hand was something Britain could not ignore, and attempts were made at once to come to an arrangement about trade. The first proposal was for all countries of Western Europe, including the Six, to join a Free Trade Area where all tariffs would be abolished; but this idea was vetoed by France. Thereupon in 1959 Britain and six other countries outside the Common Market formed themselves into the European Free Trade Area (EFTA), sometimes known as 'The Seven', and for a time it seemed that Europe, already divided by the Iron Curtain, was going to be divided yet again.

In the following years, however, more and more people became convinced of the necessity, late in the day though it might be, for Britain

---

[1] Commonwealth goods were admitted into the United Kingdom on preferential terms.

to join the Common Market. Many of the reasons for not joining were now disappearing: Britain's links with the Commonwealth countries were becoming less binding and the special relationship with the United States was becoming of less significance. Also the economic position of Britain on her own continued to be weak, and the country was no longer able by herself to exert much influence in world affairs. And so in 1961 the Conservative government of Harold Macmillan took the decision to apply for membership of the European Economic Community. This was a bold act, as it was known that many Conservative members of parliament were strongly opposed to it, and it might have led to the breakup of the Conservative party. In the event, however, there were no great upheavals as Britain's application was turned down. Previously Britain would have been welcomed with open arms, but that was before the arrival on the scene of General de Gaulle.

General de Gaulle Bars the Way

General de Gaulle, who had been in retirement for twelve years, was brought back into office in 1958 when France was on the verge of civil war over the situation in Algeria. For four years there had been an intensely bitter struggle between the French army and the Algerian nationalists; and then in 1958, when a new French government seemed to be about to come to terms with the rebels, the leaders of the European population,[1] backed by the army, took matters into their own hands. They defied the French government and even threatened an invasion of France.

In this desperate situation de Gaulle emerged as the country's saviour. Convinced that he was a man of destiny whose mission it was to save France, he proceeded to act in a way that was high-handed and skilful and, when necessary, devious. At one moment overawing his political opponents and at another lulling them into a sense of false security, he managed to introduce a new Republic, the Fifth, in which the president had more power and parliament less. Having thus strengthened his position, de Gaulle then dealt with the Algerian crisis. Previously he had given a pledge that Algeria would always be French;

---

[1] The European population of Algeria amounted to about one million as opposed to eight million Algerians of Arab descent.

but then he did an about-turn and announced that the country would be independent. This caused furious anger in some quarters, and there were a number of attempts on his life. The majority of French people, however, were convinced that he was the only person who could save France from chaos and rallied to his support. By 1961 his authority in the country was unshakeable. Already by then he had turned his attention to the subject nearest his heart – that of building up the power and glory of France in the world.

De Gaulle had not at first been favourably disposed towards the Common Market, and when he came to power he soon made it clear that, whatever the Treaty of Rome might say, in matters concerning France he was not prepared to be overruled by a majority of other countries. But, that being established, de Gaulle realised that the Common Market could serve his main purpose. It was certain that in the Treaty of Rome France had received outstandingly favourable terms, both as regards her overseas territories (colonies and ex-colonies) and, more particularly, as regards her agriculture.[1] Also de Gaulle saw clearly that in world affairs France on her own carried little weight, but at the head of the Common Market countries she would carry a great deal.

De Gaulle, then, was only interested in the Common Market provided it was dominated by France. And for this reason he was firmly opposed to the admission of Britain. If this happened the character of the European Economic Community would be changed; leadership would have to be shared and French authority diminished. Moreover de Gaulle had no great love for Britain. During the war, as leader of the Free French, he had constantly clashed with Churchill, and he had always regarded Britain as France's historic rival. Also he was suspicious of Britain's close ties with the United States and feared that British entry into the Common Market would bring with it a strong American influence which he would not welcome.

Although de Gaulle was determined to exclude Britain from the Common Market, he was a shrewd enough politician to know that he must avoid doing this too openly. He must not be held responsible for

---

[1] In France there were numerous small farmers who received large subsidies. This resulted in enormous surpluses – the so-called beef and butter 'mountains' and wine 'lakes'.

blocking the way to European unity. And so he did not veto Britain's application to join at once. Realising how divided the British people, and in particular the Conservative Party, were on the issue, he hoped that Macmillan's government would fall and the British application would lapse. But when this did not happen and negotiations began, he saw to it that these were prolonged as much as possible and that on every detail there were lengthy, quibbling arguments. However, Britain's chief negotiator, Edward Heath,[1] was a man of great ability and persistence as well as an ardent European, and in the end all outstanding questions were settled.[2] It was then that de Gaulle was compelled to reveal himself in his true colours and declare that he was opposed to British membership in principle on the general grounds that Britain was not 'European minded' and that her ties with the United States and the Commonwealth were too great.

De Gaulle's vote came as a shock to Harold Macmillan who thought, with some reason, that he had been deceived. If de Gaulle objected in principle he should have said so at the beginning of the negotiations not at the end. For some time afterwards Britain's relations with France were strained, but, in spite of his disappointment, Macmillan realised that it was important not to regard the door as being finally closed. Not even de Gaulle could last for ever.

Britain's second application to join the Common Market came six years later during the Labour government of Harold Wilson. This time de Gaulle did not allow negotiations to begin; he imposed a veto at once. By then, however, his days were beginning to run out.

Entry at Last

It was to be eighteen months later in 1969 that de Gaulle at last resigned and was succeeded by Georges Pompidou. The new president had less rigid views on the Common Market than his predecessor and was aware that the situation was changing. France's leading position in the Community was no longer assured; the power of West Germany was growing rapidly, and the admission of Britain would do something to

---

[1] Subsequently prime minister 1970–74.
[2] These included such diverse matters as New Zealand dairy produce, Caribbean sugar, even tinned kangaroo meat from Australia.

counterbalance this. At the end of 1969 the Six decided to open negotiations not only with Britain but also with Ireland, Norway and Denmark. In the following year a Conservative government came to office
in Britain under Edward Heath, and protracted and detailed talks began.
Once again Heath had to work hard to remove lingering French doubts
as to Britain's dedication to Europe, but a year later agreement was
reached and on 22nd January 1972 Britain, Ireland and Denmark signed
a treaty of accession to the European Community.[1]

The signing of the treaty was not, however, the end of the matter. It
was still necessary for it to be ratified by the British parliament, and
this was not a foregone conclusion, for in the last months considerable
opposition had been developing to British membership. A few members
of the Conservative Party and many members of the Labour Party were
strongly opposed to it. In the following months many arguments were
brought forward for 'keeping Britain out'. It was shown that membership would mean higher food prices, that British agriculture would
suffer and that British taxpayers would have to pay large sums to
subsidise less efficient French farmers. It was also argued that Commonwealth countries, like Australia and New Zealand, which had stood
by Britain so loyally during two world wars, were being let down, and
that in joining Europe Britain was joining a 'rich man's club'; increased
trade with Europe would be at the expense of the underdeveloped
world. Above all it was stressed that Britain would be giving up some
of her sovereignty and would no longer be fully independent and in
control of her own destiny.

As against these arguments the pro-Marketeers emphasised that in
the modern world it was impossible for Britain to 'go it alone', and that
her natural place was in Europe. Now that the Empire had been disbanded and Commonwealth ties were growing weaker, Britain was no
longer a world power and carried little weight in world affairs on her
own. A united Europe, on the other hand, with Britain a leading member, would be a power comparable with the United States and Russia.
It was also pointed out how great were the opportunities which would
be available to British industry if Britain were to join a dynamic, rapidly
expanding trading group of 300,000,000 people. The position was
summed up by the *Daily Mirror*: 'Britain faces the choice of languish-

---

[1] Norway also signed but later withdrew after a referendum was held.

Harold Macmillan (right) failed to convince de Gaulle (talking to Lady Dorothy Macmillan) of the case for Britain joining the Common Market.

ing in a dead end as an offshore island – or sharing the drive and the expansion of a thriving continental powerhouse.'

These arguments continued to rage for many years especially when schemes for closer union were proposed; but it seems likely that the majority of British people do not feel strongly on the issue; great popular enthusiasm for or against European union has never been aroused. But opposition did increase within the Labour Party and although the leadership was in favour of British membership in principle, Harold Wilson found it necessary to oppose the terms negotiated by the Conservatives. This, in conjunction with a number of inveterate Tory opponents, made the ratification of the treaty a close run thing. However, in the event a number of Labour pro-Marketeers abstained from voting, and British membership of the European Economic Community was confirmed by a narrow majority.

The matter was still not an end, however. When Labour returned to office in 1974 Wilson was pledged to renegotiate the treaty. This, in the course of the next years, he did to his own satisfaction, but in order to avoid a split in his party it was necessary for him to hold a referendum on the subject and to pledge himself to accept the decision of the country. A referendum was something new in British politics and it was heavily criticised as being unconstitutional and a threat to the sovereignty of parliament. Wilson was, indeed, taking a great risk, for if the vote had gone against him his position would have been impossible. However, the result of the referendum, held in 1975 showed a two-thirds majority in favour of British membership.

Towards Closer Union

It was always the contention of British pro-Marketeers that, although there were stumbling blocks to British entry into the Common Market, the best policy was for Britain to join and try to remove the stumbling blocks later. But in some cases this proved very difficult. An especially thorny problem was that of agriculture where the French were insisting on a Common Agricultural Policy (CAP) whereby farmers including their numerous, unmodernised smallholders should be paid large subsidies out of European Community funds. But this had resulted in huge overproduction and Britain, with more up-to-date farming methods, wanted the subsidies reduced. There was also strong disagreement on such matters as fishing rights, North Sea oil and the size of Britain's contribution to the European Community's budget.

In spite of these disagreements, however, the European Community continued to prosper and to grow – Greece, Spain and Portugal joined in 1986 – and there was a strong body of opinion in favour of closer union. In 1987 the Single European Act provided that in 1992 there should be freedom of movement for goods, people and capital between member states. This was as far as Britain at that time was willing to go, but others looked on it as only a beginning. They looked forward to a unified taxation system, a common currency and a common Social Charter with all countries adopting the same policy on such matters as equal pay for women, weekly working hours and a minimum wage. To them – the Euro-Federalists as they came to be called – all member states should make major sacrifices in their national sovereignty so that there should be an all-powerful central government. They also believed that there should be European trade barriers against the rest of the world to protect European industries. To these ideas Britain and a few other countries were strongly opposed. They urged that there should be only minimum relinquishment of national sovereignty and interference in domestic affairs. They also believed firmly in free trade among all nations of the world, not only those in the European Community.

Timescale

1949	Setting up of the Council of Europe.
1951	Setting up of European Coal and Steel Community.
1957 March 25	Treaty of Rome signed. Setting up of European Economic Community (EEC).

1958 General de Gaulle returns to office in France.

1959 Establishment of European Free Trade Area (EFTA).

1961 First British application to join EEC.

1963 General de Gaulle vetoes British entry.

1967 Second British application. Again vetoed by de Gaulle.

1969 Resignation of de Gaulle.

1972 Britain, Ireland and Denmark join EEC.

1975 British membership of EEC confirmed by referendum.

1986 Greece, Spain and Portugal join European Community.

1987 Single European Act (people, goods and capital to have free movement between member states).

Chapter 23

TURMOIL IN THE MIDDLE EAST

Arab–Israeli Conflict

After the 'Suez Affair' in 1956 (see p. 299) there was a period of uneasy peace between Israel and the Arab states; but these were still determined to 'drive Israel into the sea' and to restore Palestine as it had been at the beginning of the century before mass Jewish immigration and the establishment of the state of Israel. The man who took the lead in this movement was President Nasser of Egypt whose prestige since the thwarting of the British and French in 1956 had risen high in the Arab world. In 1967 he massed an invasion army on the Israeli border at the same time as the Syrians and Jordanians prepared to invade Israel from their countries. These states had been armed with modern weapons by the Russians, and it seemed that Israel must be overwhelmed. But she had had considerable military aid from the United States, and in the event it was she who struck first and with devastating effect. The Egyptian air force was destroyed on the ground and her army driven out of the Sinai. At the same time the Syrians were driven from the Golan Heights and the Jordanians from the West Bank and their part of Jerusalem. The 'Six Day War', then, resulted in extensive gains for the Israelis which they showed no signs of giving up and which the Arabs were determined to win back. Six years later in 1973, on the Jewish holy day of Yom Kippur, Egyptian and Syrian armies, with support from Jordan, Iraq and Saudi Arabia, launched attacks on Israel. Because it was a holy day the Israeli forces were caught off guard and for a time the situation for Israel was critical. But aid from America was flown in and the Israeli forces rallied and counter-attacked. As a result the invading Egyptian army was cut in two and the Israelis crossed the Suez Canal into Egypt. The Syrians too were halted and driven back. Soon afterwards the United Nations called for a cease-fire,

President Sadat of Egypt (left) and Prime Minister Begin of Israel with President Carter at Camp David (1978).

and a peacekeeping force was brought into the area to keep the opposing forces apart.

The results of the 'Yom Kippur War' were far-reaching. In the first place it made President Sadat of Egypt[1] realise that some kind of agreement must be made with Israel. Egypt was not a rich country and could not afford a state of permanent war. Also Egypt had no direct interest in annihilating Israel; there were no overriding reasons why the two countries should not live at peace. So in 1977 Sadat visited Jerusalem and suggested peace talks; and in the following year he and the Israeli prime minister, Menachem Begin, met in America under the auspices of President Carter[2] at his home in Camp David and came to an agreement which was signed in 1979. For this Sadat was bitterly attacked by other Arab leaders,[3] as also was Begin by Jewish extremists. Not all outstanding matters were settled at Camp David, but at least Israel's right to exist was acknowledged, and it marked the withdrawal of Egypt from the Arab–Israeli conflict.

This conflict was, however, carried on with great bitterness and ferocity in other parts of the Middle East, notably in the Lebanon. Lebanon had once been the richest and most civilised of the Arab states where Christians and Moslems of many different sects[4] lived peacefully together. But in the 1970s and 1980s the country was plunged into civil war and chaos. Huge numbers of Arab refugees had fled there from Palestine and later from Jordan, and these set about terrorist activities against Israel. The Palestine Liberation Organisation (PLO) under Yasser Arafat was especially active; and in 1976

---

[1] He had become President on the death of Nasser in 1971.
[2] He had been elected President in 1976.
[3] He was assassinated in 1981.
[4] There were twelve different Christian sects and three main Moslem groups.

and again in 1982 Israeli forces invaded Lebanon in an attempt to drive out the terrorists.

From 1989, following the advent of *glasnost* in Russia (see p. 350), many thousands of Russian Jews started to arrive in Israel; and this may have been one reason why more Arab leaders came to think that a permanent agreement with Israel was necessary. In 1993, after months of secret negotiations in Norway, the Israelis and the PLO came to an agreement. By this Yasser Arafat agreed to renounce violence and to recognise the existence of the state of Israel, while the Israelis agreed to the setting up of an independent Arab state in the Gaza Strip with the West Bank city of Jericho as its capital. At the time the Israeli prime minister, Yitzhak Rabin, who was bitterly attacked by some Jews for the agreement, described it as 'giving peace a chance'.

Middle Eastern Oil

The principal reason why European countries and the United States have a special interest in the Middle East is that it is the world's greatest source of oil. And in the twentieth century all countries have become increasingly dependent on oil. Until the Second World War Arab countries had been content to allow the large multi-national oil companies (such as Shell, Esso and British Petroleum) to extract the oil they needed in return for comparatively small royalties. But this situation began to change as the oil-producing countries came to realise the strength of their position. The first to take action was Iran in 1951 when the Anglo–Iranian Oil Company was nationalised (see p. 297). Ten years later the Organisation of Petroleum Exporting Countries (OPEC) was formed to help each member in dealings with the multi-nationals. Here OPEC were to gain the whiphand, and in 1973, after the Yom Kippur War, it proceeded to wield its power in an attempt to coerce the Western governments to give up their support of Israel. Between 1972 and 1974 the price of oil rose four times. This had a devastating effect on Western economies, causing great unemployment and inflation. But it had an even more harmful effect on Third World countries[1] which because of the recession in world trade, were unable to sell their

---

[1] These are countries allied neither to the capitalist West nor the Communist East. For the most part they are less rich countries from Africa and Asia.

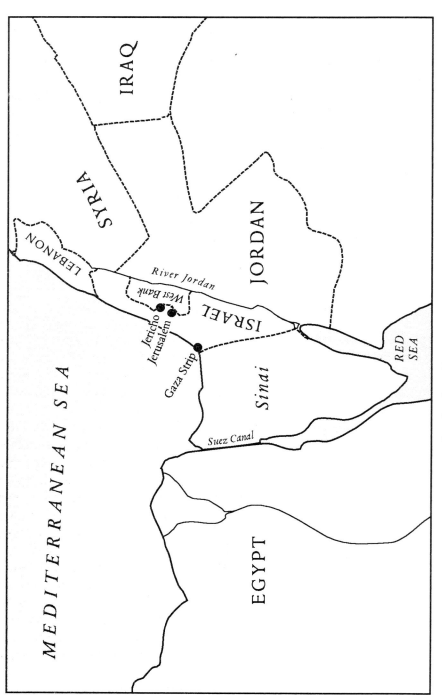

Israel and neighbours.

products; they also found that because of inflation the money they received in aid from Western countries had lost much of its value. In time new sources of oil, notably in the North Sea, Nigeria and Alaska, were developed and partly because of this and partly because of dissensions in OPEC, the price of oil was brought down which led to a revival of world trade.

International Terrorism

As well as being partly responsible for the 'oil war', the Arab–Israeli conflict also led to a great increase in world terrorism. It was the Palestine Liberation Organisation (PLO), set up in 1964, which developed new and horrifyingly effective methods of terrorism which spread to other countries, assisted by the setting up of special training camps. In the 1970s and 1980s terrorist groups proliferated all over the world – the Baader-Meinhof group in West Germany, the Red Brigade in Italy, the Basque Separatists in Spain and the IRA in Britain. Many reckless and brutal crimes were perpetrated such as the murder of eleven Israeli athletes at the Munich Olympic games, the blowing up of an airliner over Lockerbie in Scotland and the kidnapping and holding hostage of innocent victims.

Many terrorist groups received undercover aid from Russia and other Eastern bloc countries which looked on them as allies in the Cold War and knew that free democracies were far more vulnerable to terrorists than Communist countries with their autocratic powers and draconian police forces. Some governments, notably that of Colonel Gadaffi of Libya, gave open support to terrorists, and this led in 1986 to President Reagan ordering US aircraft to carry out a bombing attack on Libya. In the 1990s there have been signs of some abatement

Hooded terrorist on balcony of Israeli athletes' quarters at Munich Olympic Games (1987).

in terrorist activities. It may be that the lesson has been learned that giving in to terrorist demands causes more not less terrorism. But the threat of increasingly powerful weapons falling into terrorist hands is an extremely serious one.

The Gulf War

The vital importance of Middle Eastern oil to Western countries was demonstrated again in 1990 when the Iraqi dictator, Saddam Hussein, invaded the small but oil-rich state of Kuwait.

Saddam Hussein had come to power in 1979, bent on pursuing a 'greater Iraq' policy. In the same year the Shah of Iran was deposed and replaced by the Ayatollah Khomeini, a leader of the Moslem Shia sect which was being persecuted by Hussein in Iraq. At the time there were other disputes as well as religious ones between Iran and Iraq, and in 1980 Hussein, thinking that Iran was in chaos following the change of regime, invaded the country. In this he had support from other non-Shiite Arab countries such as Jordan and Saudi Arabia, as well as from Russia. Later too he had some support from Western countries who had no love for him but regarded him as a lesser evil than the Ayatollah Khomeini. It seemed that Iraq must be successful, but the Iranians fought with tremendous zeal and with little heed to loss of life, and the war was to drag on for nearly ten years with some 500,000 killed. At the end of it Hussein immediately embarked on another reckless venture when in 1990 he ordered the invasion of Kuwait, expecting little opposition. But he had miscalculated. By so doing he posed a threat to Saudi Arabia and the oil states of the Persian Gulf, and Western countries, notably the United States, had no wish to see the whole of this area dominated by Hussein. The United Nations Security Council, now with the support of Russia following the rise to power of Gorbachev, condemned Hussein's action and ordered the immediate withdrawal of Iraqi forces from Kuwait, and when this did not happen authorised the sending of a UN force to expel them.

The task confronting the UN force, which came mainly from America, was a formidable one. In spite of the war with Iran Hussein's armed forces had been steadily increasing and were now believed to be the fourth largest in the world, and they were armed with modern weapons including ones for biological warfare. There could have been a fearful bloodbath, but in the event this was avoided. When the UN army attacked early in 1991 it carried all before it, and the fighting was over in a few days with minimal casualties.

The Iraqis, then, were expelled from Kuwait, but the UN forces did not exploit their victory by invading Iraq and toppling Hussein who (in 1994) remains in place, a friendless and dangerous dictator.

Timescale

1964   Establishment of Palestine Liberation
       Organisation (PLO)
1967   'Six Day War'.
1973   'Yom Kippur War'.
1978   Egypt and Israel reach agreement at Camp
       David.
1979   Shah of Iran deposed. Replaced by Ayatollah
       Khomeini.
       Saddam Hussein comes to power in Iraq.
1980   Beginning of Iraq–Iran war.
1990   Iraq invades Kuwait.
1991   Iraq expelled from Kuwait by UN force.
1993   Agreement reached between Israel and PLO.

Chapter 24

THE DOWNFALL OF COMMUNISM

Decline of Russian Economy

The 1970s had been a depressing decade for the free countries of the world. As has been seen (p. 285) the American defeat in Vietnam led to Communist takeovers in neighbouring countries along with appalling atrocities. In Africa there was increased Communist activity, particularly in Ethiopia, Mozambique and Angola.[1] And the Soviet government maintained its iron hold on the countries of Eastern Europe. At the same time there had been a marked decline in America's military power relative to that of the USSR. Russian expenditure on armaments had been 50 per cent higher, and in consequence, as well as maintaining their overwhelming superiority in conventional forces, the Russians were closing the gap in American nuclear predominance; and in the late 1970s they had installed in Eastern Europe a number of intermediate-range, multiple-warhead rockets (SS20) which had altered substantially the nuclear balance.

In the early 1980s, however, the situation began to change. In 1980 Ronald Reagan, a one-time film actor and governor of California, was elected President of the United States and made it clear that he was going to give top priority, regardless of cost, to 'gaining military superiority over all potential enemies'. In furtherance of this policy he persuaded some West European countries to allow the installation of American intermediate Cruise missiles, known as Star Wars, which would give the United States a commanding lead over Russia. This put the Soviet government in a very difficult position, for to keep pace with the American programme would put an unbearable strain on the

---

[1] In these countries Russia not only provided arms and economic aid to Communist groups but also prompted and financed the sending of Cuban troops to fight alongside the guerrillas.

*Ronald Reagan and Mikhail Gorbachev at
summit meeting in Moscow (1988).*

ever-weakening Russian economy. The only alternative was to seek agreement with the United States on arms control.

At the same time momentous changes were beginning to occur in the Soviet Union. Since the downfall of Khruschev in 1964 power had lain mainly with Leonid Brezhnev, an old-time Communist dedicated to fighting the Cold War abroad and to a policy of repression at home. He had managed to stay in office until his death at seventy-six in 1982 when he was succeeded by sixty-eight-year-old Yuri Andropov, one time head of the KGB. He died after two years and was followed by another elderly Communist, Konstantin Chernenko (seventy-three) who died one year later. But then at last a younger man came to the fore. When he became General Secretary of the Communist Party in 1985 Mikhail Gorbachev was fifty-four; he was a Communist of a different generation and with a different outlook. His appointment marked a new era in Russian, and indeed in world, history.

The problems facing the new Secretary were daunting. First and foremost was that of the Soviet economy. Nearly all agriculture was still run by collectivised farms which were so inefficient that the Soviet Union with some of the best farming lands in Europe was having to rely on huge imports of grain, mainly from the United States and Canada, to avoid starvation. Russian industry too was ineffective and not keeping pace with Western countries; its rate of growth was one-third that of the United States and one-quarter that of Japan. In addition roads, railways, housing, hospitals and all public services (known collectively as 'infrastructure') were running down and in urgent need of repair and replacement. Generally the standard of living of the average Russian was one-quarter that of the average American and substantially less than that in most East European countries.

Glasnost and Perestroika

This being the case Russia was in no condition to take on America in a new bout of the arms race. If she did she must lose. To Gorbachev it was clear that great changes were necessary in the Soviet Union, particularly in the economy, and that these changes must involve a move away from Communism and tight central control towards a free market and private enterprise. He must also have realised that these economic changes would inevitably result in basic political changes. Certain it was that in order to bring about the modernisation of Russian industry massive help would be needed from the West and this would not be forthcoming unless there was a radical change in the Soviet's repressive domestic policy; there would have to be more personal freedom and more open government (known as *glasnost*). The Western powers had been urging the Soviet government to give more respect to human rights – in such matters as freedom of speech and religion and the granting of visas to Soviet citizens wishing to emigrate or travel abroad. But in the Brezhnev era these calls had been dismissed as interference in Russia's domestic affairs. At the Helsinki Conference of 1975, attended by 35 countries, Russia had agreed to acknowledge basic human rights, but it soon became apparent that this was deceptive, and brutal punishment was still meted out to anyone speaking out of turn.

During his first years in office Gorbachev talked much of the need for change, but he acted cautiously. There was no abandonment of Communism, and moves towards private enterprise were on a small scale. A little more land was allowed to be farmed privately and some industries were released from central control and allowed to move towards a free market. However, the immediate result of these changes (known as *perestroika*) were not always beneficial. In agriculture there was increased production but this was to a large extent invalidated by a totally inadequate transport system. In industry most factories continued to run down resulting in higher prices, fewer goods in the shops and higher unemployment. *Glasnost* did mean that there was more personal freedom in the Soviet Union; people could speak out more and the powers of the KGB were curbed, but an unfortunate consequence of this was that there was a great increase in crime, particularly in illicit, undercover financial dealings.

Because Gorbachev had been slow to act many in the West were at first distrustful of him. It was noted that he had made no reductions in Russia's armed forces. Was all his talk of change, they wondered, just a ploy to gain time for a Russian recovery and the survival of Communism? However, in 1987 a major arms reduction agreement was concluded with the United States, and in 1988 there was a significant development when Gorbachev announced the withdrawal of all Russian armed forces from Afghanistan. Russia had been drawn into a civil war in Afghanistan on the side of the Communist regime in 1979, and this had proved disastrous. They had found, like many invaders before them, including the British, that Afghanistan is virtually unconquerable. The war had dragged on for nearly ten years, and when the Russians finally pulled out, it was for them a disaster comparable with the American defeat in Vietnam. It was the first time that Russian Communism had been forced to make a retreat, and the significance of this was not lost on other Communist countries. It was a sign that Soviet leaders might no longer be willing to support them with armed action, as they had done in the past, to prevent political changes away from Communism To Western leaders it was an indication that Soviet leaders no longer aimed to 'communise' the rest of the world.

This feeling was enhanced the following year (1989) when a new style Russian parliament was established. This was still very different from Western parliaments: of the 2,250 seats only 395 were freely elected; the remainder were allocated to special groups which were Communist dominated. Still it was a distinct advance on the old Supreme Soviet, and of the members freely elected some 330 were to form themselves into a vocal and active opposition.

By 1990 most foreign distrust of Gorbachev had disappeared, and wherever he and his attractive and fashionable wife, Raisa, went on their foreign travels they were received rapturously. However, it was becoming clear that these warm feelings were not shared by the people of Russia. Increasingly they were becoming resentful. It seemed to them that after five years *perestroika* had brought only lower living standards and greater unemployment. To Communist hardliners this was proof that Gorbachev's policies had been mistaken and that the Soviet Union should revert to the old style Communism of the Brezhnev era. But there were other Russians who thought differently. They believed that Russia's economic troubles were caused not by too many changes but

Yeltsin mounts a tank and urges the crowds to reject the 1991 attempted coup.

too few, and that what was needed was greater movement towards a free economy and a complete break with Communism. Thus Gorbachev was caught between two fires.

Break Up of the USSR

At the same time another crucial problem was emerging. *Glasnost* was leading to some of the many ethnic groups within the Soviet Union demanding their independence. Foremost among these were the Baltic States of Estonia, Latvia and Lithuania. It has been seen (p. 255) that these had been annexed by Stalin during the Second World War; but the people of these states had never regarded themselves as Russians and were always looking forward to a time when they would be liberated. With *glasnost* this became more insistent than ever, and in 1988 Gorbachev felt obliged to give them limited independence.[1] The example of the Baltic States was not lost on other republics of the Soviet Union which had been incorporated into Russia in earlier times. Independence movements began in many of these including the two largest, Georgia and the Ukraine. With these movements gathering strength it

---

[1] They were to become completely independent in 1991.

seemed to Gorbachev that a new Soviet Union was needed, one to which all republics belonged of their own free will and one that was not necessarily bound to Communism. And so he aimed to replace the Union of Soviet Socialist Republics (USSR) with the Union of Sovereign Soviet States (USSS). It was these plans to break up the old Soviet Union and open the way to the abandonment of Communism that precipitated a crisis.

In 1991 some Communist hardliners with some army leaders conspired to overthrow Gorbachev by force and in August, while he was on holiday in the Crimea, they struck. Gorbachev was put under house arrest and it was announced that he had resigned because of ill health, and the leaders of the coup were taking over the government. In this crisis everything depended on the attitude of the army and it is surprising that the leaders of the coup did not make sure of this before taking action. Certainly there was great discontent in the army at that time partly because of defence cuts leading to demobilisation without prospects of civilian employment and partly because many units had been withdrawn from East Germany where they had been comfortably billeted back to Russia where there was only the roughest accommodation for them. And at one time it seemed likely that the coup would succeed. The leaders included the Defence Minister, the head of the KGB and the Minister of the Interior, and at an early stage they took control of all broadcasting stations and other key points, and troops were brought in to seal off the Parliament building where most of the opponents of the coup were thought to be. And yet the coup failed. It had been badly organised and lacked a strong dynamic leader. At the same time the opponents of the coup found a leader of exceptional dynamism and appeal.

The star of Boris Yeltsin had been rising rapidly lately. After being elected President of the Russian Republic by popular vote in 1991, he had become the leader of those pressing for more extensive reforms and the total abandonment of Communism. For some time he had been engaged in a power struggle with Gorbachev, and his moment of triumph came at the time of the coup. It had been a serious mistake on the part of the conspirators not to have made him a prisoner, for when the coup took place he took the lead in mustering opposition to it. At one point he clambered on to one of the tanks surrounding the Parliament building, urging the soldiers not to fire on the crowds but to join them.

Moment of truth. Yeltsin humiliates Gorbachev in Russian Parliament, forcing him to read a list of his ministers who had taken part in the coup.

When the coup was finally overcome there was a wave of anti-Communist feeling. Statues of Stalin and other famous Communists were toppled, Lenin's embalmed body was removed from the tomb in the Kremlin, and the city of Leningrad resumed its previous name of St Petersburg. Gorbachev, badly shaken, returned to Moscow, but soon realised that it was to a new situation. He had been saved by Yeltsin, and Yeltsin made him aware of this. In Parliament he was publicly humiliated when Yeltsin compelled him against his will to read out a list of his ministers who had taken part in the coup. For a time he remained in office, but by then everything was going Yeltsin's way; he had the great advantage of having been elected by popular vote. Gorbachev had to agree to complete independence being granted to the Baltic States and to the Warsaw Pact being disbanded. He also had to watch in Parliament while Yeltsin signed a decree dissolving the Communist Party in the Russian Republic,[1] an example soon followed by other Republics who then sought independence and set up their own governments. Some remnant of the old USSR was preserved when in December 1991 the Russian Republic, the Ukraine and Belorussia agreed to form a loose union to be known as the Commonwealth of Independent States (CIS). At the same time Gorbachev, realising that he had no further function, resigned and went into private life.

When Yeltsin took over Gorbachev's powers, at the same time he took over his problems and these were growing more acute all the time. Russian agriculture and industry continued to under-perform so that the standard of living of most people continued to decline. After 70 years

---

[1] This was much the largest of the republics making up the Soviet Union, comprising three-quarters of the area and over half the population.

of Communism private enterprise could not be made to work at once. In return for disarmament and the ending of the Cold War and for showing more respect for human rights Yeltsin could expect massive foreign aid, but all too often this was to fall into the wrong hands – those of black marketeers and financial racketeers bent on lining their own pockets. Also as unemployment grew and police powers were relaxed the problem of law and order became more intense. These problems, perhaps insoluble, led to a great fall in Yeltsin's popularity and to a revival of Communism. In the autumn of 1993 there was an attempt by members of the Russian Parliament, led by the Vice-President to remove him from office. In the event, however, he survived thanks to the support of the army.

The Fall of the Communist Regimes in Eastern Europe

Hungary – First Breach in the Iron Curtain

For more than forty years the Communist governments of Eastern Europe had been propped up by the Soviet army which had always intervened whenever they had been threatened by democratic forces. By 1988, however, it was becoming clear that the Soviet government was no longer prepared to give armed support to the satellite governments, with the result that it was not long before they were brought down.

Hungary had always been the most restless of the Soviet bloc countries (see p. 311) and she was now to take the lead in shedding Marxism and setting up a government elected by popular vote. In 1988 a moderate Communist government, on the Gorbachev model, took office, hoping to maintain Communist ascendancy by granting moderate reforms. But it was to discover that it had stirred up forces it could not control; the more reforms it granted the more were demanded. In 1989 the government was compelled to allow the formation of a new non-Communist opposition and the introduction of a new constitution in which no single party should ever again have sole control of government. At the same time it was ordered that the barbed wire fence on the border with Austria be taken down. This meant that there was a major breach in the Iron Curtain and thousands of refugees, not only from Hungary but from other East European countries as well, poured through to find a new life in the West. From then on the reform movement gathered momentum. More freedom was allowed to religious groups and to the press, and in 1990 a democratic government was freely elected and the Communist Party dissolved itself.

Solidarity Blazes the Trail in Poland

In Poland there had always been strong anti-Communist feelings centred mainly on the Roman Catholic Church. This had been brutally persecuted first by Hitler and then by Stalin but, as often happens, this had had the effect of strengthening rather than weakening it. In the years since the war the Catholic faith had gained ground steadily, and this came to a climax in 1978 when Karol Wojtyla, Archbishop of Cracow, was elected Pope as John Paul II – the first non-Italian Pope since 1522 and the youngest for more than a century.

Two years later an independent trade union, known as Solidarity, was established in the Gdansk shipyard under the leadership of an electrical worker, Lech Walesa. At first this had considerable success, obtaining from the government not only better working conditions but also greater freedom of speech including the broadcasting of a Catholic mass each Sunday. Later, however, on pressure from Russia, the movement was suppressed and Walesa for a time imprisoned, but in 1989 the Communist government, following popular outcries, felt itself obliged to come to an agreement with Solidarity whereby the movement was legalised, greater freedom of speech was to be allowed and partially free elections were to be held ten months later. In these 239 seats in the Lower House would remain under Communist control and 161 would be elected by popular vote as also would all the 100 seats in the Upper House. In the event all the freely elected seats were won by Solidarity supporters which led to the resignation of the Communist government and to the establishment two months later of the first non-Communist government in Eastern Europe. In the following year Walesa was elected President. But, as in Russia, the transition from Communism to a free democratic society proved thorny. In the short term the economy of the country became worse with rising food prices and higher unemployment. The result of this was that in elections held in 1993 candidates with Communist sympathies had some success.

Reunification of Germany

Of all the countries of the Eastern bloc East Germany had the strongest economy and the strongest government. Under the iron rule of Erich Honecker all freedom movements had been rigidly suppressed and all escape routes to the West closed. Honecker had even attempted to keep from the East German people the details of the Gorbachev reforms in Russia and the lapse of Communism in Hungary and Poland. But this could not be done for long and in 1989 movements for democratic reform began to grow in strength. For a time Honecker with his efficient and ruthless secret police was able to hold these in check, but without the help of the Russian army, which Gorbachev refused him, he could not do so for long. In October 1989 he was forced to resign and this was a signal for increased anti-Communist activity. For a time a new Communist government held office, but it grew ever weaker and in the following month it had to sit by while the hated Berlin Wall (see p. 315) was demolished, giving free access to the West. At the same time non-Communists were admitted into the government, the powers of the secret police were curbed and free elections promised.

It was at this time too that talk began to proliferate about the re-unification of the two Germanys. There were great difficulties in the way of this as in the last 45 years the two countries had grown so far apart. The East German economy was much weaker than that of West Germany and its industry far less efficient. In the event of unification it would need extensive economic aid, and there was likely to be widespread unemployment when East German firms failed to compete with their Western counterparts and went out of business. But when the East German elections took place in March 1990 there

The Berlin Wall comes down. Bits of it were to be sold as souvenirs.

were large majorities for the anti-Communist parties, and soon afterwards agreement was reached on the terms of reunification; and this took place on 3rd October.

After reunification problems proved even greater than expected. It had been agreed that the currencies of the two Germanys would be put on an equal basis and this imposed a tremendous strain on the West German economy as huge subsidies were needed to prop up the East German standard of living, and unemployment rose steeply. At the same time a large number of refugees from other countries poured in and these had to be provided for. As a result taxes had to go up and this led to a severe recession.

Czechoslovakia – Change Comes with a Rush

Since the crushing of the 1968 uprising by Russian troops (see p. 312) Czechoslovakia had been ruled by a hard-line Communist government. But with a softer line from Moscow and the success of democratic movements in Poland and Hungary, it was not likely that Czechoslovakia would be far behind, and when change did come, it came within a month. In November 1989, after widespread riots and a firm refusal of armed assistance from Gorbachev, the Communist government was compelled to resign and was replaced by a non-Communist administration under the playwright, Vaclos Havel, who was elected President five months later. Like all the Eastern European countries making the change from Communism to democracy Czechoslovakia was faced with great economic problems, but she was also confronted with difficult racial problems. Czechoslovakia consisted of several racial groups of which the main ones were Czechs (Moravian and Bohemian) who comprised 54 per cent of the population and Slovakians amounting to 31 per cent. There were strong differences between the two, particularly in religion, and the Slovakians considered themselves treated as second class citizens. In 1992 it was agreed that Slovakia should be partitioned off, and this occurred peacefully without bloodshed on 1st January 1993.

Rumania – Overthrow of a Tyrant

No East European country suffered so much under Communism as Rumania. Nicolae Ceaucescu became head of state in 1967 and, with the help of a ruthless and brutal secret police, became an all-powerful

'Nothing lasts forever.' Demonstrators in Prague carry aloft a toppled statue of Stalin.

dictator. In the course of the next 22 years all freedom in Rumania was stamped out and the country became the poorest in Europe.[1] Ceaucescu had his own version of Communism which sometimes brought him into conflict with Russian leaders and, for this reason, favour with the West.[2] But he inflicted fearful miseries on the Rumanian people, particularly with his schemes of 'social engineering', the most infamous of which was the destruction of some 8,000 rural villages and their replacement with 'agro-industrial complexes'. Ceaucescu's position in Rumania was very strong, but not even he was proof against the winds of change that were blowing in Europe in 1989.[3] The end for Ceaucescu (and his fearsome wife) came quickly and savagely. In December he was deposed and went into hiding. On Christmas Day he was captured, tried and summarily shot. This left a power vacuum in the country which was not easily filled; there was no well-organised anti-Communist

[1] Bread, flour and sugar were all rationed and there were other rigorous regulations about such things as the strength of electric light bulbs and owning a typewriter.

[2] He came on a state visit to Buckingham Palace in 1978.

[3] It was paradoxical that all the Communist governments of East Europe should have been overturned in 1989 which was the bicentenary of the French Revolution.

Nicolae Ceaucescu and his wife on trial for
their lives. They were shot soon afterwards.

group ready to take over as in Poland and Czechoslovakia. The government was taken over by a group calling itself the National Salvation Front which, although not officially Communist, consisted of many ex-Communists. It found itself confronted with massive economic problems but, following gruesome television reports of the plight of some Rumanians, particularly children in state orphanages, extensive aid was forthcoming from the West. But it will take many years to redress the long misrule of Ceaucescu.

Chaos and Civil War in Yugoslavia

On the whole the transition from Communism to democracy in East Europe was achieved without much bloodshed. A tragic exception to this was Yugoslavia where there has been (and still is in 1994) bitter fighting and ghastly atrocities.

As has been seen (p. 55) Yugoslavia was put together as a country after the First World War, consisting of six Slavonic states of which much the largest and most powerful was Serbia. But although they were of the same race the states differed widely in religion and culture,[1] and the union was never an easy one. Since the Second World War the country had been held together by Communism and the masterful character of its President, Marshal Tito (see p. 271) Tito died in 1984 and since then the country had been showing signs of breaking up. In 1989 Slobodan Milosevic, the Communist leader, was elected President

---

[1] The religion of Serbia was predominantly Christian Orthodox, that of Croatia and Slovenia Roman Catholic and that of Bosnia, Roman Catholic with Orthodox and Moslem minorities.

of Serbia, proclaiming a policy of 'Greater Serbia'. This greatly alarmed some of the other states who feared Serbian domination and the retention of Communism of which they were wanting to be rid. In June 1991 Slovenia and Croatia declared their independence, but this Serbia would not accept, especially in the case of Croatia where some half million Serbs were living. And so the Yugoslavian army, which was predominantly Serbian, was sent into Croatia to 'safeguard' the Serbs and to prevent the formation of a separate Croatian state. Here some bitter and bloody fighting took place, but worse was to occur in Bosnia where there was a Moslem minority and differences between the various groups were most acute. It was here that the Yugoslav army along with irregular Serb guerrillas put into practice the fearsome policy known as 'ethnic cleansing' which involved torture, massacres and other horrors.

In view of the tragic and shocking situation in Croatia and Bosnia there were loud outcries from other countries for intervention to prevent worse from happening. But to do this effectively involved great difficulties. A large neutral army would be needed among which there might be heavy casualties, and the mountainous country of Yugoslavia was admirably suited to guerrilla warfare, as Tito had shown during the German occupation in the Second World War. And so the United Nations confined itself to sending in peace-keeping forces (from 30 countries) to attempt to keep the opposing forces apart and see that supplies of food and medical aid got through to where they were needed. Sanctions on Serbia have also been imposed and a naval blockade has been set up to prevent arms from reaching the country. But these measures have had only limited success. By December 1992 the Serbs had occupied 70 per cent of Bosnia, and in 1993 the persistent efforts of the United Nations mediators to find a settlement acceptable to all parties had come to nothing.

Timescale

1979	Russian forces enter Afghanistan.
1980	Election of Ronald Reagan as President of USA.
1982	Death of Leonid Brezhnev.

1985	Mikhail Gorbachev becomes General Secretary of Soviet Communist Party.
1987	Arms agreement between USA and Russia.
1988	Russian withdrawal from Afghanistan. Limited independence granted to Estonia, Lithuania and Latvia.

1989

March	Elections for new Russian parliament.
April	Polish government comes to terms with Solidarity.
May	Slobodan Milosevic elected President of Serbia.
July	Removal of barbed wire along Austro–Hungarian frontier. Refugees pour through.
August	Non-Communist government takes office in Poland (first in Eastern Europe).
October	Resignation of Erich Honeker in East Germany.
November	Destruction of Berlin Wall. Resignation of Communist government in Czechoslovakia.
December	Downfall and execution of Ceaucescu in Rumania.

1990

May	Non-Communist government in Hungary takes office.
October	Reunification of East and West Germany.

1991

June	Boris Yeltsin elected President of Russian Republic. Slovenia and Croatia declare independence from Yugoslavia.
August	Attempted coup to oust Gorbachev.
December	Formation of Commonwealth of Independent

States (CIS).
Resignation of Gorbachev.

1992 Bosnia declares independence from
Yugoslavia.

1993
January Separation of Slovakia from Czechoslovakia.
September Attempt by Russian Vice-President and
others to oust Yeltsin.

EXERCISES

Chapter 1

Comprehension

1. Why was there unrest in Bosnia in 1914?
2. Why did Austria want to teach Serbia a lesson?
3. Why did the German government take fright when the Russians mobilised their forces?
4. What was it that finally brought Great Britain into the war?
5. Why was there rejoicing in Germany on the outbreak of war?
6. Why did Turkey come into the war on Germany's side?
7. Why did France make a treaty with Russia?
8. Why did Great Britain feel it necessary to abandon 'Splendid Isolation'?
9. Which was the one Allied power to declare war on Germany instead of the other way round?

Project

Make a detailed study of the causes of the First World War.

Imaginative

Imagine the thoughts of an ordinary citizen of one of the great powers on the outbreak of war.

Chapter 2

Comprehension

1. What advantages were there in 1914 to the side on the defensive?

2. Why did the Germans invade Belgium? What were the consequences of this?
3. Why did the French offensive fail?
4. Why was the German advance into France finally halted?
5. Why did Russia start an offensive in 1914 before she was ready?
6. Why was it considered a British victory that both British and German battlefleets remained in harbour for most of the war?
7. What were the main threats to battleships at this time?
8. Why were British and French attacks on the Western Front unsuccessful? What lessons should have been learned from these?
9. How did Marshal Joffre hope to win the war?
10. What did the British hope to gain from the Gallipoli campaign? Why did it fail?
11. Why did Italy come into the war? What effect did it have?

Project

Make a detailed study of the Gallipoli operation.

Imaginative

1. Describe the feelings of (a) a British and (b) a German soldier at the Battle of Mons.
2. Write a letter home describing life in the trenches.
3. Imagine you are a British citizen returning to London in 1915 after an absence abroad of five years. What changes would you have found in everyday life?

Chapter 3

Comprehension

1. What was the German plan for 1916? How far did it succeed?
2. Why did the Germans choose Verdun as the point for their big attack?
3. Why was the Battle of the Somme such a bloodbath? What was its effect on the British army?
4. How did the Germans hope to defeat the British fleet? What successes did they have?
5. Why was Admiral Jellicoe so cautious at the Battle of Jutland?

6. How did Ludendorff hope to defeat Britain in 1917?
7. What measures did Britain take to counteract the U-boat menace?
8. Why did the United States come into the war?
9. Why did American entry into the war not have immediate effect?
10. What were the causes of the Russian Revolution?
11. Why did the Germans provide Lenin with a special train in 1917?
12. How did Marshal Pétain restore morale in the French army?
13. How did the British eventually achieve a major breakthrough of the German trenches?
14. Why was Britain vulnerable in the Middle East? Why did some people think British operations in this area unimportant?
15. Why did the Germans need a quick victory on the Western Front at the beginning of 1918?
16. Why did the German attack in 1918 succeed at first? Why did it ultimately fail?
17. Why did Ludendorff ask for an armistice in November 1918?

Projects

Make a detailed study of:

(a) The Battle of Jutland
(b) The Russian Revolution
(c) The part played by America in the war.

Imaginative

1. Write a speech that might have been made at the end of 1916 advocating peace; and one that might have been made in answer to this.
2. Describe from the point of view of a crew member a voyage of a German U-boat and its first encounter with a convoy.
3. Describe the feelings and experiences of a British infantryman at the Battle of Passchendaele.
4. Write a letter which a German soldier might have written home just after hearing about the armistice.

Chapter 4

Comprehension

1. Where in Europe was fighting still taking place in 1919?
2. In what ways did President Wilson hope that peace making in 1919 would be different from previous occasions?
3. Why was Paris an unsuitable place in which to hold the Peace Conference?
4. Why was it necessary to make a peace treaty quickly?
5. Why were delegates at the conference not always free agents?
6. What were the difficulties in the way of self-determination?
7. Why did Clemenceau demand at first that the French frontier be extended to the Rhine? How was he later dissuaded?
8. What did Britain gain in the peace treaties?
9. What is a mandate?
10. Why was it that German ships handed over to Britain as reparations proved a doubtful blessing?
11. What territory did Germany lose by the Treaty of Versailles?
12. Why did the treaty of Versailles come in for heavy criticism later? What were the good things about it?

Project

List all the changes to the map of Europe that came about as a result of the Paris peace treaties. Find out the different races in the new countries. In which areas was there still not self-determination?

Chapter 5

Comprehension

1. Why was there a post-war boom in Britain?
2. What is meant by 'Protection'? Why were some people strongly opposed to it?
3. Why was the first Labour government's freedom of action restricted?

4. What did Stanley Baldwin achieve as prime minister? Why did his reputation later sink low?
5. What caused unemployment in British coalmines?
6. Why did the government break off negotiations with the TUC during the General Strike?
7. What were the causes of the Great Depression?
8. Why did foreigners lose confidence in the pound?
9. How did the split in the Labour Party occur?
10. What faults did Keynes find in the capitalist system? How did he propose to rectify them?
11. Why did Mr Baldwin think that it was not possible for Mrs Wallis Simpson to become queen?
12. How did the lives of women change in the post-war years?
13. Which of the Victorian values were becoming less strongly held?
14. Why was American influence in England so strong at this time?
15. What advantages did airships have at one time? Why did they eventually disappear?
16. What difficulties were there in establishing long-range international airlines?

Projects

Make a detailed study of:

(a) The General Strike
(b) The Great Depression
(c) Developments in aviation between the wars.

Imaginative

1. Write diary entries of:

(a) A miner called out on strike in 1926.
(b) An American investor driven to suicide by the Great Depression.

2. Describe a conversation between an older lady brought up in Victorian times and a 'new woman' of the 1920s.

Chapter 6

Comprehension

1. In what ways had the independence of the press been threatened since the appearance of the first newspapers?
2. What was the effect of large-scale advertising on newspapers?
3. How was the *Daily Express* different from other newspapers? In what ways did it succeed? In what ways did it fail?
4. How was it that the *Daily Mirror* achieved a larger daily circulation than any other newspaper in the world?
5. Who first demanded organised broadcasting in Britain? Who were its main opponents?
6. What were the main differences between broadcasting in Britain and in America?
7. What were the arguments in favour of the BBC monopoly? What were the arguments against it?
8. What was the influence of John Reith on broadcasting?
9. How did the 'star system' in the cinema come into being?
10. Why was the cinema so popular? What effect did it have on entertainment in general?
11. Why might it have been expected that hard times would come to the theatre in the inter-war years? Which part of it was worst affected?
12. What was new about the plays of George Bernard Shaw?

Projects

Make a detailed study of the history of:

(a) British newspapers.
(b) The cinema.
(c) Broadcasting in Britain.

Imaginative

1. Describe the scene in a British home when the first radio signals were picked up.
2. Describe the first visit of a family to a cinema in the 1920s.

Chapter 7

Comprehension

1. What was the essential difference between the British Empire and the Commonwealth?
2. In what ways were the dominions still not completely independent after the war?
3. What were the difficulties in the way of granting self-government to India?
4. What were the main differences between India and the British dominions which had already been granted self-government?
5. What were the main achievements of British rule in India?
6. What hastened the end of British rule in India?
7. What methods did Gandhi employ to bring about the end of British rule? Why did he call them off?
8. What were the difficulties in the way of granting full independence to Egypt?
9. What caused the Egyptians in 1936 to be less eager to see the departure of British troops?
10. What caused British troops to return to Egypt three years after moving out?
11. Why have there been so many wars and disputes about Jerusalem?
12. What difficulties and dangers did Jews encounter when they settled in Europe?
13. What made it easier for Jews to be absorbed into their adopted countries?
14. Why had the Jews not been able to set up a National Home in Palestine before 1917? What difficulties were there then?
15. How did Britain come to be involved?
16. What caused Jewish immigration into Palestine to increase greatly during the 1930s?

Projects

Make a detailed study of:

(a) The events leading to the setting up of the Irish Free State.
(b) The life and achievements of Mahatma Gandhi.

(c) British rule in Egypt.

(d) The setting up of a Jewish National Home in Palestine.

Imaginative

1. Write a letter that might have been written by one of the first Jews arriving in Palestine to set up a National Home.

2. Write a letter by an Arab inhabitant of Palestine saying what he thought of Jewish immigration into Palestine and describing all the changes that had occurred in that country.

Chapter 8

Comprehension

1. How did British and Turkish forces nearly come into conflict in 1919?

2. What became of the territory which Germany had taken from Russia by the Treaty of Brest-Litovsk?

3. What was the importance of the battle of the Vistula?

4. What did Karl Marx think of (a) religion and (b) man's conscience?

5. What did Karl Marx say would have to come before the setting up of a Communistic society?

6. Why did France feel insecure in the 1920s?

7. Why was it becoming increasingly difficult to enforce the Treaty of Versailles?

8. Why did Germans feel resentment about reparations demanded of them?

9. Why did the French occupy the Ruhr in 1923?

10. What brought America back onto the European scene?

11. How did the League of Nations hope to keep the peace of the world?

12. What was the basic weakness of the League of Nations?

13. Why did the League of Nations fail to keep the peace of the world.

Project

Make a detailed study of the League of Nations – how it came into being, its successes and failures.

Chapter 9

Comprehension

1. Why did Italians feel aggrieved after the war?
2. Why was Italy not granted all the territory promised to her in the Treaty of London?
3. Why did it seem likely after the war that Communism would gain the upper hand in Italy?
4. How did the Fascists gain power in Italy?
5. How did Mussolini build up his power?
6. In what ways did Mussolini abuse his power?
7. Why did Lenin not set up a Communistic society in Russia immediately?
8. In the Russian civil war what were the main disadvantages of the 'White' Russians?
9. In what ways did Bolshevik rule become dictatorial?
10. Why did Lenin give more freedom to private enterprise in 1921?
11. Why before the war did Lenin break away from other Communists and form his own party?
12. What promises to the Russian people did Lenin fail to fulfil?
13. How did Stalin differ from Lenin?
14. Why did Lenin on his deathbed try to prevent Stalin from becoming his heir?
15. What was the main disagreement between Stalin and Trotsky?
16. How did a new class system emerge in Russia? Who were the new top people?
17. Why did Stalin come to believe that all farms should be collectivised? What were the consequences of this?
18. What were the reasons for Stalin's purges?
19. Why did Stalin make a treaty with Hitler; and Hitler with Stalin?
20. How did the civil war in Spain begin?
21. Why did the policy of non-intervention in the Spanish civil war work out to the advantage of the Fascists?
22. Why did people from outside Spain come to fight for the Republicans?
23. Why did Stalin not give full support to Spanish Communists?

24. How did Russian intervention change the nature of the Republican forces?

Project

Make a study of the Spanish civil war. Find out which sort of people fought for the Republicans and for the Nationalists. What were the things about which Spanish people felt most strongly? Why did the Nationalists win? What were the consequences of this? Find out about the people from abroad who came to fight in the civil war – why they did it, why some of them were disillusioned.

Imaginative

1. Describe the feelings of a well-to-do Italian on hearing of Mussolini's 'march on Rome'.
2. Describe the feelings of an Italian soldier taking part in the invasion of Abyssinia.
3. Describe the fear which some Russians felt for their lives during the 1920s and 1930s. Describe their arrests and what happened to them afterwards.
4. Describe, as you imagine it, how a group of Russian smallholdings were collectivised? What were the attitudes of the peasants before and after it happened?

Chapter 10

Comprehension

1. What brought Adolf Hitler into politics?
2. Why did his oratory have such power?
3. What were the main stages in Hitler's rise to power?
4. How did Hitler make use of the Reichstag fire?
5. What especially caused Hitler's prestige to soar during his first year in office?
6. What was the significance of 'The Night of the Long Knives'?
7. Why was the occupation of the Rhineland a rash undertaking? What made Hitler think he could get away with it?
8. What methods did Hitler employ for incorporating Austria into Germany?

9. What were the consequences of the *Anschluss*?
10. How did Hitler at first hope to bring about the collapse of Czecho-slovakia?
11. Why did Chamberlain give in to Hitler at Munich?
12. Why was Chamberlain unwilling to make an alliance with Russia?
13. What caused Chamberlain to change his mind about Hitler? What was the main consequence of this which led eventually to war?

Project

Make a study of Hitler's early years in power. Why did so many Germans vote for the Nazi party? Why did they later come to look on him as the saviour of the country and were willing to accept his extremist views and illegal acts? Find out about the people who were opposed to Hitler and were working against him. Why were they unavailing? Find out from where Hitler drew his main support. What was the attitude of the churches and the trade unions? Study the character of Hitler. What evidence is there of insanity and a split personality?

Imaginative

1. Describe as you imagine it a meeting of the German Workers' Party being addressed by Hitler in the early 1920s.
2. Write a letter by a German churchman after 'The Night of the Long Knives' giving his feelings and fears about the state of the country and its future.
3. Write a series of diary entries by a Czech citizen during the events leading up to and including the Munich settlement.

Chapter 11

Comprehension

1. Why did Germany have such a quick and complete victory over Poland?
2. How was the German use of tanks different from that of other countries?
3. What were the main features of the 'blitzkrieg'?
4. Why did Russia invade Poland in September 1939?

5. Why did the French not invade Germany at the beginning of the war?

6. How was everyday life in Britain affected in the opening months of the war?

7. Why were the Germans successful in their invasion of Norway?

8. How did it come about that the BEF in France was nearly trapped? What saved it?

9. Why was French resistance so weak? What other reasons were there for the German victory?

10. What were the principal difficulties in evacuating the BEF from Dunkirk?

11 What might have been Hitler's reasons for ordering the Panzers to halt before reaching Dunkirk?

12. Why did the Royal Navy sink French warships in 1940?

Project

Make a study of the fall of France. Give an account of the German plan of campaign. Why did the Maginot Line do more harm than good? Contrast the leadership of France and Germany. Why was there so much defeatism in France? Describe the reaction of various French people to defeat.

Imaginative

1. Write a letter home from a member of a German tank crew after the invasion of Poland recalling his experiences.

2. Describe the feelings of (a) a young man of military age and (b) an old man who had fought in the First World War on hearing the news of Britain's declaration of war on Germany.

3. Describe the plight of French refugees forced to leave their homes by the German invasion and the ordeal they suffered on the roads while trying to make their way westwards.

Chapter 12

Comprehension

1. What effect did the danger of invasion have on the British people?

2. Why did Churchill have to resign from the government during the First World War?
3. Why was Churchill out of office for a long period in the years between the wars?
4. What were the disadvantages of the Royal Navy in protecting Britain from invasion?
5. Why did Hitler try to make peace with Britain after the fall of France?
6. Why did the German invasion of Britain have to be put off?
7. What advantages did the RAF have over the Luftwaffe in the Battle of Britain?
8. Why did the Germans switch their attacks from the English airfields to London? How did this save Britain?
9. What were the main lessons to be learned from German air raids on British cities?
10. What advantages did Italy have in the war in the Mediterranean?
11. Why was Malta so important to Britain?
12. What disasters befell Italy in the early part of the war? What were the reasons for this?
13. Why did Rommel have quick success in North Africa?
14. Why did Britain go to the aid of Greece?
15. Why without the command of the seas were the Germans able to capture Crete?
16. Did the British forces in Greece achieve any useful purpose?
17. How was it that German U-boats had such easy targets in the Atlantic?
18. What were the main disadvantages of the British in countering the U-boats?
19. Why did German surface raiders do comparatively little damage?
20. What was the main lesson to be learned from the sinking of the *Bismarck*?

Projects

Make a detailed study of one of the following

(a) The Battle of Britain.
(b) The Battle of the Atlantic.
(c) The Blitz.

Imaginative

1. Write diary entries for a member of the Luftwaffe during the Battle of Britain.
2. Write diary entries of a member of the crew of a German U-boat.
3. Write diary entries of a member of the crew of the *Bismarck*.

Chapter 13

Comprehension

1. Why was Russia unprepared for the German invasion?
2. What other reasons were there for German successes?
3. What caused the Germans to be checked in front of Moscow?
4. What was the effect on Hitler of this defeat?
5. What were the main stages in America becoming involved in the war?
6. What were the immediate results of the Japanese attack on Pearl Harbour? Why did it not do permanent damage?
7. What were the main causes of the British collapse in Malaya?
8. Why was Singapore surrendered so soon?
9. In what ways was the Battle of the Coral Seas an American victory?
10. What advantages did the Americans have in the Battle of Midway?
11. What were the results of the Battle of Midway?
12. What were the main differences between Generals Montgomery and Rommel?
13. What were the main reasons for the British victory at El Alamein?
14. Why did the British think it impossible to open a second front in France in 1942?
15. Why were American military chiefs opposed to the North African operations?
16. What were the great strengths of General Eisenhower?
17. Why did the RAF switch to night raids on Germany?
18. How did Air Marshal Harris aim to end the war?
19. What was achieved by the bombing offensive of Germany? What did it fail to achieve?

20. Why did shipping losses rise steeply after America came into the war?
21. Why did Russian convoys incur such heavy losses?
22. How did the Allies eventually overcome the U-boats?

Projects

Make a detailed study of:

(a) The war in the desert.
(b) The war in the Pacific.
(c) The bombing of Germany.

Imaginative

1. Write a letter home from a German soldier in front of Moscow in 1940 as winter begins to set in.
2. Write a letter home from one of the Japanese pilots who took part in the attack on Pearl Harbour.

Chapter 14

Comprehension

1. Why was the main German attack in Russia in 1942 made in the south?
2. Why did Hitler want to capture Stalingrad at all costs? Why did he fail?
3. Why did Churchill want an invasion of Italy? Why were American war leaders opposed to it?
4. Why did it take so long for the Allies to capture Rome?
5. Why was the decision taken to destroy the monastery of Monte Cassino?
6. What conditions had to be fulfilled before an invasion of France was possible?
7. What was the difference of opinion in the German high command about defending Europe from invasion?
8. How did the Allies hope to break through the Atlantic Wall?
9. How did the Allies deceive the Germans about where they were going to land?

10. Why were large German forces kept in other parts of France long after the invasion of Normandy?

11. Why were the Germans not able to move large forces to Normandy quickly?

12. What special measures did the Allies take to land supplies in Normandy?

13. Why was it some time before the Allies broke out of the Normandy bridgehead?

14. How did the Germans nearly lose their whole army in Normandy?

15. Why were the Germans able to stage a recovery on the Western Front in September 1944?

16. Why was the capture of the port of Antwerp intact of no immediate use to the Allies?

17. Why did Hitler fight on to the last? Why did most Germans support him in this?

18. Why did Churchill want to reinforce the Allied army in Italy? Why did Roosevelt disagree with him? Why did Stalin?

19. Why in September 1944 did Eisenhower want to advance on a 'broad' front? Why did Montgomery disagree with him?

20. Why was the Battle of Arnhem unsuccessful?

21. Why at first were the Germans successful in their attack in the Ardennes?

22. Why did Eisenhower halt Allied forces on the Elbe?

23. Why did some Japanese leaders realise that Japan had no chance of winning a long drawn out war? How did they hope to bring the Allies to terms?

24. What was the strategy of General MacArthur in winning the war in the Pacific?

25. How were the British able to recapture Burma?

26. What was achieved by the Chindits?

27. What were the considerations which induced President Truman to authorise the use of atomic bombs?

Projects

1. Make a study of the war on the Eastern Front. Show how, after colossal early defeats, the Russians were able to turn the tables on the Germans. Why was Stalingrad of such importance? Why was the German position growing ever weaker? Assess the importance of Anglo–American help to Russia.

2. Make a detailed study of the D-Day operation and the battle of Normandy. Assess the generalship of Montgomery.
3. Make a detailed study of the war in Burma. How did the Fourteenth Army overcome fanatical Japanese resistance?
4. Make a detailed study of the Italian campaign. Assess the disagreements between Allied war leaders on the subject. Why was the campaign undertaken? What failures of leadership were there?

Imaginative

1. Write a letter from a German soldier fighting at Stalingrad describing the battle and his fears of being captured.
2. Describe, as you imagine them, the experiences of a German prisoner of war in Russia.
3. Write as might have happened a conversation between Rommel and Von Runstedt about the defence of France from invasion including telephone calls to and from Hitler.
4. Imagine the thoughts of a British soldier going in on the first wave of the attack on D-Day.
5. Describe the feelings of a citizen of Paris when American and Free French troops entered the city.

Chapter 15

Comprehension

1. Why was Churchill so anxious at the end of the war?
2. Why was Stalin so suspicious of the Western powers?
3. What was the effect of making concessions to Stalin's demands?
4. What promise did Stalin break concerning Poland?
5. What difficulties were there after the war in charging Nazi war leaders with waging aggressive war?
6. What was it that brought about a revival of the West German economy?
7. Why in the closing months of the war did the Allies not occupy Vienna and Prague?
8. What was the usual pattern of Communist takeovers in Eastern Europe?
9. Why did some people believe that it was necessary for Russia to create tension abroad after the war?

Project

Make a study of the Communist takeover of Eastern European countries after the war.

Imaginative

1. Describe the experiences, as you imagine them, of a displaced person in Europe after the war.
2. Write diary entries of a non-Communist member of the Polish (or Czech or Hungarian) government at the time of the Communist takeover.
3. Write a letter from a German struggling to exist in the ruins of Hamburg after the war.

Chapter 16

Comprehension

1. What were the main reasons for Labour winning a massive election victory after the war?
2. Why was Britain in such great economic difficulties after the war?
3. How did Sir Stafford Cripps aim to solve Britain's economic problems?
4. Why did Beveridge insist that rich and poor alike should receive the same benefits?
5. What were Beveridge's five giants which had to be overcome?
6. Why were some doctors opposed to the setting up of the National Health Service?
7. Why were Labour's achievements in housebuilding less than those of the Conservatives?
8. What were the disadvantages of the eleven-plus exam?

Project

Make a study of the achievements of the post-war Labour government.

Chapter 17

1. What was the first step taken by the US government to help European countries to resist Communism?
2. What was the basic purpose of Marshall Aid?
3. What were the consequences of Marshall Aid?
4. What was the importance of the Berlin airlift?
5. Why was Yugoslavia expelled from the Cominform?

Imaginative

Write diary entries of a West Berliner at the time of the blockade of Berlin.

Chapter 18

Comprehension

1. Why did the Chinese Communists receive little help from Russia?
2. Why were the Chinese Communists ultimately victorious?
3. How did the Communist takeover differ from those in other countries?
4. What were the reasons for the failure of Mao Tse-tung to increase significantly agricultural production in China?
5. What were the main reasons for the hostility that existed between Russia and China?
6. What were the causes of the Korean War?
7. Why was General MacArthur dismissed?
8.. What advantages did the Vietcong have in the war in Vietnam?
9. Why did the Americans ultimately lose the war in Vietnam?
10. What were the consequences of this defeat?
11. Why did Mao launch the 'cultural revolution'?
12. What were the results of the 'cultural revolution'?
13. Why did President Nixon decide to end US hostility in China?

Imaginative

Give an eye-witness account of the arrival of the Red Guards in a Chinese city and what happened subsequently.

Projects

1. Make a study of the life and achievements of Mao Tse-tung.
2. Make a study of how America became more and more involved in Vietnam and the methods of warfare used by both sides subsequently. Trace the main events of the war and how it ended.

Chapter 19

Comprehension

1. Why was India partitioned?
2. How were the Communists overcome in Malaysia?
3. What had been a great blow to British prestige in the Far East?
4. Why after the war did the British feel it necessary to maintain their position in the Middle East?
5. Why did the British and French resort to armed force in Egypt in 1956?
6. Why did the Suez operation fail?
7. What were the consequences of the 'Suez Affair'?
8. What were the difficulties about Cyprus becoming an independent country?
9. Why did South Africa leave the Commonwealth?
10. What were the advantages of the Central African Federation? Why did it fail?
11. Why was Ian Smith compelled to accept the principle of black rule in Rhodesia?

Project

Make a study of events leading to Indian independence.

Imaginative

1. Imagine the feelings in a letter or diary of one of the following on Indian Independence Day: (a) a maharajah (b) a disciple of Gandhi (c) a schoolteacher (d) a Moslem living in a Hindu city.
2. Write a letter from a Jew living in Palestine expressing his feelings on the setting up of the state of Israel.

Chapter 20

Comprehension

1. What were the consequences of the death of Stalin?
2. What were the consequences of the denunciation of Stalin by Khruschev?
3. What lessons were to be learned from the Hungarian revolt?
4. What induced Khruschev to indulge in 'adventures' in foreign policy? What forms did these take?
5. Why was the Berlin Wall built?
6. What caused hostility between the United States and Cuba?
7. During the Cuba missile crisis what was President Kennedy careful to do?

Project

Make a study of the events leading to the Cuban missile crisis and how the matter was resolved.

Imaginative

1. Imagine the feelings of an average Russian on hearing of Khruschev's denunciation of Stalin.
2. Describe the experiences and feelings of a Hungarian taking part in the 1956 rebellion.
3. Describe the feelings of (a) a West Berliner and (b) an East Berliner about the building of the Berlin Wall.

Chapter 21

Comprehension

1. How was it that the Russians were able to catch up so quickly in the development of nuclear weapons?
2. What are the advantages of nuclear power over other fuels (coal, oil, gas) in generating electricity? What are the disadvantages?
3. What were the main problems to be overcome in manned space flight?
4. Why were some people critical of space flight? How were their criticisms answered?

Project

Make a study of the development of space flight.

Chapter 22

1. Why was Churchill in favour of European unity?
2. Why did the British Labour government hold back?
3. What were the ideas behind the setting up of the European Coal and Steel Community?
4. Why did Britain not join?
5. What were the main provisions of the Treaty of Rome?
6. What were the difficulties for Britain in joining the Common Market?
7. Why did the British government eventually feel obliged to join?
8. Why was de Gaulle opposed to British entry into the Common Market?
9. What enabled Britain to join eventually?
10. Why was there strong opposition in Britain to joining the Common Market? What were the opposing viewpoints?

Project

Make a study of the events leading to the establishment of the European Common Market.

Chapter 23

Comprehension

1. Why did the Israelis have such quick and overwhelming success in the 'Six Day War'?
2. What induced President Sadat of Egypt that he must come to terms with Israel?
3. What caused the disintegration of Lebanon?
4. What persuaded Yasser Arafat to come to an agreement with Israel?
5. Why did the price of oil go up four times between 1972 and 1974?
6. Why was the Third World so badly affected by this?
7. What led to the price of oil coming down?
8. Why were democratic countries worse affected by terrorism than Communist countries?
9. Why did Saddam Hussein invade Iran in 1980?
10. Why did he receive some support from the West?
11. Why did Western countries react so strongly to Iraq's invasion of Kuwait?

Projects

1. Make a detailed study of the Arab-Israeli conflict between 1948 and 1993. Show how Israel has managed to survive against all odds. Show the milestones by which some measure of peace and agreement has been brought about. What have been the effects of the conflict on the rest of the world?
2. Make a study of the impact on world history of the increasing importance of oil. How has British history been affected by it? Study the changes it has brought about in oil-producing countries.
3. Make a study of the growth of international terrorism and how it has been countered.

Imaginative

1. Describe the scene in an Israeli family when first news came through of the Yom Kippur War.

2. Describe as you imagine them the feelings and experiences of Arab refugees in Lebanon.

Chapter 24

Comprehension

1. What put pressure on the Soviet Union to seek an arms agreement with the United States?
2. What were the conditions on which Russia would receive economic aid from the West?
3. Why at first were some Western leaders distrustful of Gorbachev?
4. Why was the war in Afghanistan a turning point in the Cold War?
5. What were the unfortunate results in Russia of *Glasnost* and *Perestroika*?
6. Why did the attempted coup in 1991 fail?
7. What were the main problems in making the transition from Communism to a democratic society?
8. Why was it that Communist governments in East Europe were toppled in 1989 whereas all previous attempts to do so had failed?
9. What were the difficulties in the way of the reunification of Germany?
10. Why was Czechoslovakia split up?
11. Why did President Ceaucescu temporarily find favour with Western governments?
12. What were the basic causes of civil war in Yugoslavia?

Project

Make a study of the collapse of Communism in Russia or one of the other countries of Eastern Europe.

Imaginative

1. Imagine the feelings of a Hungarian (or Pole or Czech) as he sees the toppling of a gigantic statue of Stalin.
2. Imagine the feelings of an East German and a West German as the Berlin Wall was being demolished.
3. Describe the feelings and experiences of a Russian citizen during the attempted coup of August 1991.

INDEX